The Invasion of France, 1814

The Invasion
of France,
1814

The Memoirs of a Russian Artilleryman

Translated and edited by
Alexander Mikaberidze and Peter G A Phillips

Pen & Sword
MILITARY

AN IMPRINT OF PEN & SWORD BOOKS LTD.
YORKSHIRE – PHILADELPHIA

First published in Great Britain in 2025 by
PEN AND SWORD MILITARY
An imprint of
Pen & Sword Books Limited
Yorkshire – Philadelphia

Copyright © Alexander Mikaberidze and Peter G A Phillips, 2025

ISBN 978 1 39904 260 4

The right of Alexander Mikaberidze and Peter G A Phillips to be identified as
Authors of this work has been asserted by them in accordance with the Copyright,
Designs and Patents Act 1988.

A CIP catalogue record for this book is available from the British Library.

Typeset in Times New Roman 11.5/14 by
SJmagic DESIGN SERVICES, India.
Printed and bound in the UK by CPI Group (UK) Ltd.

The Publisher's authorised representative in the EU for product safety is
Authorised Rep Compliance Ltd., Ground Floor, 71 Lower Baggot Street, Dublin
D02 P593, Ireland.
www.arccompliance.com

For a complete list of Pen & Sword titles please contact
PEN & SWORD BOOKS LIMITED
George House, Units 12 & 13, Beevor Street, Off Pontefract Road,
Barnsley, South Yorkshire, S71 1HN, England
E-mail: enquiries@pen-and-sword.co.uk
Website: www.pen-and-sword.co.uk

or

PEN AND SWORD BOOKS
1950 Lawrence Rd, Havertown, PA 19083, USA
E-mail: uspen-and-sword@casematepublishers.com
Website: www.penandswordbooks.com

FSC
www.fsc.org

MIX
Paper | Supporting
responsible forestry
FSC® C013604

Contents

Maps   vi

Preface   viii

Chapter I   The Blockade of Mainz   1

Chapter II   From Mainz to Châlons   11

Chapter III   From Reims to Laon   29

Chapter IV   From Laon to Paris   47

Chapter V   From Paris to Sainte Menehould   79

Chapter VI   From Sainte Menehould to Nuremberg   93

Chapter VII   From Nuremberg to Dresden   105

Chapter VIII   From Dresden to Białystok   122

Chapter IX   Permanent Quarters   146

Chapter X   The Reconnaissance Mission   155

Maps

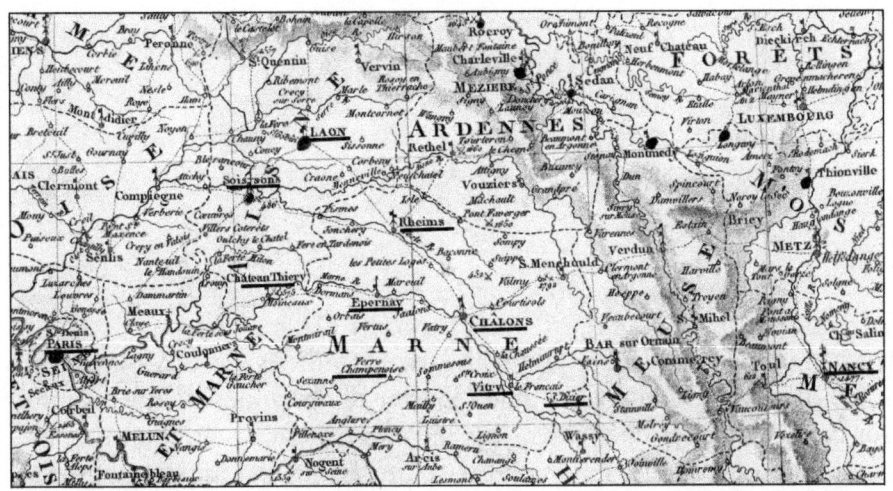

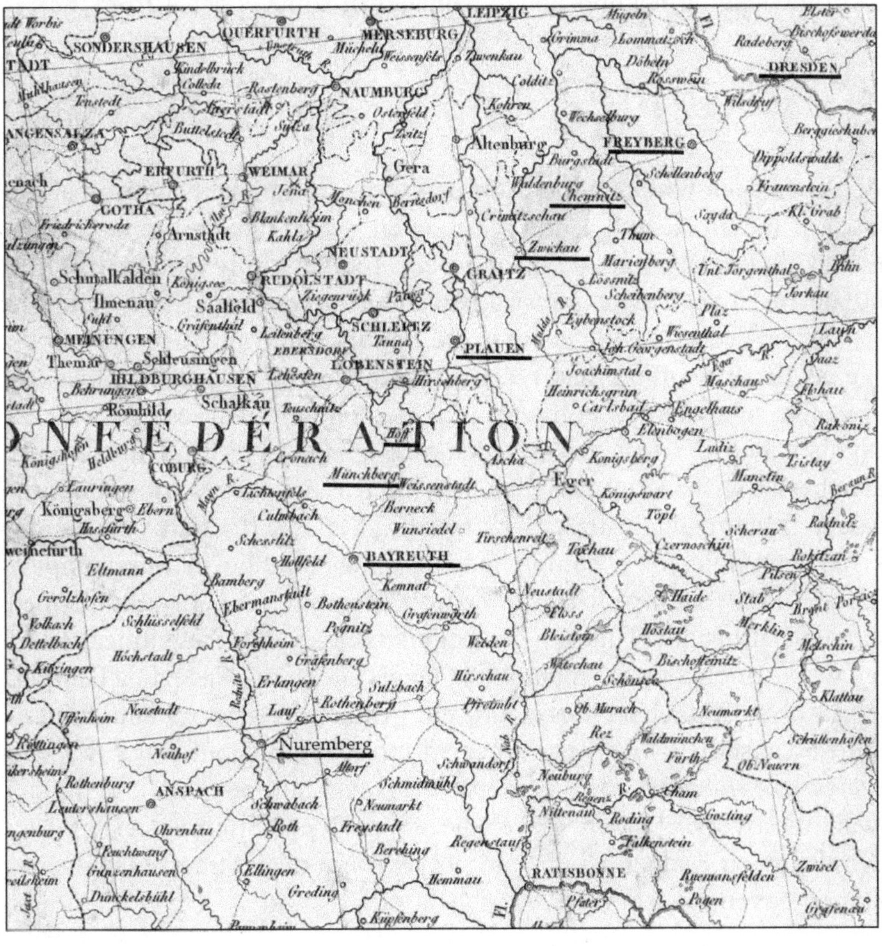

Preface

Human life is short and fleeting, and many millions of individuals who share in it, are swallowed by that monster of oblivion which is waiting for them with ever-open jaws. It is thus a very thankworthy task to try to rescue something – the memory of interesting and important events or the leading features and personages of some epoch – from the general shipwreck of the world.

Arthur Schopenhauer,
'Art der Literatur'

Much has been written about Europe's struggle against Napoleon at the dawn of the nineteenth century. Yet, even within this vast landscape of human experience, many crucial aspects remain dimly explored. While the shelves of any decent library groan under the weight of works detailing British and French involvement in the Napoleonic Wars, Russia's pivotal role in these conflicts has received scant attention outside Russian-language scholarship. Political and ideological rivalries, as well as linguistic barriers, have ensured that only a handful of Russian memoirs have been translated into English, leaving Russian voices conspicuously absent from many historical narratives. Yet the Russian perspective is indispensable for a comprehensive understanding of this complex era, and the wealth of Russian memoir literature remains an untapped reservoir of insight. This gap has begun to close with the publication of key works, including the memoirs of Denis Davydov, Nadezhda Durova, Moritz von Kotzebue, Boris Uxkull, Alexey Yermolov, and Eduard von Löwenstern, as well as the recent three-volume anthology *Russian Eyewitness Accounts*. Still, dozens of fascinating memoirs and diaries await discovery. Among these, the expansive reminiscences of Ilya Timofeyevich Radozhitskii stand out as some of the finest Napoleonic memoirs ever penned.

PREFACE

Born on July 17 (Old Style)/28 (New Style), 1788, Radozhitskii would rise to become a major general, but little is known of his early life. He lost his family at an early age and studied at the Imperial Orphanage (*Imperatorskii voenno-sirotskii dom*) as the Napoleonic wars raged in Europe and Napoleon crushed the Third and Fourth Coalitions. In late 1806, while Russia was still at war with France, the 18-year-old Radozhitskii joined the Kherson Artillery Garrison as a sub-lieutenant, where he served for two years before transferring to the 2nd Field Artillery Brigade in 1808. His persistence and exemplary service earned him a promotion to lieutenant in 1810, and by 1812, he was serving with the 3rd Light Company of the 11th Artillery Brigade in the 6th Infantry Corps.

Napoleon's invasion of Russia in 1812 marked a turning point in Radozhitskii's life. From the war's earliest days, he was in the thick of the fighting, distinguishing himself at the Battle of Ostrovno (July 25), where he was wounded and awarded the Order of St. Anna (4th class) for gallantry. He went on to witness pivotal battles at Smolensk, Valutina-Gora (Lubino), and Borodino, sharing the heartbreak of Moscow's surrender and the triumphs at Vyazma and Krasny. In the catastrophic retreat of the Grande Armée from November to December 1812, he bore witness to scenes of human and military devastation, vividly chronicled in his memoirs.

In the subsequent War of the Sixth Coalition (1813–1814), Radozhitskii fought in campaigns in Germany and France that culminated in the Allied triumph at Paris, where he celebrated the end of the long conflict on the Champs-Élysées in March 1814. Promoted to staff captain in 1815, he barely had time to rest after the long march home before being assigned to the Russian Expeditionary Corps sent to confront Napoleon following his escape from Elba. Although the corps arrived too late to see combat at Waterloo, Radozhitskii relished his time in France and Germany, indulging in the arts, theatre, and nature.

After the war, Radozhitskii continued to rise in his military career. Promoted to captain in 1817 and lieutenant colonel in 1819, he commanded artillery brigades and served in the Caucasus during the Russo-Ottoman War. There, at Erzurum, he met and befriended the great Russian poet Alexander Pushkin. Later, he directed the Tula Armament Factory, earned the Order of St. George (4th class) for 25 years of exemplary service, and was promoted to major general in 1850. He retired that same year, spending his final years in Voronezh, where he died in April 1861 and was buried at the local Pokrovskii Monastery.

Beyond his military exploits, Radozhitskii was a prolific writer and intellectual. He corresponded with leading literary figures and contributed to prominent journals such as *Severnaya pchela* and *Otechestvennye zapiski*. His literary output included a four-volume memoir on the Napoleonic Wars, a multi-volume account of the Russo-Ottoman and Caucasian Wars, and numerous ethnographic essays offering rich insights into the cultures of the North Caucasus. An avid botanist, he amassed one of Russia's largest private botanical libraries and laboured over an ambitious, illustrated 15-volume encyclopedia of world flora, though it was never published.

Radozhitskii's memoirs, based on meticulous notes he kept during his campaigns, began appearing in Russian periodicals in the 1820s. His four volumes on the Napoleonic Wars are structured by campaign, offering a ground-level view of a soldier's life during this turbulent period. The present volume begins with the Allied occupation of Frankfurt am Main and the subsequent invasion of France. Radozhitskii describes his experiences with vivid immediacy, blending contemporaneous notes with retrospective narration. France, for him, was a land of contradictions: its picturesque landscapes enchanted him, but the French people failed to meet the idealized image he had formed from books and journals. His memoirs brim with details of campaign life, from the rigours of the march to the cultural curiosities of occupied towns. They also recount his firsthand experiences in battles such as the disastrous confrontation at Rheims, where Napoleon routed a Russian corps. Radozhitskii's observations extend beyond the battlefield, reflecting his love for theatre and offering incisive commentary on German and French society.

Though coloured by strong biases – including his evident disdain for the French and his antisemitic views – Radozhitskii's writing provides a window into the personal and cultural attitudes of his time. Written with narrative flair and a keen eye for human drama, Radozhitskii's memoirs rival the historical novels of his era, painting a vivid panorama of Russia's epic struggle against Napoleon through the eyes of a humble artillery officer, hardened by war yet unyielding in his humanity.

Alexander Mikaberidze
Shreveport Louisiana

Chapter I

The Blockade of Mainz

During their stay at Frankfurt [am Main], the Allied Sovereigns had decided to invade France. They knew Napoleon's inexorable arrogance, indomitable enterprise, and enduring ambition to reclaim what he had lost. They knew he would not accept a peace deal that would humiliate him; therefore, they gathered vast resources to defeat him inside his realm. The Kings and Princes of the Confederation of the Rhine[1] committed twice the number of troops that Napoleon used to demand from them; even Saxony, which had been utterly depleted by the [last] campaign, deployed 20,000 more men, who joined some 12,000 who had already deserted Napoleon's banners. In total, German troops amounted to an army of some 145,000 men. Prussia was the first to set an example of raising a martial spirit in all of Germany. Thus, after so many centuries [of disunity and squabble], the Germans, inspired by the cause of national independence, united as if to form a single nation and, in doing this, discovered a possibility of creating one strong polity out of many [German] ones.

The rapid mobilization of the forces of the German Confederation[2] supplied the three main Powers, who had challenged Napoleon's hegemony, with the much-needed reinforcements; their army rears had been secured and the supply system organized. Furthermore, these powers received their fresh reinforcements. In the Russian army,

---

1 An alliance of three dozen German states that Napoleon had created in 1806 to serve as a satellite and major military ally of the French Empire.

2 The German Confederation (*Deutsche Bund, Germanskii soyuz*) was established in June 1815 as a successor to the Confederation of the Rhine and served as a political association of German states until 1866.

Prince Lobanov-Rostovskii[3] led 30,000 men out of the Duchy of Warsaw while another reserve force, some 20,000 men under General Bezobrazov,[4] had reached the Vistula River. Prussia also reinforced her forces with new troops from the territories she had occupied on the left side of the Elbe River, while Austrians received strong reserves from Vienna.

The Allied forces were divided into three armies. The main one comprised the former Army of Bohemia, [augmented by] two corps from the German Confederation, and was commanded by Prince Schwarzenberg.[5] The second army, formerly that of Silesia, consisted of the Prussian corps of Yorck[6] and Kleist,[7] which were strengthened by the Russian corps of Count Langeron[8] and Baron Osten-Sacken,[9] and two more corps from the German Confederation under the command of Prince Blücher.[10] The third army, of the North, included only two corps, those of Russian General Wintzingerode[11] and Prussian General Bülow.[12] The [Swedish] Crown Prince,[13] with the Swedes and the Russian detachments of Counts Vorontsov[14] and Stroganov,[15] marched against Hamburg and Denmark. Bennigsen,[16] with his Russian troops,

---

3 General Dmitrii Lobanov-Rostovskii (1758-1838) was given command of the Reserve Army in March 1813.

4 Major General Nikolai Bezobrazov I (1770-1833).

5 Austrian Field Marshal Karl Philipp Fürst zu Schwarzenberg (1771-1820).

6 Prussian General Johann David Ludwig Graf Yorck von Wartenburg (1759-1830).

7 Prussian General Friedrich Emil Ferdinand Heinrich Graf Kleist von Nollendorf (1762 – 1823).

8 Russian General Count Louis Alexandre Andrault de Langeron (1763-1831).

9 Russian General Baron Fabian Gottlieb von der Osten-Sacken (1752-1837).

10 Prussian General Gebhard Leberecht von Blücher (1742-1819).

11 Ferdinand Karl Friedrich Freiherr von Wintzingerode (1770–1818).

12 Friedrich Wilhelm Freiherr von Bülow (1755-1816).

13 Crown Prince Karl Johan, Formerly Jean Baptiste Bernadotte, French general and Marshal of the Empire, became the crown prince of Sweden in 1810.

14 Russian Lieutenant General Mikhail Vorontsov (1782-1856).

15 Russian Lieutenant General Pavel Stroganov (1774-1817).

16 Russian General Levin August Gottlieb Theophil Graf von Bennigsen (1745-1826).

was approaching Magdeburg. Meanwhile, Wellington[17] had already invaded the south of France.

Thus, about 600,000 warriors, led by experienced commanders, had prepared to overthrow the Emperor of France.[18] At the very heart of this enterprise was Russian Emperor Alexander, whom the Providence itself had chosen to liberate the peoples of Europe. He had decided to exploit the enemy's weakness to invade [France] during winter, with which the robust warriors of the North [Russians] were familiar while the enemy was least prepared for it.

Napoleon, abandoned by his allies, was compelled to resort to forceful measures to raise a new army within his realm. He sought to rally the ordinary people to defend his power, but the [French] people, discouraged by earlier disasters and hopeful of deliverance from tyranny, remained aloof [to Napoleon's appeals] and awaited the victors. Nonetheless, Napoleon, resorting to threats and severe measures, raised some 300,000 soldiers quickly.

By January 1 [January 13, 1814], the main Allied army was at Vesoul, while on 4th [January 16], without facing any obstacles, it reached Langres. The Allied forces gathered here for a few days, expecting to clash with Napoleon, who was massing his troops near Châlons[-en-Champagne]. On January 5 [17], Blücher, facing almost no resistance, entered the town of Nancy while Toul, with its small garrison, was seized without a fight. Thus, by early January, the Allies had invaded the Champagne region in just six days, with two main armies, of Schwarzenberg and Blücher, uniting.

The French people, suffering from the devastation brought about by the invasion of foreign troops, gradually became embittered and began to arm themselves. The Allies were compelled to disarm the residents and issue announcements that anyone caught with arms in hand would be executed; any city or village that tried to resist was threatened with fire and depredation. Yet, such threats only further antagonized ordinary people, who came close to rising in a national war [natsionalnaya voina].

While the Allied armies were advancing deeper into France, Count [Alexander] Langeron's corps remained near Mainz, maintaining

---

17 British General Arthur Wellesley, Duke of Wellington (1769-1852).

18 Napoleon's title was Emperor of the French.

the blockade of the local fortress. All the while, I was in Frankfurt, preoccupied with my drawings.

The 1st of January! New Year! New Year! But this time, these are just empty words. Back at home, in our beloved Mother Russia, we usually spent the last evening of the old year in the circle of relatives or friends or with our benevolent superiors, celebrating New Year with loud salutations and to the sound of music and joyous clinking of glasses. But in this foreign land, everything is quiet and dreary... [and] as ill luck would have it, I did not have a single coin in my pockets. Oh, money, money! Seneca[19] spoke the truth when he proclaimed that this world has no greater wickedness than gold. Yet I am more inclined to side with Rabbi Hirsch,[20] who stated that gold can be the greatest blessing in the world... Indeed, a wise man's preaching cannot buy you bread, while with money, I am always fed and happy. Money can encompass all wisdom and virtue. The question is, where to find them? Their value is appreciated only when they are all gone. With such thoughts, I eased myself in Frankfurt, having lost hope of going to the theatre where [Wolfgang Amadeus] Mozart's glorious opera *The Magic Flute* was played. Alas, to live in Frankfurt and to be confined to a cold room filled with boredom on the very first day of a new year – I felt that this was a punishment befitting Tantalus[21] himself. [But] later that evening, I unexpectedly acquired a *Thaler* and, thrilled by such a bit of luck, I hastened to the theatre.

[Radozhitskii devotes the following five pages to discussing local theatre plays]

[After a weeklong] stay in Frankfurt, I learned that my artillery company was passing through the city towards Gross-Gerau. This unexpected turn

---

19 The great Roman philosopher Lucius Annaeus Seneca (d. 65 CE).

20 Probably Rabbi Samson Raphael Hirsch (1808-1888), German Orthodox rabbi best known as the intellectual founder of the Torah im Derech Eretz school of contemporary Orthodox Judaism. The source of this quote is uncertain and might reflect Radozhitskii's innate antisemitism.

21 Tantalus was a Greek mythological figure, most famous for his eternal punishment in Tartarus: he was made to stand in a pool of water beneath a fruit tree with low branches, with the fruit ever eluding his grasp, and the water always receding before he could take a drink.

of events excited me. I rushed to my apartment to inform my host that I was departing... The artillery was required to march for over 30 *verstas* [20m]. I caught up with my company on the seventh *versta* [4.6m] from the city and did not find a single officer with it. Our lieutenant colonel stayed behind to have fun in the city, and all the other officers also stayed there.

On 7 [19] January, I was already on the left bank of the Rhine, near the village of Nierstein, on the road from Mainz to Oppenheim. Looking out of the windows of my apartment, I enjoyed the view of the river's quiet flow that bathed the walls of the house I was lodged in. Large packs of ice, like a flock of swans, drifted over the entire expanse of the river, speedily outrunning each other as if hurrying to inform our enemies, still residing inside Mainz, about the arrival of the formidable Russian forces that had persistently scattered their [French] hordes to the winds. And soon, the Rhine, having never seen such foes except for the few prisoners of war, would wail under the weight of the Russian rumble and bayonets. But at this time of the year, when everything seemed melting, flooding, or getting soaked, nature itself appeared mourning with the Rhine. Winter deprived the river of its beauty and left only bare vineyards that, like remnants of crops in harvested fields, revealed occasional vines from underneath the snow. The Oppenheim and Nierstein wines are considered among the best of the Rhenish wines, and this nectar soon satisfied my thirst. So, the greatly esteemed Rhine, was there any other time that the Russians have saddled you!? Until now, you have marked the boundary of the German might and carried [the German] tribute to the conquering Gauls, knowing no other burden. Your riverbanks, flourishing with abundance, ensured the well-being of their inhabitants, who cultivated juicy grapes next to your glistening waters, sang hymns of joy and amused you with their happiness. And now? Now, only wailing and misery rein on your banks while damnations, instead of blessings, can be heard everywhere. Despite your [French] overlord's efforts, foreign peoples have come to cross your boisterous waters. You have armed yourselves with swift currents and heavy ice flow in vain. The rumble of the Russian tsar will reach deep into your heart and make you bend timorously to our might. Weep, the mighty Rhine, weep! Like Napoleon, whom Providence has deprived of all his earthly glory! Weep, just like our Niemen and Dnieper did not that long ago! May your wails reach the shores of the chaste Seine! And may your formidable overlord, who has caused so much suffering, also cry bloody tears!

Below Oppenheim, where we crossed the Rhine, the river became narrower than the Vistula is at Warsaw, but further downstream, at Mainz, it was extensive, especially below the estuary of the River Main. The twelve cannons of our artillery company required two full days to cross the river on boats. The crossing was dangerous and had to be carried slowly and cautiously. Consequently, my men and I got both chilled and wet to the bone. Accompanying the cannon, I crossed the river several times and enjoyed the view of its banks, which, although bare, still offered charming sights. The right bank was flat, while the left – elevated. We were accompanied by the 12th Division during the crossing, and its wagons constantly hindered us. The division was tasked with blockading Mainz from the left side of the Rhine while Count Langeron led the rest of his forces to Blücher. On the third crossing, the Prince of Coburg[22] accompanied my cannon. I have rarely met such a handsome man; his eminent face conveyed such nobility of his soul. It seemed that no female beauty could compare with the face of such a fine-looking man, conveying all the superiority of one gender over another […].[23] The Prince of Coburg, commanding the German 5th Corps, was dispatched to replace Langeron at Mainz but did not have [enough] officers. Although he was given a few Prussians, he was now travelling to Count Langeron to ask for Russian officers to train his Landwehr troops.

Our new quarters proved to be worse than before. I, leading two cannons protected by jägers, was assigned to the village of Ober-Olm on the left side of the Rhine, about six *verstas* [6.4km/4m] away from Mainz. The remaining cannons were deployed as follows: four, commanded by Captain Zhemchuzhnikov, were at Leubenheim, and two – at Hechstheim. The troops of the 9th Corps closely blockaded the fortress [of Mainz] on all sides. Residents assured us that Mainz would surrender soon because its [French] garrison had no more than 8,000 men, most of them sick, many of whom were dying daily, while some healthy soldiers were going over to the besieging side. So, we waited for

---

22 Radozhitskii is using a wrong title – the commander of the German V Corps was Duke Ernest of Saxe-Coburg (1784-1844), the future father of Albert, Prince Consort of Queen Victoria of Britain.

23 Radozhitskii goes on to elaborate on female and male beauty.

siege artillery, seemingly intending to capture this fortress in a proper siege.

For ten whole days, I lived in this monotonous solitude. Days passed without any occurrences. But I was alone, and this had some advantages too. Conversing with muses, as well as with Schiller, Goethe, and La Fontaine,[24] I did not notice the passage of time. After a dissolute life in Frankfurt, one found a different kind of enjoyment at Ober-Olm, less for senses and more for cultivating mind and heart.

On 18 [30] January, I travelled to Mainz. Snow was melting, and it seemed like spring was trying to appear. About four *verstas* [4.28km/2.6m] from Ober-Olm, I found a Cossack outpost deployed in the devastated village of Marienborn, and another *versta* away from them was a French outpost. Compared to Hochheim on the opposite bank, it was not easy to get a good view of Mainz from this direction due to its fortifications. I enjoyed the view of Hochheim and observed the tower of Höchst.[25] Peering at the blue horizon, I could guess the location of Frankfurt, where I had experienced so many joys. The French controlled the four closest villages on that side of the river, although I could not see or hear anything. What a dreary enterprise it is to maintain a blockade!

Four days later, I again decided to go to Hochheim, where our Sub-Lieutenant Baron Ungern-Sternberg was deployed with two cannon. The village was located on the right side of Mainz, about three *verstas* [3.2km/2m] away from the fortress. Travelling along the road, I enjoyed the views of snow-covered plains and the city skyline visible on the left. The fields between the fortress and the road where I travelled were immaculately clean! The Cossacks very rarely rode along the front line. And how simple-minded the Frenchmen are. It had already been some time since we quietly took positions around the fortress and lived as if in canton quarters. If only they had sent a cavalry column across this field – it might not have caused much harm to us but would have produced great distress and might have gotten to my guns as well! I would have met them near the hill with jägers in close support. What a strange way of capturing a fortress – through patience! The enemy could not be seen

---

24 Reference to the great German and French writers Fridriech Schiller, Johann Wolfgang von Goethe and Jean de La Fontaine

25 Reference to the tower of the Höchster Schloß, originally built in the fourteenth century and repaired in the sixteenth century.

at all. On both sides, troops sit in their quarters, amuse themselves, and strike up affairs until the appearance of that all-consuming monster – hunger. And then...

Such were my thoughts as I approached Hochheim and heard musket fire coming from Mainz's direction. 'It is probably just skirmishing at advance posts,' I thought. 'Probably someone got bored.' Having seen no bullets or cannonballs fired since the battle of Leipzig, I looked around to see if I could determine where the clash was taking place. Maybe I could go and witness it, I thought. There were two cannons in front of the village. Horses were about to be taken away, and a group of cannoniers gathered around an open caisson. Not far from them stood an outpost of soldiers whose muskets rested on trestles near a straw hut. Several merry chaps sat around a bonfire. 'Cheers, lads!' I told them. After the usual greetings, one of the *feurwerkers* told me, 'Your Honour, we had a busy day today.' – 'How come!?' – 'Mikhailov has been killed, and one of our limbers got damaged.' Without waiting for further explanations, I went to [Baron] Ungern, who told me what had happened. About 6,000 French made a sortie directly at this village and almost reached the heights of Laubenheim. They dug in amidst the ruins of a monastery, deployed six cannons there, and, under their protective fire, advanced in thick columns of infantry and cavalry. We hastily gathered some 4,000 men between Hochheim and Laubeheim. But just as [Baron] Ungern made several successful shots at the enemy columns, they stopped and retreated. Our skirmishers did not even get to take part in the clash. The Ukrainian Cossacks captured an enemy cannon but had to relinquish it because they could not overcome the enemy cavalrymen [who came to the infantry's support]. Thus, it appeared that some 6,000 Frenchmen were turned back by just two of our cannon. They evidently hoped to surprise us but failed and had to beat a hasty retreat to the fortress. It would have been better, of course, if we had lured them further away and cut them from Marienborn's direction.

I soon received three "For Saving the Fatherland" medals:[26] one for me and two for *feurwerkers*. Earlier, while in Frankfurt, I bought this medal,

---

26 The Medal in Memory of the Patriotic War of 1812 was established on 17 February 1813, following the Russian victory over Napoleon. Nobles wore bronze medals on the ribbon of the Order of St. Vladimir, merchants – the tape of the Order of St. Anne. In 1814, all participants of the 1812 Campaign received silver medals on the ribbon of the Order of St. Andrew the First Called.

albeit not Russian-made, from a Jewish merchant. I closely examined the new medal that was issued to commemorate that most important event: on the front side, it showed the All-Seeing Eye inside a triangle with emanating rays of lights and "1812" inscribed at the bottom; on the reverse, there was an inscription, "Not unto us, but unto Thy Name,"[27] so familiar from the coins of Emperor Paul I. Nowadays, wherever you look, everyone has a blue ribbon in a buttonhole; yet twenty years later, they would be rarely seen, and another twenty years later, the future generations would esteem their bearers far more than contemporaries ever did because warriors with medals are the representatives of national honour in the grand historical events. In this regard, medals have an advantage over decorations.

At last, the winter almost completely disappeared. Snow melted and rushed in overflowing streams from the hills down into the valley. All fields turned black, with occasional white scars of snow. They presented a rather depressing sight. It seemed as if the creation of the world began with this. Nature is not always beautiful. I would have laughed at any artist who tried to find something pretty and worthy of a paintbrush in these muddled features of the earthly landscape. Winter is beautiful only when it is accompanied by fluffy snow, gleaming sunlight, the fields sparkling and bewitching one's eye with a diversity of colours; when curly trees are covered with white frost as if with sugar dust; when sunlight shimmers in icy mirrors that resemble crystals; and, when the blue shadow of white hills pleases the eye just like a young woman's face does. That is when winter, with its white mantle, can truly compete with the delights of the splendidly adorned summer.

It is 1st [13] of February, Sunday. I went to the village church to observe religious service and the residents attending it. Women sat dressed in blouses and white hats with flaps, so it was impossible to distinguish married women from single girls except by looking at their faces. In the choir sat men in blue and grey coats and books in hand. The orchestra – a pipe organ, to be precise – began to play just as the priest, in white clothing, proclaimed, 'Dominus vobiscum! In saecula saeculorum!'[28] The orchestra sometimes played allegro, which amused

---

27 The inscription is an excerpt from Psalms: "Not to us, O Lord, not unto us, but unto thy name Give the glory of thy mercy and thy truth "(Ps. 113, 9).

28 "The Lord be with you! Unto the ages of ages!", an ancient salutation and blessing customarily used during Catholic liturgies.

the attendees. Occasionally, a venerable *küster*,[29] sitting in the upper gallery, got carried away by the enthusiasm and began to sing a hymn in alto, accompanied by a choir of descant and bass singers below and above him. 'Oh, what voices they have!' I told a jäger officer standing next to me, who got all red in the face and bit his lip. It seemed rather strange to see a German with a Latin book in hand inside a Catholic church since I got used to seeing them in simple Lutheran churches. I wondered if everyone understood what needed to be comprehended in this impenetrable service.

I received an order to depart with two guns to the village of Nieder-Olm, which served as the gathering point for forces blockading Mainz. I eagerly packed my belongings and bid goodbye to the canary bird, which got used to me. If it were springtime, I would have taken her with me, but the winter still held its sway, deceiving the eye with the greenery of some grass and the newly rising grain sowed in the autumn.

My new quarters were with a good peasant, who was a miller and baker. He had a good house and gave me his best room while he himself lived constrained. His joyous but unattractive daughter brought me some food. She frequently welcomed her friends, very adroit and cheeky girls, who did their best to overcome my indifference and warm up my cold heart. But their efforts were futile. My intellectual exercises and rather different frame of mind distracted me from their exuberance and merriment. One of the girls even dressed in a jäger officer's frock coat and appeared before me to introduce herself. This charade greatly entertained everyone. I must say, I did not expect such deftness from a simple village girl.

On 2 [14] February, at noon, I arrived at Nieder-Olm where I was told to wait for my company. However, General Karpenko advised me to continue my journey, supposing that my company proceeded by a shorter route to Wörrstadt. So, I moved forward and indeed encountered my company in that village. After a prolonged seclusion, I was thrilled to get back together with my comrades. Prince of Coburg's troops replaced the 9th Corps, and we, led by Count St. Priest, hurried to rejoin the rest of our forces, who, it was said, were working miracles in France.

---

29 A sacristan or church attendant who was usually charged with care of the sacristy, the church, and its contents.

Chapter II

From Mainz to Châlons

While we were marching to the Rhine, the Allied forces were already on their way to Paris but Napoleon, despite his extreme position, then gained many victories, disordered the Army of Silesia, and forced the Allies back.

Late in the evening of 2 [14] February, we arrived at Alzey, located about 60 *verstas* [about 40 miles] from Mainz. Alzey, surrounded by walls and towers, features ruins of an ancient castle but everything appears here as if in miniature, like Rome would have looked at its founding when Remus could [easily] jump over the city moat.[1] Looking at these walls, I thought about those ancient times when people fought with arrows, stones, boiling tar, battering rams, and siege towers. How many transformations these ruins had witnessed?! Inside Alzey, buildings were built of wood and the residents, of German Brabant origin, appeared to be rather staunch supporters of Napoleon. To lure them to his side, [Napoleon] spared them more than the Rhineland Germans. But now, the plight of the residents was miserable indeed. To collect the debt that Prussians claimed from France (about 60 million [roubles]), Prince Blücher exacted dreadful contributions from every village and settlement that he encountered. Furthermore, these villages had to satisfy Russian troops and then save enough to survive themselves. The land seemed to be fruitful, but locals showed no signs of industry or well-being.

I was billeted with a Jew, but local Jews are completely different from ours in their way of life, education, and appearance. I would not comment on their souls – everything the scions of the Hebrew tribe do

---

1 According to the Roman tradition, Romulus and Remus built cities on various hills, the former choosing the Palatine and the latter the Aventine hill. Romulus drew a furrow around the Palatine, the turned-up earth symbolizing the future walls and the furrow – the moat. To ridicule his brother's intentions, Remus jumped over the "wall" and the "moat" at one bound. Enraged Romulus leaped on him and killed him.

is based on deception and the acquisition of money through the most accessible means possible. In my host's cabinet, I found many French and German books, old novels, and portraits of three European emperors.

The locals received us well and trusted us more than they did the Prussians. But we could not trust their welcome after learning about the proclamation that Napoleon issued to his people: he appealed to them to slaughter and poison us everywhere. It was said that such attempts had already been made against soldiers of Baron Osten-Sacken's corps. On the other hand, our Emperor issued a general order to the armies demanding treating the [civilian] populace as amicably as possible and winning them over through our generosity rather than vengeance. Quite a contrast to the French behaviour in Russia...

On 5 [17] February, we passed by the mountain Mont-Tonnerre, after which this entire province was called.[2] The city of Kaiserslautern was larger than Alzey but very poor. The residents were half-Germans or Brabants and received us very well.

The following day we had a long march of 40 *verstas* [26.5 miles] across mountains. We passed through Landstuhl and Homburg, where houses were rather decrepit. The further we advanced, the more wretched and poor residents we encountered: they wore rags covered with filth, and their faces showed signs of emaciation. At least the area near the town of Zweibrücken was picturesque, and many places were worthy of an artist's paintbrush. We rested there and found good quarters already prepared for us. My friend and I were billeted to a baker while our lieutenant colonel stayed in the apartment of a widow, a certain Duchess Lewenhaupt, of Swedish ancestry.

Zweibrücken is located between the two fortresses of Saarbrücken and Bitt [Bitche?] and was bordering with Lotharingia,[3] where we are supposed to enter the following day.

Count St. Priest commanded our detachment. Locals organized a ball in his honour and invited all officers to attend. At 4 o'clock the

---

2 Mont-Tonnerre was the name of a département of the French First Empire. It was named after the highest point in the Rhenish Palatinate, the Donnersberg.

3 Lotharingia was a region comprising the Low Countries, the western Rhineland, and what is now western Switzerland. It was established in the tripartite division in 855, of the kingdom of Middle Francia, itself formed of the threefold division of the Carolingian Empire by the Treaty of Verdun in AD 843.

following morning, I was sent to Sarreguemines to prepare quarters for my company. At sunrise, I was already at Blieskastel, behind which I observed a telegraph tower on a mountain.[4] Under the Bourbons, French soil began at Sarreguemines, a town on the Saar River that separates Lotharingia from Brabant. Upon arriving here, I appeared in front of the local commander, Lt. Col. V., a rather polite Guard officer, to receive an assignment of quarters. I took this document to the local city hall (*municipalité*) that still bore the symbol of the French imperial eagle and found myself surrounded by the representatives of that very nation that had caused so much harm to all of Europe and my Fatherland in particular. I experienced remarkable first impressions: in German towns, I got accustomed to seeing slow, mostly quiet, and important-looking burgomasters who went about their business; but here, to the contrary, I saw talkative, polite but sombre Frenchmen, whose swarthy faces alternately manifested all passions and moods. I thus witnessed *Liberté et Égalité* under the burden of unlimited despotism. Inside the meeting hall, everything attracted my attention, even golden bees on the blue wallpaper that covered the walls. Three mayors, all wearing glasses, fussed about assigning quarters while other municipal officials, wearing caps or hats and smoking pipes, walked around the room. Many other [officers] were seeking quarters, so I had plenty of time to observe and examine everything. Citizens, displeased with the mayors' decisions, constantly came in holding billet assignments and demanding changes to be made...[5] Suddenly, there appeared a swarthy, skinny but agile Frenchman in sailor's dress, and rather brashly declared to the mayors that he could not support troops billeted to him and that their decision was contrary to all existing laws. The mayors refused to consider his appeal, so he began to bang his fists on the table, cursed, and shouted at them until he was forcefully removed from the room. All of this was utterly startling to me, especially when I saw an old lady, wearing a large bonnet and shouting at the top of her lungs, loudly chiding the mayors and proclaiming her readiness to scratch their eyes out at the first opportunity; she was followed by the charming dark-eyed

---

4 Radozhitskii is referring to the famous mechanical telegraph developed by Claude Chappe in the 1790s. Napoleon built an extensive network of such towers to maintain control over his growing empire.

5 Ellipsis are original to the text.

French women whose gentle voices besought the mayors to help them... Others might have been swayed by these cries and appeals but these dispassionate officials, immersed in their work, paid heed to nothing and simply continued issuing billets. They appeared utterly heartless.

I finally obtained billets for my artillery crews and went to inspect houses. At the lieutenant colonel's billet, I found a rather adroit and quick-witted French woman who anticipated all my questions and showed me three excellently furnished rooms, even though she was just the wife of a cuirassier who served in Napoleon's [Imperial] Guard. Her sister, an adorable girl, kept unintentionally showing her legs and seemed to be voluptuousness personified. 'What a vacation our lieutenant colonel will have here,' I muttered to myself... At the captain's billet, I was met by a madame, who was a Jew, and her entire family, but they were of such different appearance and so well dressed that one would have easily mistaken them for genuine French people. My hostess, a baker, tried to bribe the mayors with ten sous while her husband kept offering me as much to change a billet, which required him to host three officers. I declined and saved them from additional expenditures.

During these first encounters, I found French women very pretty and adroit. Many were beautiful; all had enchanting and alert black eyes that suggested a burning sense of passion; their features, voices, words, and glances all conveyed a sense of love, and it seemed they lived and breathed this emotion. Only then did I understand how different was the appearance [fiziognomia] of French women from the German! The former combined liveliness, bluster, levity, inconstancy, and fervour, while the latter stood for slothfulness, thoroughness, distrustfulness, constancy, and coldness. The women closest to the French were the Poles.

We were uncertain about what the future held for us, but this first [French] town received us well; during the passage of our troops, locals marvelled at our grenadiers. Still, there were rumours that further inland, deeper in France, locals were massacring our quartermasters. It must be said that even here, some French looked at us rather gloomily, with their frowned brows straightening only when they remembered Moscow's burning and Russia's desolation. Fortunate enemies indeed! We treated them as friends and only sought out those who raised arms against us. Hurrah to the Russians! May we serve as an example to all other nations through our gallantry and generosity!

On 10 [22] February, we arrived at Château-Salins,[6] which is named after salt-producing manufactories that dot the region and produce enormous quantities of salt. Between Zweibrücken and Château-Salins, the population is a mixture of Germans and French and speaks a particular dialect that is rather difficult to understand.

Château-Salins proved to be a destitute town, its residents impoverished and worn down by repeated misfortunes. Their demeanour suggested a deep fear, so pervasive that the thought of conspiring against us seemed unimaginable. I found it peculiar to see a man in a tattered blue coat, a woman in a filthy dress, or a young boy begging in the street, all speaking French. Back home, French is a language reserved for the elite, spoken only in the circles of high society. Yet here we were, listening to the common rabble converse fluently in that same tongue. Nothing better illustrated the superficiality of our own infatuation with all things French.

Large crowds were a rare sight, and when we did encounter them, they consisted mostly of older men, boys, and women, conscription having taken nearly all able-bodied men. Beyond Sarreguemines, we noticed a striking change in the architecture. Houses grew wider, their shutters became latticed, and fireplaces replaced the ovens we had seen before. The soil in this region appeared rocky and heavy with clay, making it less fertile than the land we had traversed earlier. Despite this, the locals consumed good-quality wheat bread. The terrain beyond Sarreguemines was notably flatter compared to the hilly region between Mainz and Zweibrücken, which had made for a more arduous march.

At last, we arrived at Nancy. It is a major commercial city, larger than Frankfurt, and located on the plain that the Meurthe River intersects. It used to be the capital of Lotharingia but is now the main city of the department of Meurthe. It is considered one of the best cities in France and has a palace, a bishopric, and numerous beautiful buildings. Its streets are straight, wide, and decorated with trees. The best of the city squares was named after Napoleon, featuring fountains and sidewalks. In the middle of it stands the bronze statue of Henry IV. Local shops are built in a particular style and present a view of a long row of glass doors. Each home has an inscription or sign. The Polish King Stanisław

---

6 Château-Salins is located about 60km west of Sarreguemines.

Leszczyński, who was related to Louis XV,[7] resided here after losing his kingdom[8] and decorated the city with many beautiful buildings. This philosopher-king and his spouse are buried at the cathedral seven *verstas* from here.[9]

Our troops moved by a parade march through Nancy. The French watched them in the streets with amazement. But who were these people? Almost all of them were poor residents. A common Frenchman is dressed worse than a Russian peasant. He wears a blue linen coat on top of his shirts and pantaloons, a cap on the head, and wooden shoes, called sabots, on his feet. Such was their usual clothing.

My friend and I received quarters on the *place carrée* in a building that used to be a restaurant, but its owner recently went bankrupt and then died; his widow mourned him deeply and was, probably out of deep grief, rather drunk when we arrived. I went to see local shops and found everything too expensive – I had to pay five francs for a pound of sugar. Such high prices were caused not as much by war as by heavy taxes that merchants paid to the government not just for colonial goods but everything else. All the tobacco in France was produced at mills Napoleon established, and this tobacco monopoly was as profitable for him as alcohol taxes are in Russia, for you will not find a single Frenchman who does not smoke or sniff tobacco[...] In addition, Napoleon collected taxes on doors, windows, and chimneys. Such was the price the French had to pay for their liberty and equality! Such was Liberty for which they condemned their good king. But now Napoleon stands among them like a stork amidst frogs and devours them as he pleases.

The theatre in Nancy was as large as the one in Frankfurt, but, considering the circumstances, it had poorer music and a more meagre wardrobe. The theatre staged the opera *La Folia* in three acts, but the audience consisted almost entirely of our officers, and even these were a few. No Frenchmen, except for some boys, attended the play. Almost

---

7 Louis XV was married to Stanisław's daughter Marie.

8 Stanisław was twice deposed from the Polish throne in the first half of the eighteenth century.

9 Stanisław died at the age of eighty-eight in 1766. His body was buried in the church of Notre-Dame de Bonsecours in Nancy while his bowels were placed in a cenotaph inside the church of Saint-Jacques in Lunéville.

all the boxes and seats were empty; the Cossacks and Prussians stood in the parterre. The opera had pleasant music, and some of its arias were charming indeed. The actors sang and played well, but it was obvious that they were not in the mood to perform. And how could they be when their fatherland was perishing!? Yet they were forced to go onto the stage because the city refused to organize a ball [for the Allies]. A theatre buffet resembled an open market, and after each act, we had to wait for more than half an hour before the curtain was raised. The French, playful and capricious by nature, walked with their heads bowed and deeply immersed in thoughts about impending misfortunes. But the younger lads were still talkative. After getting my seat in the first row, I would have been all alone if not for youngsters, in dress coats, hands stuck inside their trousers as was the custom [in France] and hats on their heads, who approached me. They sat on the balustrade in front of me and, during intermissions, frequently asked me questions about the theatre, the city, and what I liked there. Finally, one asked me, 'Do you really think you will be able to reach Paris?' – 'Of course, just as your troops reached Moscow.' – 'And you will burn Paris?' – 'I do not know.' – 'Please, do not burn Paris. You will be ashamed of it later...' The curtain rose then, but I did not pay attention to the play as much as I looked at these children who were already concerned about politics and the fate of their fatherland. It was clear how much earlier youth matured in France.

Blücher entered Nancy on 8 [20] February and was greeted by the members of the municipality and honorary citizens, who presented him with the city keys that [Blücher] immediately sent to our Emperor. We soon learned that Blücher's entire Army of Silesia, having been concentrated on the road to Paris, was routed by Napoleon and that Blücher himself barely escaped French captivity; that the Prussian infantry, forming a square, had to fight its way through the enemy cavalry for some 15 *verstas* [10 miles] under incessant attacks. At one point, the French surrounded Blücher, whose death seemed imminent. The gallant officer Ried and the cannoniers from Colonel Shusherin's horse artillery company saved Blücher and helped him fight through the enemy cavalry toward Etoges. In just six days, the Army of Silesia lost 18,000 men and 43 guns, which forced Blücher to fall back to Châlons while Napoleon turned towards the main Allied army. Prince Schwarzenberg was forced to retreat to Troyes. Napoleon's rapid successes, coupled with considerable losses of the Allied armies, sicknesses that raged among our troops, devastated countryside that had no provisions to supply armies, the growing discontent of the people in the occupied regions, and, finally, the corps of General Augereau, some 40,000 strong, at Lyons in our rear – all of these factors caused the Allies to offer peace terms to Napoleon. But he was so proud of his last victories that he rejected the offer with the words, 'I am now closer to Vienna than to Paris.'

We expected a day of rest at Nancy but were instead ordered to advance at once to replenish losses caused by Blücher's excessive haste and desire for the quick capture of Paris. On 12 [24] February, we entered the city of Toul, some fifteen *verstas* away from Nancy. The area would have been in some places impassable if not for the [French] ability to construct levies to raise the roads, in some places as high as 20 *sazhens* [40 metres] and turn them into pleasant alleyways. We encountered numerous donkeys laden with firewood and enormous two-wheeled carts pulled by a single horse. Horses and oxen were famished all around this region. We also met numerous carts carrying the wounded from the defeated corps of the Army of Silesia. They confirmed earlier news, adding that all the generals had been captured, all the artillery had been lost and that they were retreating with the remnants of our corps. Such news obviously deprived us of any desire to march on Paris.

The city of Toul can be observed from a distance of 10 *verstas* [6.6 miles]. It is about four times smaller than Nancy and is surrounded by an earth rampart with bastions. Given a good garrison, it could have resisted us, but Napoleon left here only an invalid commandant with some 400 disabled troops, who surrendered upon the arrival of the first Prussian troops. The fortress was now garrisoned by the Spaniards whom [Napoleon] had left in Nancy but who defected to our side.

I was billeted with a Royalist, or to be precise, a former grenadier in the royal army who was discharged at the start of the Revolution. He told me many detailed stories about the Revolution and assured me that it was the English who incited Prince d'Orléans[10] and the rabble to kill King Louis XVI and his family, hoping to exploit France's domestic

---

10 Louis Philippe Joseph, Duc d'Orléans was a member of the Orléans branch of the House of Bourbon. Influenced by the ideas of the Enlightenment, he actively supported the French Revolution, adopted the name Philippe Égalité and voted for the execution of his cousin King Louis XVI.

turmoil to their advantage. The grenadier also told me that Napoleon was mistaken in seeking to destroy Russia's power when it would have been easier to defeat the English in alliance with the Russians. He believed that [Maximillian] Robespierre and [Honoré de] Mirabeau restored order and law, which Napoleon then perfected. He was also convinced that Napoleon's victories exalted France and enriched her through conquests. How saddened this veteran was to recall the gallantry and beauty of Napoleon's army on the eve of the Moscow Campaign![11] His face shone when he reminisced about the glorious past of the French nation, which had dominated Europe for the past twenty years. The French must now desire peace, he told me. Only a durable peace would revive the exhausted nation. 'Indeed,' I replied, 'Napoleon and his supporters are like soap bubbles, still sparkling and floating around but about to pop.'

The buildings of Toul were old and grimy, with all the shops closed. Notices posted on many homes indicated they were for sale or rent, reflecting the town's decline. The streets were littered with trash and filth, a testament to what seems to be a national habit of untidiness in France. The only noteworthy structure was the local cathedral, celebrated for its Gothic architecture and intricate stone carvings. Few residents remained in the town, but among them were idle young men who, by all rights, should have been conscripted by Napoleon. The size of the houses and the quality of their old but sturdy furniture led us to hope we might find abundant supplies in Toul. Alas, only misery and scarcity greeted us here. The desperate locals resorted to various tactics to extract even a single *sous* from the pockets of Russian officers – men turned to buffoonery, while the women resorted to…[12] Unfortunately for them, we had already spent all our money.

On one of the town's squares, a performance was taking place, featuring an assortment of animals and birds. For half a *franc*, a young French woman – beautiful, fresh, and healthy-looking – entertained the crowd with her lively explanations of the animals' names and traits. Her voice was clear and ringing, drawing the attention of even the most disinterested passersby. Of the three monkeys she presented, one was particularly attached to its mistress. At the mere sight of her, it would

---

11 The Russian Campaign of 1812.

12 Radozhitskii implies that women resorted to prostitution.

jump, yell, and play excitedly with a garlic bulb in its paws. Beyond the monkeys, her menagerie included a seal, an Alpine eagle, two eagle owls, a horned rooster, pheasants, a bear, a badger, and a wolf. Such was the merry company that accompanied this beautiful girl as she travelled freely through those turbulent times, collecting contributions from none other than the conquerors of France themselves.

[The town of Toul] also had a theatre, and judging from the placards, the opera *La Fausse Magie*[13] was performed there. But after the cheerless performance in Nancy, I had no desire to attend another show.

The village of Void [Void-Vacon] was located on the left side of the Meuse River, which was no wider than five *sazhens* [10 metres] at this location. The area was mountainous again, and our quarters were paltry once more. Here, I saw, for the first time, wooden jackboots attached to the saddle of a postal courier; if a horse falls, the boots protect the rider from any harm even if he has been galloping at full speed.

The road to Ligny [Ligny-en-Barrois] was mountainous. Approaching this town, we observed vast vineyards on the slope of the mountains on our right side. Between Toul and Ligny, the soil was sandy and rocky and should not have been very fertile, yet the local red wine was superb. A pleasant view of Ligny was presented as we came across the mountain. A river flowing through the valley and ancient towers on battlements added rather picturesque elements to this panorama. The town gates bore an inscription, 'À l'Impératrice Marie Louise' [To Empress Marie Louise]. It might have been that the locals resorted to this placard to spare the town from pillaging, but it was also said that the town belonged to Marshal Oudinot. The town was almost completely empty; all homes bore inscriptions 'à vendre' [for sale] and 'à louer' [for rent]; most windows had shattered glass. Earlier, there was a relentless combat here as Prince Sherbatov dislodged the French troops from the town. So, as a precaution, we were billeted two or three men per apartment. My friend and I found ourselves assigned to the home of a ninety-year-old *mademoiselle*[14] who greeted us with fear and apprehension. She served us as well as circumstances allowed, but we still did not trust the old witch [*staraya ved'ma*].

---

13 It was composed by André Grétry in 1775. Jean-Francois Marmontel was the librettist.

14 Radozhitskii is using this word ironically.

On 15 [27] February, we arrived at Saint-Dizier. The road from Ligny was a newly built paved road, a *chaussée*. It was cut into the hill slopes, and it surprised us with its builders' daring vision and skill in construction. Travelling along this road, our eyes feasted on countless pleasant sights, all worthy of an artist's brush.

For the third day already, we encountered Prussian wagons with numerous wounded; this time, men were coming from the battle at Champaubert [fought on 10 February].[15] While we were resting, a certain person, travelling with his wife and children in a carriage from Châlons[-sur-Marne], passed by us. Upon being stopped, he produced a document, signed by Count [Alexander] Langeron, identifying him as an Englishman. He told us that Châlons, where he resided, suffered greatly from the recent battle; that [the Prussian] General Yorck's attack resulted in half of the city being burned down before it surrendered; that Blücher's Army of Silesia suffered considerable losses, and that the main Allied army had retreated beyond Troyes to Chaumont. We occasionally encounter old bivouacs suggesting we are getting closer to the front line. Rumours claimed that the locals were ambushing and massacring the Prussians and that Blücher shot anyone caught with arms in hand and threatened entire families with exile to Siberia.

The city of Saint-Dizier was larger than Toul and stretched along the Marne River. Its streets were almost empty, with very few people, and even those hiding. Inside most homes, we found only women. At the apartment where I was billeted, I encountered three women, one of whom had her husband captured by the Russians; another had her brother in our captivity. They fed us well here, but we always had misgivings that they might harbour ill intentions toward us. Local houses bore no signs of orderliness, cleanliness, or neatness that we found in Germany. Entering one of these houses, I saw three women sitting near the fireplace, one of them reading aloud the French translation of the Russian book describing the life and exploits of Yemelyan Pugachev.[16]

---

15 The opening engagement of the Six Days' Campaign, the battle involved Napoleon's army and a small Russian corps commanded by Lieutenant General Count Zakhar Olsufiev. After putting up a good fight, the Russian corps was routed, losing half of its men. Champaubert is located almost 50 km/29 mi west of Châlons-en-Champagne.

16 Yemelyan Pugachev was the leader of the Yaik Cossacks who led a great popular insurrection during the reign of Catherine the Great in 1773-1775.

For me, it was both startling and gratifying to see them doing this. I understood that they wanted to read something to understand better the Russians, whom locals were beginning to perceive differently from what they had been told for so long... Rumours claimed that the French guerrillas surrounded us, so we remained constantly on guard: six of our cannons, protected by the Polotskii [Infantry] Regiment, moved ahead of our column; all transports were with the Ryazanskii [Infantry] Regiment in the middle, while another six guns, supported by the 33rd Jägers, stayed in the back awaiting our reserve parc.

The road to Vitry[-le-François] reminded us of Saxony in the environs of Leipzig: vast open plains dotted with groves of trees and white houses or picturesque estates. Unlike the area between Ligny and Saint-Dizier, where we saw hills, forests, sands, rocks, and numerous vineyards, we saw vast grain fields and little water here. On the approaches to Vitry, we encountered devastated villages, empty homes without doors, windows shattered, and, inside, all the property broken and scattered around. The locals were all hiding in the woods and occasionally appeared in groups some distance from the road.

The ancient Gothic church of the Holy Mother[17] added much grandeur to the city of Vitry, which was surrounded by an earthen rampart. A Prussian garrison of 3,000 men was stationed here. Napoleon stayed here on 14 [26] January before launching his campaign. Upon learning that the Russians were nearby, he ordered to drive them back to Saint-Dizier, intending to cut off Blücher from Nancy, and then attack the flank and rear of the main Allied army. But having learned that Blücher was at Brienne, Napoleon decided to attack there, and the ensuing battle, known as the battle of La Rothiere, proved unsuccessful for him.[18]

The city had very decent buildings. Its vast main square was filled with Prussian wagons. There were numerous residents, including local peasants gathered to repair fortifications because a military depot and supply magazines had been established in the city. During the night,

---

17 Collégiale Notre-Dame de Vitry-le-François is a collegiate church built in the 17th-century and is considered the largest classic church in the Marne.

18 The battle was fought on 1 February 1814, amidst a snowstorm that hampered both sides. Unable to break through the Allied positions, Napoleon ordered his men to fall to Lesmont where the French destroyed a bridge. Owing to the state of the roads and the lethargy within the Allied headquarters, no pursuit was attempted, resulting in the Battle of Champaubert which Napoleon won (see above).

the French guerrillas roamed around the fortress intending to get inside like wolves into a sheepfold. Our one half-company was deployed outside the fortress under protection of jägers while another was with the [reserve] parc and had not arrived yet.

I got such an excellent apartment that I had never seen before: two rooms with Chinese wallpapers and luxurious furniture, a spacious bed with a purple canopy, an antique bronze clock on a table, a fireplace with a mirror, and large Venetian windows leading out into a garden. The sun shone in my room all day long. I was served three excellent dishes and a bottle of superb wine at lunch. My host was a respected member of the municipal authority, whom I rarely saw except for occasional greetings, and barely had time to talk to him. I experienced the pleasure of domestic life and belongings for the first time, and caught myself thinking: 'Will I ever own an apartment like that, filled with possessions chosen to my taste. If only... How far I am from this moment! First, I must learn how to earn, then how to save, and, finally, how to manage and enjoy things. It is rather satisfying to live in an environment where our every wish is anticipated and fulfilled, where our self-esteem is constantly flattered. It is a very gratifying experience indeed! But how long will it last? Maybe tomorrow, I will be forced to sleep in rain, wind, and mud, and gnaw a coarse biscuit soaked in a dirty puddle of water! The lot of a military man is patience as he struggles with every passion and experience, be it hardship and pleasure, grief and delight, a perpetual fusion of good and bad. Fortunate is he who, amidst this chaos, endures all these trials and emerges with an unblemished heart!' Such were my thoughts as I lay on a beautiful double bed, wrapped in a satin blanket and my head resting on a round satin pillow with large tassels. But the other half of my bed was vacant – I stared at it for a while, saddened and feeling emptiness in my heart.

Count St. Priest received orders to command another 10,000 Prussians marching behind us. Together, we comprised a corps of some 14,000 men. He was supposed to unite this mass of men and advance to Reims. During our day of rest, I took a stroll through the town and across the Marne in the morning. The beautiful stone bridge had been destroyed by an explosion that collapsed its middle arch. Therefore, a parapet was built here, and a Prussian howitzer was deployed on the main road behind it. Beyond the bridge, there was a paved road lined with poplar trees. The road was covered with trees – about an *arshin* [28 inches or 71cm] wide and three *sazhens* [6 metres or 21 feet] in circumference, with deep furrows carved by their age – that have been tumbled like proud giants who have been conquered by a mightier hand. The French lumberjacks, acting rather aloofly, were busy cutting them down and shaping poles. 'What are you doing?' I asked them, hoping to see some anguish on their faces. 'Making palisades,' they replied coldly.

Upon hearing bells tolling, I rushed to the magnificent Cathedral of Notre Dame, which looked imposing on the outside. Entering it, I saw a sentry standing at the door while the vast space inside the building was filled with straw and hay. 'What is this?' I inquired. 'A supply store!' the soldier replied as he shrivelled up. I pitied these immoral Frenchmen. Will we continue to emulate these charming buffoons, these courteous flatterers, who, anticipating our words and thoughts, shower us with the most obsequious greetings while sharpening their daggers so at the first opportunity, they could strike them straight into our hearts, still bearing that same gentle smile?

Leaving the church, I went to the square. A battalion of R. [the Ryazanskii?] Regiment was conducting a parade or drill in a narrow space that was left in between transports. Idle Frenchmen and Prussians came from various directions to gawk at the cleanliness and beauty of the Russian soldiers' uniforms, appearance, and gallantry. The grenadier platoon was fit for the Guard: its men were cheerful, young, and healthy. Their commander was an excellent lad who observed everything and corrected everyone. Most bystanders watched with their mouths agape while some, wearing tailcoats, compared French soldiers' drill to the Russian and seemed to prefer the latter. There was indeed a significant difference between a Russian and a French soldier! No one can surpass a Russian soldier in patience and obedience. One must know Russian soldiers to be able to lead them to victory: Suvorov knew them, and he did wonders with them; that's why in his hands, a bayonet is a Russian lad while a French bullet is a fool.[19]

A local prison housed six French villagers who had mistreated our couriers and stragglers. The order had been given to shoot them.

On 18 February [2 March], we arrived at Châlons. Once again, we were in a major provincial town in the Champagne-Pouilleuse region that was

---

19 Radozhitskii refers to Suvorov's famous saying, "The bullet is a fool, but the bayonet is a good lad."

famous for its sparkling wine; yet, some people kept saying that the best wine was actually produced in the Provence region. This city was once a fortress, which could still be seen in surviving stone walls and towers. Between Vitry and Châlons we observed signs of terrifying devastation everywhere. Crowds of unfortunate locals wandered in the woods or hid amidst the ruins. At the entrance to Châlons, an entire suburb had been destroyed and presented a view of homes without roofs, with straw, rags, burned timber, shattered glass, bricks, and ashes scattered all around. The city walls were broken through in several places, and palisades were erected in front of the city gates. Marshal Macdonald wanted to defend this city, but the Prussians, led by General Yorck, set the town on fire with incendiary shells, and the residents begged Macdonald to surrender the city on condition that it would be spared. Nonetheless, the Prussians rushed in and plundered it. The impoverished residents walked fearfully amidst the ruins, many crying bitterly that they could no longer recognize their homes... What a miserable fate this war had cast on them!

Inside the walls, the town is rather ancient, and some buildings appeared on the verge of collapsing; streets were uneven and crooked. The main square housed a vast, magnificent building where municipal and departmental government, as well as authorities handling military affairs, resided. Four stone lions stood at the entrance to a spacious staircase, and beautiful statues adorned its walls; portraits of distinguished men born in Châlons hung at the entrance into a large hall. Numerous rooms were filled with writing desks[...], and crowds of people were going back and forth everywhere: French frockcoats and round hats mixed with military uniforms and blue coats; one could frequently catch a glimpse of female bonnets or grenadier mustaches sticking from under the shakos and pushing through the crowd. The best of these rooms were decorated with magnificent paintings. I stopped in front of one showing a winter landscape and, examining it, almost felt cold. I admired a painting showing chained Prometheus being tormented by a kite, and observed, with great pleasure, a sleeping Eros who was so lovely that I was ready to kiss him myself. I was amazed by the agility of a jäger who carried away a fowl and smiled to a Jew who was looking out of a tavern window... This was a veritable feast for my eyes, which have long been starved for such sights.

Soldiers bivouacked near the empty church in the suburbs. What a sight it was! The former place of worship now had fires burning before its entrance and kettles cooking meat; nearby were stored muskets while the tired soldiers were sleeping next to the church wall. Not far from them were others, with pipes in their mouths and airing their shirts over the fire or warming their backs. What a sight! How cruel a war can be!

Upon reaching the apartment I had been assigned, I found one grief-stricken monsieur and several mademoiselles and madams sitting around a large table. Glancing at my billet, an old lady quickly stood up and led me to the second floor, where I found a large apartment with many beds. 'Why are there so many beds?' I wondered as I came down to the ground floor. After lunch, one of the ladies asked me, 'Will there be many officers in town today?' – 'You will see them yourself when you will witness the arrival of four thousands of our men.' – 'Oh, you will have a splendid spectacle then.' – 'What is it?' I inquired. 'This madam is a theatre director,' responded another woman, pointing to a lady. 'And she wants to stage an opera to entertain Russian officers.' 'Oh, I see,' I replied, realizing the nature of the company I found myself in. 'So how many officers do you think will come to the theatre?' the theatre director asked me again. 'What difference does it make,' interjected monsieur. 'Indeed. Just stage a cheerful opera and do not overcharge for it,' was my response as I left the room. When I returned, the hostess introduced me to a woman who had lived in Russia for fifteen years and had the honour of entertaining St. Petersburg high society in the French theatre. This lady showered me with questions about Russia, but I excused myself on the grounds of fatigue and promised to talk to her after the dinner.

Later that night I had the pleasure of seeing all these individuals in their miserable theatre. There were just four musicians and about twenty people in the audience, with me sitting in the front row. Both plays – first *L'épreuve villageoise*, followed by *La famille d'innocens* – were poorly performed; the music was dreadful. Two actresses and one actor sang decently, but the other actor kept roaring with a hoarse bass voice. I did not expect to find such a pitiable theatre at Châlons. But it should have been expected – the French had no time for entertainment, and whoever was the best, most cheerful, and lively was then carrying a musket in Napoleon's army.

We remained here for another day, waiting for the entire corps to concentrate here. I stayed with the actresses. All around me were people learning their roles, singing, dancing, and performing. Somebody else in my place would have considered himself the happiest person and might have courted favours from these beauties. But on the first day I pretended to be a simpleton and kept observing everyone. I noticed that the faces of actresses were attractive only by the candlelight and with theatrical makeup on them. But on a sunny day and up close, they looked frightening [*strashnymi*] – cold, weary, exhausted by their nocturnal exertions, with eyes that were drained and always cast down, towards pockets… I must admit, none of them looked enticing to me. "You only need to knock on the doors directly across from your room; they belong to your delightful neighbour," the hostess said with a glint in her eye. "Knock and the doors will open for you." "Knock? With what, a gold coin?" I replied wryly. The thought of love at the price of gold repels me, for it denies me any opportunity to express myself in such relations. The hostess' daughter, a lovely girl about thirteen years old, frequently visited me inquiring if she could help. I only welcomed her with polite greetings, which she received with pleasure.

A deaf girl was at our lieutenant colonel's apartment. She was the daughter of Count Girancourt who had seven children but only three of them were not disabled, while the rest were either blind or deaf. It was even said that one of his daughters was born with a calf-like head and licked herself with a long tongue, like animals do; she supposedly lived until age twenty-four and wanted to find a husband, going as far as to chase after men, so her father was forced to place her at a monastery, where she fell asleep in front of the fireplace and burned to death. There is a convent for educating girls at Châlons.

[Radozhitskii proceeds to discuss various plays performed at a local theatre.]

[After several days spent in Châlons], we received the news that the French troops, assisted by locals, captured our Prince N. with 380 Bashkirs and 150 jägers in Reims. So, our corps' advance guard, consisting of the Polotskii [Infantry] Regiment, four cannon, and two squadrons of dragoons, under the command of General Emmanuel, was ordered to depart for Reims... Farewell to pleasures – no more warm apartments, soft beds, or delicious meals! Goodbye, beautiful women! The time had come for soldiers to return to the fields and smoky bivouacs, where they would be called upon to perform a different kind of theatre before the eyes of the world. With fires burning and a martial spirit coursing through their ranks, the troops found a grim vitality amidst the ruins of devastated homes. A wild delight animated men as they tended kettles of boiling porridge around the bonfires or smoked pipes by the fireplace inside burned-out houses, surrounded by the wreckage of war. Everything was infused with war, a monstrous, all-consuming war!

Chapter III

From Reims to Laon

On 22 February [6 March], we found ourselves bivouacked just 12 *verstas* [8 miles/12.8 km] from Reims, in the already pillaged village of Bonnome. Everything that had escaped the initial looting – save for the stone walls and roof tiles – was now fed to our bonfires. Oh, the tragic misfortunes of war! How they turn once-pleasant villages into mere wreckage and cemeteries! Places where peaceful civilians, surrounded by their families, once lived contentedly, far removed from the ambitions of powerful men, were now engulfed by the thunderous roar of cannons that spread death in their wake. Terrified and helpless, the villagers fled to the woods and mountains, abandoning their homes to the mercy of ravenous foreign soldiers, who brought fire and destruction to those who, in peacetime, might have been their closest friends.

The road from Châlons to Reims wound through a valley that resembled the steppes of our native Elizavetgrad province. The soil was heavy with limestone, making it unsuitable for grain cultivation but ideal for the grapevines that produce the sparkling wine that has made the Champagne region famous – and, some might say, enriched it at the expense of Russians. The fields were still grey and soggy, with no sign of grass anywhere.

The following morning, at six o'clock, we broke camp and began our march. We left our supply trains at Sillery and advanced in battle formation towards Reims. Our advance guard, which had approached the city the day before, was greeted with cannon fire. Our force numbered no more than 6,000, including Prussian troops, but Reims was defended by a weak garrison under the command of General Corbineau. So Count St. Priest, confident in the strength of our forces, decided to launch an assault to capture the town.

About four *verstas* [2.6 miles/4.3 km] from Reims, we caught sight of the town's bell towers and heard gunfire from our advance guard.

As we approached to within artillery range, our troops halted behind a hill that concealed the fortress. Count St. Priest took the time to survey the area to prepare for the assault. Following his example, I decided to conduct my own reconnaissance. My experience had taught me that an artillery officer, more than anyone else, must carefully examine the terrain in front of and behind his position to make informed decisions about where to position cannons, how to move them, and where to retreat if necessary.

Riding along the Châlons road, I quickly ascended the hill that concealed the town and, from the windmills, observed the vast panorama of Reims stretching for some three *verstas* [2 miles/3.2 km] in the valley below. The rooftops of houses, shrouded in a blue-tinted haze, were interspersed with bell towers and church spires. The most prominent feature was the great cathedral where the French kings were once crowned; it loomed like a two-headed giant, towering over all the other buildings. Beyond it, I could make out other tall and beautiful structures, the ruins of ancient triumphal arches, and a Roman amphitheatre. The town was encircled by a stone wall dating back to the age of knights, with a deep moat at its base. Cannons protruded from embrasures, and I noticed people – among them, women bearing arms – gathered around them.

As I traversed the hill, I inadvertently came within musket range, but the French did not fire, allowing me to continue my observations undisturbed. Reims appeared more expansive than Châlons and as large as Nancy. Beyond the town, on the far side of the Vesle River, a rolling plain dotted with villages extended toward the hills covered with vineyards. I spotted numerous cavalry units scattered across this landscape; it was Tettenborn[1] with our Cossacks.

As I returned from the hill, I noticed a dragoon officer, accompanied by a trumpeter, making his way toward the town as a truce-bearer on behalf of Count St. Priest. The officer's left arm was wrapped with a scarf, and in his right hand, he held a piece of paper high above his head so that it could be seen from the town walls. The two men rode up to the Châlons gate, followed by a few curious onlookers from our side who kept their distance. When they were within pistol-shot range

---

1 Friedrich Karl Freiherr von Tettenborn (1778-1845), Austrian officer who served in the Russian army during the 1813-1814 Campaigns.

of the fortress, the trumpeter blew his trumpet, but no one responded. Hoping this was just a matter of French aloofness, the truce-bearer edged closer and began speaking to those on the town wall while displaying the paper. Meanwhile, more of our soldiers gathered, eagerly watching what would happen next. Suddenly, a cannon fired from the town wall, and its projectile whizzed past our ears! In an instant, the truce-bearer, trumpeter, and all the onlookers scattered, and our troops began advancing toward the fortress.

Just as I moved forward, a hare ran across the road. 'Your Honour, this is a bad omen,' the nearest cannonier told me while others began to shout and drive the hare further away from us. Old mustached artillerymen told me that we would most certainly suffer some misfortune because the hare crossed our path. 'Misfortunes will befall those who believe it,' I replied to them and began moving my cannon up to the windmills. Just then an enemy cannonball, fired from the fortress, buzzed over our heads. It did not touch us but proved to be deadly for the Prussian column that was marching behind us; it claimed more than ten men, injuring six in the legs, the rest in the head and many were simply thrown to the ground. Thus, the hare foretold death for the Prussians, not us.

The Ryazanskii regiment, supported by four cannons and two squadrons of dragoons, moved to the right, attacking the suburbs from the Charleville road. Simultaneously, the Polotskii regiment, accompanied by four Prussian howitzers, marched directly toward the windmills, leaving the Châlons gate on their left. An intense firefight erupted on both sides. The Prussian howitzers, however, did not last long. The French, firing accurately from the embrasures, managed to kill a company commander, along with several men and horses, causing the unfortunate howitzers to become disordered and retreat hastily. I was then ordered to advance with two licornes[2] and two guns to replace them.

My previous reconnaissance proved invaluable as I positioned our cannons on a reverse slope, effectively concealing them. While we fired canisters at the town walls, the enemy guns, lacking obvious

---

2 Licorne (edinorog in Russian) is the French term for a type of Russian artillery piece that combined the features of howitzers and traditional cannon. It was a muzzle-loading howitzer that had a longer barrel, giving its shells a flatter trajectory but longer range.

targets and seeing only the heads of my cannoniers, the tips of our gun barrels, and the puffs of smoke rising after each shot, could not cause any damage to my crews; their cannonballs mostly flew over us, and I only lost one crew member. The windmills sheltering our artillery bore the brunt of the damage. To our right, near a stone mill, stood Count St. Priest, who, exposing himself to danger, bravely surveyed our assault through his spyglass. The attack commenced around 10:30 a.m. and seemed poised for a quick resolution until around 3,000 enemy cavalry appeared unexpectedly on the road from Soissons; moving in a dense column, they hastily descended from the heights on that side of the town, where the residents heralded their arrival with ringing bells. Their appearance disrupted our assault and compelled us to make an orderly retreat to Sillery where we hoped to entice the enemy into open terrain. However, the French halted their pursuit, content with reclaiming the heights that we previously held in front of the town.

That night, we found a respite amid the ruins of Sillery. Anything flammable was burned at our bivouacs; there were almost no residents left, and the only locals we encountered were a few elderly men in blue coats, wandering wretchedly among the smoldering ruins. Our lads discovered a cellar containing nearly 30,000 bottles of champagne, which we proceeded to consume along with sixty remaining barrels of wine. I watched soldiers roll out these barrels, break their lids, and cheerfully gulp down wine; the soldiers indulged themselves heartily, some even cooking porridge in champagne. We joked that this devastation would surely double champagne prices in Russia, and that for all the wine we consumed during the war, the French would make us pay twice over in peacetime.

Between 24 and 28 February [8–12 March], for four whole days, we held our position without engaging the French, who were stationed merely eight *verstas* [5.3 miles/8.5km] away. The Count [St. Priest] awaited Prussian reinforcements from Châlons, intending to concentrate his forces and take the town by a formal assault. During this lull, we prepared for the upcoming battle by assembling fascines and ladders, while maintaining a cautious distance from the town. And so it was that the French did not dare to foray out of town while we avoided attacking before completing our preparations for the assault.

What do soldiers do on the eve of the battle? Some sleep, others rest, and still others clean weapons; most officers occupy themselves playing cards. All this takes place amidst billowing bivouacs, in or around straw huts or amidst ruins of burned-out buildings, thus creating a surreal, almost hellish, scene. Here, detached from the societal shackles, a soldier experiences a profound freedom of spirit, embracing the present, disregarding the past, and not thinking of the future. His emotions seemingly transcend the physical boundaries of this world – the proximity to death heightens his disdain for danger; with a wild delight, he observes the smoldering ruins of his enemy's houses and contemplates the corpses of the fallen enemy soldiers of whose demise he is the chief cause; and the more he observes this, the more eager he becomes to confront fate and thus become a victim of his own unrestrained ambition.

On 28 February [12 March] we were at Reims, transitioning abruptly from desolation to luxury. Such are the vicissitudes of military life! Once again, we found ourselves cast from the smoldering ruins into beautifully arranged rooms; instead of porridge and animal joints, we enjoyed French sauces and spilled champagne from our glasses! The city, weakly defended, fell to us quickly and with minimal losses due to the prudent arrangements of Count St. Priest. Everything was prepared the day before. We approached the city around two o'clock in the morning [on 12 March]. The first jäger columns, commanded by General Bistrom,[3] moved to the right towards the Charleville suburbs. The second column, consisting of the Polotskii regiments and my four cannon, under the command of General Pilar,[4] proceeded to the Châlons gate. The third column, comprising of the Prussians under General von Jagow,[5] advanced along the opposite bank of the Vesle river, along the road from Epernay. A general assault was scheduled to start before sunrise, around five o'clock in the morning. However, our column was delayed due to the mistake of a particular cavalry general who stumbled onto the path of the second column and whom we took for an enemy force. Peering through the darkness, our General P. [Pilar?] observed some

---

3 Adam Otto Wilhelm von Bistrom (Bistram) (1774-1828).

4 Georg Ludwig Pilar von Pilchau (1767-1830).

5 Friedrich Wilhelm Christian Ludwig von Jagow (1771-1857)

cavalry moving before us and immediately ordered us to stop and open fire. Before determining that these were the Chernigovskii Dragoons, we remained uncertain about what to do next and thus approached the city only after sunrise. By then, the French already knew our intentions and greeted us with artillery fire.

I quickly moved my cannon directly to the windmills, where they had previously been deployed, and was the first to return fire. I was reinforced with two heavy cannon and two Prussian howitzers. My entire battery of eight guns unleashed a fierce bombardment. The force of the discharging cannon shook the ground and deafened us; smoke billowed all around while our projectiles struck the embrasures and flew over the town walls and the roofs of the houses. Four enemy cannon, deployed in embrasures against us, fought back but very feebly. They did not realize that all our efforts were just for show since this attack, from the direction of Châlons, was just a diversion. Half an hour later, we saw, to our right, jägers shouting 'Hurrah' and charging in open order directly to the city walls. Moments later, the enemy guns fell silent, and the enemy disappeared from the walls. Our jägers climbed the fortifications and scattered around, some of them running directly in front of us. Seeing them passing through the embrasures, we initially mistook them for the French and fired a few cannonballs before the running troops stopped and waved their hands. General P. then told us proudly, 'Cease fire! They are asking for mercy!' After learning that our first column had broken into the city, General P. led us towards the Châlons gate. The soldiers charged, shouting, towards it, but encountered an obstacle. The accursed French had brought so much earth and rubble to block the gates that we spent nearly two hours removing it to clear the road. A ditch dug across the road also delayed the advance of our artillery. Meanwhile, some infantry officers and soldiers crawled through the breach near the gates to enter the city and scattered to look for the enemy inside homes, shops, wine cellars, and stables, from where they soon returned with trophies, which belonged to them by right of conquest.

Despite our efforts, we were unable to clear the Châlons gates. So, I was ordered to move my cannon through the Charleville suburbs, where the city was protected by a weak wall and palisade, which the jägers broke through without resorting to ladders. In this part of the city, the streets were jammed with transports. If the French had a stronger garrison and defended the town properly, we would not have seized it so easily. Our assault produced almost no casualties; the Prussians, however, lost about twenty men. In the Soissons suburbs, on this side of the town, we saw several French and Prussian corpses, men who had been killed in a cavalry melee that took place here: the former were caught trying to escape from the town while the latter sought to prevent them. Most of the French garrison managed to depart downstream on the Vesle River, though the Prussians sabred and drowned many of the [French] lancers. We captured about 200 French wounded, including a general, and found another 2,000 sick soldiers at local hospitals. We also took eight bronze cannons that were abandoned on the city walls. The [French] garrison included many armed civilians.

Entering Reims, we found the streets deserted, the residents hidden in cellars and lumber-rooms and fearing imminent pillaging and murder. We naturally could not ensure that none of the victorious troops would enter homes and shops to claim whatever was to their liking. Several Frenchmen later complained to me about this, but I only shrugged my shoulders and told them that I could do nothing since such was the reality of war. All our infantry concentrated in the city's main square, where I brought my cannon. The streets were soon crowded with our troops, and the atmosphere quickly shifted from tension to celebration. Plenty of clamour, movement, and joy everywhere; men congratulated each other on the successful turn of events. At last, the city residents slowly emerged from hiding and the victors began to disperse to their billets. The Prussians moved out of the city to the nearby villages.

In the afternoon, I took a leisurely walk around the city. I encountered a municipal official, accompanied by the rhythmic beating of a Russian drum, walking through the streets while reading Count St. Priest's proclamation at various street intersections. French men dressed in blue coats and wooden shoes, along with women adorned in bonnets, congregated to hear the announcements. They were commanded to surrender all weapons immediately, along with any remaining French troops. "We are all prisoners of war, including our women!" exclaimed one Frenchman emphatically.

The town of Reims is quite large, and its buildings are tall and well built. The front of the [famed] Cathedral, built in Gothic architecture, is decorated with exquisite and skillful carvings that resemble lace. On the main square there is the statue of [King] Henry IV, with a pool and fountains around it. The square is surrounded by three- and four-storey buildings without columns or frontons; the yellow stones from which they have been built have darkened from old age. There were numerous shops and market stalls, but that day, they were all closed. At the corners of buildings and street junctions, proclamations were calling upon the French people to arms and resistance; some of these posters claimed that the Allies had been defeated, and that for their complete defeat, every Frenchman had to take up arms. There was also a broadsheet with the news of the defeat of our 9th Corps... I was infuriated at this sight and tore it down at once. A Frenchman, who passed by then, noticed my action and said laughingly, 'Misérable Napoléon!'

Upon returning home that evening, I was informed that General Pilar, the commander of the second column, had been inquiring about me. I decided it was my duty to meet with him. He welcomed me warmly, expressing his gratitude for the commendable performance of my battery at the mill. He also mentioned that he had put forward my name for the Order of St. Anna of the second class. I respectfully bowed and left, buoyed by the prospect of receiving such an honour. However, in our rapid conquest and subsequent billeting throughout the city, we were blissfully unaware of the sinister schemes that preoccupied the French. It was only the next day that we became aware of their machinations, which led us to Festieux on March 2 [14]. There we stood, in battle formation on soggy ground, bracing for the enemy at a distance of 35 *verstas* [about 23 miles] from Reims and ten *verstas* [about 6.6 miles] from Laon. Such are the unpredictable twists and turns in the life of a soldier!

[Here is how it happened.] Yesterday [March 13], that is the day after the capture of Reims, Count St. Priest came up with a dazzling idea of gathering all Russian forces outside the city, between the roads to Charleville[6] and Neufchatel[7] where they were deployed in a large square to hold a *Te Deum* service to celebrate our victory. After the parade and ceremonial procession, the regiments returned to their

---

6 Probably Charleville-Mézieres.

7 Probably Neufchatel-sur-Aisne.

quarters in the city suburbs, except for the Ryazanskii [Infantry] Regiment, which marched to the city square to assume guard duty. Meanwhile, I joined Captain Zhemchuzhnikov and Pioneer Captain Belusovich for a Mass at the cathedral church. We were struck by the immense size of the church, capable of accommodating an entire brigade, and its ornately crafted architecture. A long series of columns divided the central part of the cathedral from its walls, and between these columns, in front of the altar, there was an elevated area where a royal throne was placed during coronations. Nearby, solemn monks seated by the altar blew silver trumpets at intervals, producing an eerie and subdued sound. The altar itself was simple yet accessible. As I explored the interior of this magnificent cathedral, I was particularly captivated by a large painting of the Crucifixion, noted for its detailed depiction of muscle anatomy and the interplay of light and shadow. The French also pointed out a marble tombstone intricately carved with scenes of wild lion hunts… They assured us that the cathedral had stood here for over a millennium.[8] Unfortunately, its interior decorations had suffered significant damage during the Revolution. At the front of the sanctuary, large round stained-glass windows cast a kaleidoscope of colourful images that delighted all who viewed them.

As we immersed ourselves in the atmosphere, Count St. Priest, accompanied by Lieutenant-Colonel Malinovskii, entered the cathedral. Malinovskii soon excused himself, while St. Priest lingered to engage in conversation with several ladies seated on chairs before the altar. After a few moments, the Count summoned Captain Zhemchuzhnikov, imparted some instructions, and sent him on his way. Curious, Belusovich and I moved closer to the altar, now encircled by numerous women clad in black dresses and bonnets, each holding a prayer book. The religious service proceeded with solemnity and strict decorum. Just as I settled in to observe the Mass and listen to the monks' muted chanting, accompanied by the sounds of violins, organs, and the somewhat off-key serpents,[9] Malinovskii reappeared. He quietly relayed a message to Count St. Priest, who sent him away

---

8 The original church was indeed established in the fifth century, but the great cathedral was built in the thirteenth century.

9 A brass wind instrument.

once more before resuming his discussion, leaning casually against a chair while speaking with a woman. Suddenly, I was summoned and given a command to deploy my cannon at once. Confused and alarmed by this unexpected order, I could not help but suspect that something secretive was unfolding, perhaps a deception or a covert operation was in motion.

As I stepped out of the cathedral, the streets were engulfed in chaos, with soldiers hurrying to and fro. It dawned on me then – the French must be near. And indeed they were – at the city gates! Being the duty officer for my company that day, I swiftly instructed my feldwebel[10] to assemble all our men and horses at the parc, strategically located outside the city on the hill slope near the Soissons gate. This position meant the French would only see our guns after approaching this suburb. Amidst the urgency, I hastened to my apartment, where I found my friend, Baron von Schlippenbach. Our young and attentive hostess had prepared a splendid lunch, with the table laden with champagne bottles and an array of sumptuous dishes that tempted all our senses – a truly mesmerizing sight. However, my friend and I were preoccupied with thoughts about the looming threat and, I must admit, were fearful that the food might be poisoned. So instead of partaking, we left abruptly, but not before instructing our batman to pack some pies and wine for the road. I then made my way to the artillery parc. Beyond the gates, a fierce skirmish unfolded as the jägers, positioned in front of our parc, engaged the advancing enemy cavalry. General Bistrom had ordered four guns to be moved forward, but our artillery crews, pampered by their generous hosts, were too sluggish in their preparations, a foreboding sign of impending trouble.

With no other officers in sight, I rushed back into the city and encountered Baron von Schlippenbach leading his two cannons, fully prepared, out of the city. As he ascended the hill in front of the parc, he faced a column of French cavalry but managed to check their advance with his initial volleys. Captain Zhemchuzhnikov, commanding four guns, took position on the left side of the Epernay road while I, with another four cannons and accompanied by our company commander,

---

10 Feldwebel was a rank of non-commissioned officer.

Lieutenant-Colonel Timofeev, advanced along the road between the two main thoroughfares.

Upon realising their attempt at a surprise attack had failed, the French began to retreat, allowing a clear battle line to form. Along the Soissons road, the Ryazanskii Regiment, supported by Prussian howitzers, successfully pushed the French forces back. Jägers scattered in front of them while two squadrons of Leib-Hussars and Leib-Dragoons, joined by a squadron of Prussians, formed a separate detachment under the command of General Albrecht, positioning themselves between my cannons. To our left, on a hill, were two battalions of Prussian infantry and Schlippenbach with his two guns. Although the French continued to fall back, our troops refrained from pursuing them too aggressively and instead halted about three *verstas* [approximately 3.2 kilometres, almost 2 miles] from the city. Flankers from both sides kept up their skirmishes.

At that time, our forces were spread along every road leading to the city but acted with a perplexing lack of urgency. The deployment of our troops, particularly on the side facing the enemy attack, was minimal. Rumours circulated that we were up against Marshal Marmont and his 15,000 men, who had received strict orders from Napoleon to seize the city at any cost. We, however, dismissed these rumours with laughter.

By three o'clock in the afternoon, our troops remained poised and calm near the city. The enemy had a substantial cavalry presence. Suddenly, we observed puffs of smoke from artillery fire in the distant hills ahead of the enemy line. This marked the capture of the two unfortunate Prussian battalions and their howitzers, who had been quartered in the village of Rosnay following our capture of Reims, and were now completely overrun by the French. Additionally, the French captured three more battalions near the city itself, and only half a battalion managed to retreat to my cannons. It was at this point that we fully grasped the French intentions. We were exceedingly fortunate that our regiments had not been dispersed in various villages but were instead congregated that morning for the *Te Deum* service. There were allegations that the city mayor had covertly informed Marmont of our positions, leading to his arrest and subsequent confinement under strict guard, pending execution post-battle. Had we been slightly more negligent, the French could have easily overwhelmed us piecemeal as we lay scattered in villages. This incident underscores the peril of quartering so close to an enemy force. While the intention was to provide better care for the soldiers during a harsh time of year, this cautious approach ultimately proved disadvantageous.

The French made limited manoeuvres. Their entire cavalry force pressed against our left flank, leaving the Soissons road almost completely empty. With artillery fire ceasing on both sides, I seized the opportunity to survey our deployment. The apparent vulnerability of our position on this side of the city suggested that either we did not plan to maintain our positions for long or that the French were reluctant to launch a significant assault in this direction. Most of our troops were on the opposite side of the city. I went to the right flank, where Count St. Priest and his entourage stood near the Prussian artillery. Upon my arrival, I overheard a hussar, sent by Count Wittgenstein, seeking instructions from St. Priest. The Count responded calmly, "Be patient, lad. I will call you when everything settles down."

As the situation on the left flank evolved, Count St. Priest observed the enemy cavalry's manoeuvres and decided to inspect the situation personally. Driven by curiosity, I accompanied him and witnessed the French chasseurs à cheval, adorned in their distinctive bearskin caps, adeptly evading our Cossacks whom they lured back into ambushes and captured. Upon returning to my cannon, my attention was caught by a significant number of troops emerging on the road from Soissons. I speculated that these might be reinforcements from Blücher's Army of Silesia, based in Laon, coming to our aid. With both sides mobilizing, I hastened back to my position, ready to engage.

Calmness is often a prelude to chaos on the battlefield, and our experience was no different. That afternoon, just as we were easing into conversations about our quarters and nearly drifting off, we were jolted awake by a sudden assault at four o'clock. The initial thrust came on the Soissons road, with a cavalry column charging at the Ryazanskii Regiment stationed on our right flank and which was closest to us. Under the valiant leadership of Colonel Skobelev,[11] the Ryazanskii soldiers repelled two fierce enemy attacks, maintaining cohesive battalion fire and receiving solid support from our batteries. However, the enemy cavalry then pivoted towards our left flank, replaced by an eight-gun battery that advanced swiftly and unleashed a barrage of cannonballs

---

11 Ivan Nikitich Skobelev (1778-1849).

and explosive shells upon us. The enemy's artillery presence quickly increased to thirty cannons, overwhelming our positions. Meanwhile, my four cannons, positioned centrally, were reinforced by six Prussian howitzers, setting the stage for a gruelling artillery duel that spread death and destruction indiscriminately. Shells kept exploding with hellish shrieks around us - one splinter whizzing past mere inches from my head while another struck our company commander, Lieutenant-Colonel Timofeev, in the leg, forcing his evacuation. Amidst this chaos, some of our artillerymen faltered, prompting me to dismount and take personal command of the cannon fire. The relentless enemy barrage eventually proved too much for the Prussian howitzers, prompting them to abandon their positions. Our entire line then began a hasty retreat, and soon our left flank was overwhelmed. As a half-battalion of Prussians near my cannon prepared to withdraw, I urged their officer to stand firm, exclaiming, "Courage, Kameraden! Französisch kaputt!" Yet, despite my encouragement, he shook his head while his soldiers, evading enemy cannonballs, turned left and marched off without a command.

As our positions crumbled, two squadrons of Guard cavalry from General Albrecht's detachment passed through our battery, leaving behind *flanquers* who were hard-pressed by the advancing enemy. Even as French cavalry crossed the stream in front of my battery and closed in menacingly, I resolved to hold my ground with four cannons and provided cover for the retreat of the remaining city troops. It was only when Captain Zhemchuzhnikov arrived and insisted that we vacate the position that I decided to move. As I did, I spotted some infantry charging towards the Soissons gate, with the French cavalry hot on their heels. To avoid capture, I directed my guns towards the gates amidst a mad rush of troops. To the left of me, coming from the suburbs, were the Prussian howitzers that the French were about to overtake. Anticipating a terrible misfortune if I allowed the Prussian artillery to get to the city before me, I rushed forward, seized the reins of the lead horse of the first howitzer and, brandishing my sabre, commanded, 'Halt! Der Teufel!' The howitzers stopped, which allowed me to move my cannons across the bridge just in time. This was a desperate move but if I had not done this, my own battery would have been captured by the French, who were already attacking the Prussian gun crews. As it was, my men escaped while all that remained behind, including the entire Prussian artillery, my caisson, and one cannon deployed with skirmishers fell into French hands.

I barely managed to escape across the bridge into the city amid shouts, shoving, pushing, musket fire, and the swish of sabres wielded by French troops in red and green. Never had I witnessed such tumult, chaos, or peril. Those who could not reach the bridge in time attempted to ford the river, and tragically, some drowned. Count St. Priest, critically wounded early in the attack by a cannonball that severed his shoulder, was moved across the river but his grave injury triggered our disorganized retreat. As the French reached the bridge, General Bistrom ordered the city gates shut and, with his jägers defending the approaches, managed to prevent the enemy from entering the city.

As I manoeuvred my cannon through a wide street, a sudden uproar erupted behind me. Our dragoons, with sabres drawn, thundered down the street, their shouts of "They are here! They are already here!" injecting terror into all of us. This alarm spurred a frenzied exodus from the city, as we scattered into the surrounding fields in desperate disarray. The scene was chaotic: an artillery limber raced alongside a sutler's wagon; batmen, burdened with bags, dodged among the galloping dragoons. Some fled toward Laon, others went to Rethel, and a few – to Châlons. I found myself with seven cannons heading to Châlons, after noticing that the Polotskii Regiment was left behind at the Châlons gate, presumably to cover our retreat. As the old proverb goes, fear has a hundred eyes.[12] This widespread panic, it turned out, was triggered by a rather minor incident. During the retreat, a lone French cavalryman had inadvertently found himself amidst our dragoons and slipped through the gates with them. Initially, he concealed his identity with a cloak, quietly blending in until someone detected his presence. Our dragoons engaged him, but he resisted fiercely; the leading dragoons, hearing the commotion and mistakenly believing that the French forces had penetrated the city defences and attacked them, fled and sparked the alarm that led to the widespread panic.

As night descended, I noticed that only a few of our troops were retreating along the Châlons road, prompting me to turn back and head through the Charleville suburbs, where the bulk of our forces were

---

12 U strakha glaza veliki, literally, "fear has big eyes", meaning that people who are afraid of something often overestimate the danger or tend to see the danger everywhere.

still attempting to escape. The city gates in this area were protected by jägers and four guns from our company. As a sole officer, I guided seven cannons towards the Laon road where we came upon a cavalry outpost to the left and two resting Prussian battalions in a vale to the right. To the far left, near the river, was an open area where enemy bonfires flickered in the distance. As the artillery fire subsided with the setting sun, sporadic musket shots still pierced the evening quiet. While observing the enemy bonfires to my left, I grew concerned about a potential cavalry attack and proceeded with caution. The Prussians informed me that many Russians had taken the road to Berry-au-Bac. Shortly thereafter, I ran into the brigade of Prince Gurielov,[13] who dispatched the Rylskii [Infantry] Regiment to provide protection for my artillery. Alone and vulnerable, my fear of falling into French hands intensified to the point where I mistakenly identified our dragoon outposts as enemy positions. However, my concerns were not baseless. As I neared the village of Saint-Thierry, musket fire erupted behind me, forcing me to halt. Panic ensued as shouts of 'The French! The French!' rang out, and everyone began to flee once again. True to my fears, French cavalry had indeed crossed a nearby rivulet, seized control of the road, and launched an attack on the infantry. They inflicted heavy casualties on many idle Prussians and captured their three howitzers. Our infantrymen greeted the enemy with a volley that effectively checked the French assault. Miraculously, for the second time that day, I managed to escape with my cannons intact, narrowly avoiding capture or worse amidst the chaos and confusion of the battlefield.

I struggled to comprehend the extent of chaos that reigned within the city. Under the cover of darkness, the French managed to repair a bridge at the village of Saint-Brice [Saint-Brice-Courcelles] and sent their lancers across the river in a sudden assault on our troops stationed at the Laon gate. This attack was devastatingly effective – the lancers slaughtered many defenders and forced their way into the city, causing our jägers and the Polotskii [Infantry] Regiment to withdraw in haste along the Châlons road. As a result of this bold manoeuvre, the French captured Reims from the north and took prisoner everyone who had not managed to flee the city in time. Among those captured were Captain

---

13 Ivan Stepanovich Gurielov commanded the 1st Brigade of the 23rd Division.

Zhemchuzhnikov and Lieutenant Katomin from our company. Amidst this turmoil, I also lost track of our wounded company commander, adding to the confusion and uncertainty of the moment.

As various transports, cavalry, and infantry began to pass us at night, I urged my crews to hasten their pace. The din of shouts and noise only intensified our pervasive sense of terror. We spent most of the night moving and took a quick respite around a bonfire, where many of our scattered troops had also congregated. We then joined a small detachment led by General Panchulidzev,[14] which made its way to Berry-au-Bac where a small rivulet marked the end of our retreat as we encountered the outposts of General Yorck's Prussian corps. Exhausted by the harrowing events, we halted at dawn and slept for three hours. During this pause, I was joined by Lieutenant Baron von Schlippenbach, who managed to rescue four cannons. I took the opportunity to replenish my ammunition from a reserve parc. The following day, General Panchulidzev approached me with a sympathetic demeanour, expressing his gratitude for preserving our guns and lamenting the heavy losses we had endured. [In a gesture of camaraderie and perhaps to lift spirits], he offered me a glass of very good champagne.

Thus ended this unfortunate battle at Reims. Count St. Priest succumbed to his injuries shortly after. Our losses were heavy: approximately 3,000 were captured, another 1,000 were killed, and about twice as many wounded. The Prussians bore the brunt of these losses, including ten cannons and howitzers, compared to just one of ours. The remnants of our defeated corps dispersed along the roads leading to Châlons and Rethel.

And so it was that March 2 [14] found us regrouping at Festieux. We halted near this village, arranging ourselves in battle formation at the forest's edge. Our scattered units gradually rejoined, among them a battery company led by Captain Vyrubov, which had undertaken a long and arduous march through Witry [Witry-lés-Reims], Bourgogne, and Neufchatel-sur-Aisne to reach Berry-au-Bac, bringing our wounded company commander, Lieutenant-Colonel Timofeev. Timofeev, now afflicted with a burning fever, required immediate transportation to Laon for medical care. With Captain Zhemchuzhnikov now a prisoner of the French, command of the entire company fell to me...

---

14 Ivan Davydovich Panchulidzev (1758-1815).

That night, we found shelter in a barn that, given the circumstances, felt almost palatial. Amidst the chaos, I had managed to save around fifteen bottles of champagne. We shared these in a jovial conversation with my surviving companions, granting us a reprieve from our recent trials. Naturally, our talk drifted to the peculiar incident with the hare that had crossed our path on the eve of our capture of Reims, a moment that now seemed ominously prophetic. As we discussed the events and missteps of the previous day's battle, we often found ourselves dismissing any pretence of deep military insight. Were we really in a position to critique our generals' decisions or dissect strategic intricacies? Our perspective was limited, confined to the immediate chaos around us. Moreover, as Montecuccoli[15] famously said, the general who makes the fewest mistakes wins. Great military leaders like Turenne[16] and le Grand Condé[17] also faltered at times. Even Frederick the Great acknowledged that success in battle often hinges on unpredictable circumstances that must be seized upon when they arise. A good general prepares with reasonable prudence and then awaits the favour of Fortune, for she influences all outcomes, rendering even the most cunning plans subject to her whims.

Our conversation also turned to the lamentable loss of Count St. Priest. We spoke of him fondly, recalling his virtues and merits. He was, unfortunately, misled by circumstances and failed to anticipate that the French, freshly defeated at Laon, would launch an immediate assault on Reims. Prince[18] Blücher, having withstood Napoleon's forces at Laon with significant casualties, remained there calmly and restfully, while St. Priest, commanding a relatively weak

---

15 Raimondo, Count of Montecuccoli (1609-1680), was a distinguished Italian-born military commander who rose to fame commanding Austrian armies.

16 Henri de La Tour d'Auvergne, vicomte de Turenne (1611-1675) was a French general, widely considered one of the best military commanders of his tumultuous age.

17 Louis II de Bourbon, Prince of Condé (1621-1686) was a member of the Condé branch of the Bourbon dynasty of France, who earned the moniker le Grand Condé for his military skills.

18 Blücher was not a prince yet. In 1814, after the end of the Napoleonic Wars, King Frederick Wilhelm III of Prussia granted him the title of Prince (Fürst) of Wahlstatt for his role in defeating Napoleon.

corps, formed the only fragile link between the two Allied armies. And yet, in hindsight, who could have foreseen that Napoleon's capture of Reims would have such consequential effects, and that by breaking through to Châlons and beyond, he would effectively open the road to Paris for the Allies? As the saying goes, every cloud has its silver lining.

Chapter IV

From Laon to Paris

On the evening of March 4 [16], we were informed that we were coming under the control of the Army of Silesia and that Prince Blücher had decided to review us. We began preparations for a parade. The town of Laon, perched on a hill, is visible from far away. As we approached, we encountered numerous signs of a vicious battle that had recently taken place: the corpses of men and horses, cannonballs, rags, damaged transports, straw, and, finally, burned villages all came into view.

Upon reaching the town, we were given such a long respite that my men managed to catch a solid nap while I went to explore the surroundings. Laon, as mentioned earlier, is located on a steep hill that overlooks a vast plain dotted with small villages. It could have been transformed into a major fortress, but the French had neglected it. Blücher exploited this oversight, capturing the town and entrenching himself so securely that even Napoleon, despite his best efforts, could not dislodge him. The town is surrounded by a stone wall with towers that were near collapsing. In spring, this area probably offers many picturesque views from the hill, but then, everywhere you looked, there were only dreadful sights. The suburbs were so devastated and plundered that only stone walls remained standing; even the roofs had been dismantled. Trash of various sorts, mixed with human filth, mud, and billowing smoke, served as grim reminders of the fierce battle waged here on February 25-26...[1]

Laon is not a large town. Its buildings are quite outdated and covered in age-old grime; the local church resembles a Chinese pavilion more than a cathedral. The overcrowded streets, filled with soldiers, horses, carriages, and transports all struggling for space, reminded us that Blücher's headquarters were established in the town. Occasionally,

---

1 Radozhitskii offers a brief account of the battle of Laon fought on March 9-10; since he was not present there, this passage has been omitted.

47

we saw residents – they were stripped bare, emaciated, and hungry, wandering around to gather rags, fragments of weapons, or struggling to move abandoned horses left by the wayside. Sometimes, we saw old women moving like ghosts amid the ruins, clothed only in rags, disfigured by their misfortunes, and starving to death. Clutching their chests, they gazed at the enemy troops passing by, as if pleading for mercy for their devastated city, already reduced to ashes and rubble. The younger and prettier girls were more cheerful and smiled at us – their circumstances were more favourable, although what they had to endure could hardly be called good fortune.

Blücher cancelled the parade, claiming ill health, so we were moved through the narrow passages around the city and past the entire corps of Count Langeron, which was bivouacked near the devastated villages. However, our guides became confused and mistakenly led us into such narrow paths, overgrown with brushwood, that we barely managed to find our way out and took a position beyond Laon, on the road to the village of Coucy. In this area, the terrain was hilly and partly wooded; the locals lived in small villages, where homes were dug into the ground or the hill slopes. There were numerous vineyards. The hill of Laon was the tallest in the area, offering a view of a vast plain stretching to Reims.

As we approached Coucy, soldiers tore the entire village apart in just a few minutes. They dismantled fences, roofs, walls – everything made of wood. Like ants carrying heavy burdens, they dragged their spoils back to their bivouacs. The few sheep that the residents had left behind were quickly caught and turned into meals.

The weather was turning towards spring – larks began to sing, and the sun shone brightly. But we were short on provisions and struggled to find enough meat and straw; only a few biscuits remained. Life in the bivouacs is much like a gypsy's life – sometimes joyous, at other times filled with hardship. Yet, as long as there is something to eat, this life in the open air and constant motion is healthier than city living, which confines you to a room.

At six o'clock in the morning on March 6 [18], Blücher's forces – consisting of the Russian corps of Count Langeron, Baron Osten-Sacken, and General Winzingerode, as well as the Prussian corps of Yorck, Kleist, and Bülow, totalling no more than 45,000 men – broke camp and advanced. General Winzingerode, with 8,000 men, was in the advance guard. As the troops departed, they set fire to their bivouacs. The sight of billowing smoke, plains strewn with corpses and debris, locals wandering in rags amidst the ruins, and troops marching in columns presented an astonishing picture of the calamities of war, one that would have overwhelmed any observer.

Passing by one of the ruins, I witnessed a very poignant scene inside a ruined house. An old woman, exhausted and mourning, lay dying on the pile of stones of a collapsed wall. A younger Frenchwoman, pale as death, deeply mourned her, bitterly crying, embracing and kissing the old woman. Nearby stood an old and drained man in rags who also loudly grieved the woman. They did not hear the clamour of the troops passing by and did not even notice curious onlookers who stopped by fleetingly to look at them before moving on. I also halted and stepped over the doorway. The Frenchman, as if awakened from slumber, shouted at me, '*Barbare! Achève notre malheur! . . . C'en est fait!* [You, barbarian, come and finish our misfortune! It is all over!]' This dreadful shout from an unarmed man could not frighten me but it awoke such deep compassion in my heart that seeking to do something to alleviate their suffering, I quickly took the last of my money out of pocket and put it in the poor man's hand . . . His eyes, gazing directly at me, became moistened with tears . . . and I departed, long to be haunted by the visions of this heartbreaking scene.

General Rudzevich[2] was appointed to replace Count St. Priest as our corps commander. We veered left from the main road and stopped for the night at the village of Royancourt that was sixteen *verstas* [10miles/17km] away from Laon and eight *verstas* [5.3 miles/8.5km] from Berry-au-Bac.

At eight o'clock the following morning, we resumed our march towards the village of Corbeny. At Berry-au-Bac, I saw Blücher's entire army for the first time: the whole area was covered with troops. Count Langeron's corps stopped near Berry-au-Bac while the rest of the troops began crossing the river on the pontoon bridges or across the fords. The French had destroyed the bridge and their outposts withdrew towards Reims. Bülow's corps departed at Corbeny towards Soissons while Yorck's corps left at Berry-au-Bac in the direction of Château-Thierry while Kleist proceeded to La Ferté-Sous-Jouarre. Napoleon marched against the main Allied army while the royalists agitated in Paris.

2   Alexander Yakovlevich Rudzevich (1776-1829).

The weather was beautiful and evenings – pleasant. Our bivouacs were full of fun – everything clamouring and moving; everywhere music and songs; dawns by the side of the cannon.

Count [Alexander] Chernyshev once again occupied Reims while the French partly retreated towards Soissons. The Prussians led our advance while Count Langeron's corps remained in reserve.

After crossing the river at Berry-au-Bac, we turned right and proceeded along the left bank of the river towards the village of Fismes. We halted about six *verstas* [4 miles/6.4km] from it and dispatched foragers to nearby villages... Woe to the unfortunate residents! Our foraging continued for twenty-four hours. The foragers of Colonel Magdenko's battery company returned with forty horses while our men brought back ten. Instead of issuing any provisions, Blücher ordered entire villages to be assigned to each regiment and artillery brigade. Whoever arrived first could claim more of anything. The success of foraging thus depended on how industrious a particular officer was. Infantrymen never shied away from marching further away than prescribed and almost always uncovered provisions in cellars, wells, and under heaps of trash, where the locals usually concealed their possessions. This was a terrible misfortune but one that was unavoidable in what has become a ruthless national [*zhestokaya natsionalnaya*] war. While in quarters our troops endured guerrilla attacks and the locals, suffering from devastation and pillaging, soon became active participants in this war, taking up arms and attacking us. In this region, the war almost reached the extremes we witnessed in Russia.

Count Langeron's corps marched through Fismes on the way to Reims on the same road that Napoleon marched with his terrifying forces to destroy St. Priest. The road was pleasant due to its location. It runs along the left side of the Vesle River, whose banks are dotted with villages amidst vast fertile plains.

About seven *verstas* from the city, we saw Reims, adorned with its cathedral and surrounded by walls. We passed through the same position that the enemy troops held when they attacked us ten days earlier. To the left of the road, there was a hill where Marmont waited for Napoleon, while on the right is the village where flanquers were having fun. On the other side of the rivulet, near the city, we could see our position. All traces of the day that was disastrous for us had disappeared. At the gates – where during the battle there was a terrible crush and crowding;

where the Ryazanskii regiment had to fight its way through the enemy cavalry in order to save the mortally wounded Count St. Priest; where the Prussian artillery was jammed in several columns; where our soldiers jumped into the river as they kept shooting back at the enemy while the Prussians kept running way from the enemy cavalry – everything was clean and well-ordered, although [some] buildings in the suburbs were completely destroyed and the windmills, on a hill on the other side of the city, were burned down. Yet, large Prussian wagons and horses were still laying in the ditches. On the first street from the gates, which was defended by the 33rd Jäger Regiment, all buildings were peppered with bullet holes and windows were missing glass.

We made a ceremonial march through Reims. All streets, squares and houses were packed with spectators, most of whom were women; [men's] blue coats and caps could be rarely seen. Their faces conveyed a wide range of emotions: old women appeared frightened and tearful, younger ones joyous; [some] men hid behind women or gazed at us from behind corners. Frenchmen in coats, with gloomy faces, moved back and forth while the children danced to our regimental music. Some residents recognised their former lodgers and greeted them. My host and his stern beauty nodded their heads from afar. The city was crowded, full of noise and commotion. Generals and their entourages took over all the homes. What a contrast this was to last time! When we stormed this city, there was not a French soul in the streets; all homes and stores were closed. And yet, now, all residents were out and about, trading and fussing around. The city is so vast that it took us half an hour to march from the Soissons gates to those of Châlons, a distance of just three *verstas*. Our cavalry deployed at Sillery while we went with the infantry to Saint-Leonard, a village north of the Vesle River, surrounded with poplar trees. Bonfires soon lit up the bivouacs and smoke billowed towards the heavens.

On 12 [24] March we advanced towards Châlons. This movement seemed inexplicable to many of us. Some argued that Napoleon had moved all of his forces to Saint-Dizier in the rear of the main Allied army and that we were rushing to join it; others claimed that General Wrede and the Prince of Württemberg had routed two French corps marching from Châlons and that we were in fact pursuing Napoleon and intending to cut him off from Paris; finally, there were also those who opined that the Austrians were already in full retreat after their Emperor

Francis had reconciled with Napoleon and left the army for Vienna. I could not figure out which of these claims was true and so waited to see how things turned out.

About one and a half *verstas* [1.6km] away from Châlons, our corps bivouacked at the village of Recy on the Marne River.

The following day we made a ceremonial march through Châlons and across the Marne and then turned to the main road to Paris. Generals Winzingerode and Count Vorontsov continued to follow Napoleon. Meanwhile our Emperor had made the decision to march directly on Paris and the main Allied army was already on its way there while Napoleon wandered around in its rear.

At the village of Chaintrix,[3] the cavalry commanded by Baron Korf and the 8th Corps moved left across the fields. We soon saw smoke billowing in the distance – this was Korf attacking the French. The rest of our corps proceeded on the main road. We were in the process of converging with the main Allied army when we stumbled upon two enemy corps, under Marmont and Mortier. The former had just reached the town of Vertus, where he discovered the advance guard of our main army, which defeated him and drove him back to Sezanne.

[Radozhitskii offers a short account of the battle of Fère-Champenoise in which he did not participate.]

By nightfall we halted amidst a vast plain, close to marshlands, near Montmirail, between Fère-Champenoise and Étoges. The fields were covered with corpses of horses that had been killed in the earlier battle.

On 14 [26] March we again turned towards the main road, leading to Étoges. From here we marched through the day and most of night along the main road to Paris and covered almost 35 *verstas* [37.3km]. It was clear that we were in a rush to get to Paris before Napoleon did.

"We are advancing on Paris!" the generals proclaimed. "Moscow will be avenged! We will overthrow the usurper from the throne he seized. We will free France from this tyrannical despot!" The exhilarating thought of marching on Paris lifted the spirits of the troops and quickened their steps; no one lagged behind, for we feared that Napoleon was marching just behind us. "We're heading straight to Paris!" officers kept telling us.

---

3 Probably Chaintrix-Bierges.

"We will find plenty of joys and pleasures there! Palais-Royal, here we come! Gentlemen, do we have enough money to enjoy ourselves? No? That's fine, we'll just have to levy a contribution..." And so the talk continued. "We are marching on Paris, lads!" soldiers repeated, waving their hands. "The war will end there. Our Sovereign will give each of us a ruble, a pound of meat, and a measure of wine! We will finally take up quarters." "To the right, to the left!" the troops in the rear shouted to those ahead whenever one of the generals needed to pass through the column. Soldiers would quickly move aside, only to see... a goat, accustomed to marching with our troops, running down the middle of the road. "Just look at that! He is also marching to Paris! Move to the right, to the left!" The resulting laughter only sped up our advance.

The main road to Paris, on which we marched, was a chaussée or a paved road but it was in a very bad condition as if someone had intentionally dug up large stones to complicate our movements. The magnificent poplar trees that lined the road on both sides were cut down in places and lay like vanquished giants by the wayside. We occasionally stumbled on stripped carcasses of horses and tattered remains of shakos and knapsacks.

After passing through Montmirail, our troops halted for the night. Prince Blücher's headquarters stayed inside town while our troops were deployed around it. At night, the bivouac fires created a scene of one giant light show.

On March 15 [27] we reached the town of La Ferté-sous-Jouarre, which is located on both banks of the Marne River. At this spot, on the left side, the smaller river, Petit Morin, flows into the Marne, which is not that wide but is meandering and fast flowing.

Between Châlons and La Ferté-sous-Jouarre we marched through vast plains that were intersected by hills at Etoges and Montmirail. But La Ferté-sous-Jouarre presented a much more picturesque location: on the right side of the Marne River there were tall banks covered with vineyards; buildings in local villages and settlements are much larger and cleaner; the soil is more fertile. Fruit trees and the budding wheat revealed minor and surreptitious natural splendours and looked ready to unfurl all their attractions with the first signs of the springtime. As we marched on the left bank of the Marne River, we admired these picturesque views on the right side of the river, which flows in a meandering fashion in this vale. However, we soon heard the sound of gunfire: Napoleon had left behind

Marshals Marmont[4] and Mortier,[5] with some 30,000 men, to halt two Allied armies that counted up to 120,000 soldiers. The marshals resisted persistently. As the darkness descended, we halted near the village of Jouan. At night, we were awakened by the sound of the thunderous explosion of the gunpowder magazine at Meaux.

The following day, we marched along the Marne riverbank and approached a pontoon crossing that was arranged near the village of Trim. Count Langeron's entire corps converged at this location and we had to wait for a long time before the troops of the 9th and 10th Corps crossed the river; once they moved, it was the turn for our artillery. A local stone bridge had been blown up and destroyed. After the crossing we advanced on a rather good, paved road to Meaux. This town is in the valley of the Marne River, surrounded by its tall banks. It is smaller than Châlons but is as large as Toul. Passing by this town, which was on our right side, we could see numerous stones that had been scattered by the explosion of the gunpowder store the previous night. After passing Meaux, we turned right and proceeded to move on local roads, gradually getting closer to Paris. To celebrate this all officers and soldiers decorated their shakos with tree branches to imitate laurels leaves that victors wear. Our main army advanced directly on Paris; Baron Osten-Sacken's corps was left at Meaux to cover our rear.

At 9 o'clock in the morning, on 17 [29] March, we resumed our advance, marching along local roads. We rested at the village of Mitry.[6] Here we already could see first signs of approaching the capital of France: more frequent settlements, more fertile soil, numerous forests and streams; larger and stone-built homes; large wagons laden with bread standing in courtyards. And yet, no residents could be seen. Foraging was no longer allowed and outposts were deployed everywhere to protect villages.

Upon reaching the main road connecting Soissons to Paris, we observed gun smoke billowing in the city's suburbs. It was General Rayevskii, who commanded the advance guard of the main army and

---

4 Auguste Frédéric Louis Viesse de Marmont (1774-1852).

5 Adolphe Édouard Casimir Joseph Mortier (1768-1835).

6 Probably Mitry-Mory.

had passed through the Bois de Bondy at Villette, forcing back the French who put up feeble resistance and kept retreating to Paris.

The hill of Montmartre, which serves as an elevated suburb of Paris on the road to St. Denis, could be seen, with its windmills, from a distance of fifteen *verstas*. 'There it is, Paris!' shouted soldiers excitedly. 'Greetings to you, Father [*batyushko*] Paris! How will you atone with us for our Mother Moscow?' they said, hurrying forward. The city environs are flat and dotted with groves. We halted for the night not far from Le Bourget.

March 18 [30]. An important day for the glory of the Russian Army and for Emperor Alexander! A doleful day for France and a dreadful one for Napoleon. Paris, defended by no more than 30,000 men and exposed on all sides, presented a weak obstacle for the 400,000 men-strong Allied army. If our Sovereign [Emperor Alexander] decided to seek vengeance with sword and fire, the Russians would have obliterated the French capital to avenge the mother Moscow. But our Sovereign waged war only against Napoleon and our victory augured less bloodshed or disastrous consequences.

Paris, situated predominantly on the right bank of the Seine River, is encircled by heights where its suburbs are located. Among these, Montmartre, perched on a prominent hill, is the most important, followed by Belleville and others. These crucial points became the primary targets for the Allied forces.

At six o'clock in the morning, General Rayevskii launched an attack on Pantin and Romainville, while Blücher advanced with his army, including the corps of Count Langeron, Yorck, and Kleist, towards St. Denis. Despite being outnumbered, the French fought with great determination. Napoleon's brother Joseph, the former king of Spain, took command of young troops stationed at Montmartre, while [Marshals] Marmont and Mortier defended the heights of Belleville. Believing only a small portion of the Allied forces was approaching Paris, the French commanders misjudged the scale of the attack. The situation changed dramatically when Count Langeron's corps appeared in the valley of Aubervilliers, followed by the Prussians, who joined the fray. Gunfire erupted around the city. Alarmed at the possibility of being captured, King Joseph fled Paris, leaving the defence in Marmont's hands.

At Pantin and Romainville, the French resistance was so fierce that Commander-in-Chief Barclay de Tolly had to reinforce Rayevskii with two grenadier regiments and the Prussian Guard. Even these reinforcements proved insufficient, necessitating the deployment of a guard division. A ferocious battle ensued, with both sides suffering heavy casualties. Ultimately, the French were forced to retreat to Belleville and Ménilmontant.

The Russians paused their advance, awaiting coordinated attacks by Blücher on the right flank and Württembergian troops on the left. This temporary lull emboldened the French, who launched a counterattack on the villages of Romainville and Pantin. However, the charge was repelled by two regiments of Russian cuirassiers, who helped us and the Prussian guard troops to hold on to our position. This marked the final effort of an exhausted French force.

Meanwhile, Count Langeron's corps had marched through Clichy, supported by Kleist and Yorck, whose Prussian troops advanced on La Villette. After suffering significant losses from French skirmishers and artillery fire, they were reinforced by Russian troops and, together, they dislodged the French defenders and seized the farm of Rouvroy.[7]

Count Langeron's forces, comprising of the 8th, 9th and 10th Corps, advanced in battle formation, in columns. While the Prussians were fighting at La Villette, my artillery company followed the jägers of the 8th Corps. Leaving the Prussians, we turned right and began deploying. The 9th Corps was sent towards St. Denis, where a small enemy force was holed up, while the 8th and 10th Corps moved towards the heights of Montmartre; the 8th corps advanced along the St. Denis road while the 10th corps was further to the left. The jägers, behind whom I was moving, scattered in a skirmisher chain; my battery deployed behind them and opened fire at the enemy cavalry and infantry that stood, with a few cannon, at the bottom of the Montmartre hill. Assailed with cannonballs and shells, the enemy retreated disorderly half way up the hill where they could hold ground under the cover of local buildings. Skirmishers could not be employed. To the left, in front of us, there was a [French] battery with four cannon. I directed most of my [battery's] fire at this target, forcing the French to move back. Soon, we were just three hundred sazhens [~700 yards] from the hill of Montmartre and remained at this position, without much action, for some time, waiting for the capture of St. Denis in our rear, where the gunfire was still raging

---

7 Rouvroy was located in the commune of Pantin.

and the French were fiercely resisting. To the left of me was deployed Colonel Magdenko's battery company while behind us, for protection, stood the Ryazanskii regiment.

The French occasionally fired cannonballs at us but none of them reached its target; French skirmishers also sporadically approached our batteries and their flanquers intermittently approached and shot at us, but our canister shots forced them to withdraw. I moved my light cannon forward to the skirmisher chain, but the Prussian howitzers, which were deployed at a farm on the left, mistook us for a French battery and opened fire with shells. Fortunately, they caused no harm to us. I was forced to ask Colonel Skobelev to send his adjutant to the Prussians and convince them that we were Russians.[8] Afterwards I moved to the right, towards the road to St. Denis. A dense column of French cavalry attempted to charge my battery, but I opened fire with all eleven of my cannon and, without letting it approach me to a canister range, I disordered and forced it to fall back. The French then sent a dense cloud of skirmishers, who, keeping to the alleyways, approached my battery but several rounds of canister fire halted their progress. Meanwhile, a fierce fighting raged to the left of us. The Russian and Prussian guards seized the heights of Belleville; Yorck and Kleist, with their Prussians, marched out of La Villette towards the Parisian suburbs.

Finally, we were ordered to move as well. General Rudzevich, with jägers, marched on the right side of the St. Denis road and began moving around the hill of Montmartre; I followed him then with my battery, which I deployed and advanced, by pelotons [*plutongami*], to engage enemy cavalry, which was forced to ride up the hill, leaving behind the dead. Suddenly, a French colonel, wearing a blue uniform, appeared from behind the house at the bottom of the hill and, waving a handkerchief, rode directly towards my battery. I ordered not to fire at him and rode out to greet him. "What do you want?" I asked him. "Where is Count Langeron, or Blücher?" – After pointing to the rear and left, I was about to turn my horse and return to the battery when he told me, "Halt! We surrender!"

---

8 Radozhitskii's note: "I was involved in a similar incident at Bautzen, the year before. The Prussian artillery cannot be praised for its skill; it often took up positions at a great distance [from the front line] and fired across our positions, [occasionally] hitting our batteries or troops protecting us".

Meanwhile, gunfire was still raging. To the left of us, French shells hit two Prussian caissons, causing a loud explosion and sending columns of smoke high into the sky. This event apparently served as a signal for our assault and General Rudzevich sent his jägers up the hill; his men, shouting "Hurrah!" rushed into the Montmartre suburbs; Colonel Magdenko, with his battery company, passed, at a trot, by my battery and began ascending the hill, following in the jägers' footsteps; I then dashed forward with my cannon. Shouts of "Hurrah!" and drums beating could be heard in all directions. [It seemed as if] everyone was rushing up that hill. The French got frightened and, without fighting, they fled further up the hill; only their cavalry remained on the left side at the bottom of the hill. As I moved, I fired several rounds at the cavalry, then loaded my cannon with canister and ordered them to get closer to the enemy. The Starooskolskii regiment was moving behind me, deployed into a line, so I was not worried about a cavalry counterattack and instead wanted to get closer to these cavalrymen and fire a volley at them. But then, suddenly, General Kaptsevich appeared, shouting, "Halt! Do not shoot!" He had received Count Langeron's order to halt all movements because a ceasefire had been reached. Nevertheless, General Rudzevich's troops continued to shoot and climb up the hill. General Kaptsevich had to convey the news to him and soon everything calmed down. Thus, on the heights of Belleville and Montmartre, the Russians established themselves as the vanquishers of the Napoleonic armies, the conquerors of Paris and the restorers of the Bourbon dynasty.

I approached the French cavalrymen whom I targeted with my artillery fire just moments earlier. They were beautifully dressed in light-blue uniforms and tall busbies. "Greeting, monsieurs! The war is over," I told them. "Yes, it is unfortunately over," responded an officer. "But will it be for better for the French?" – "Time will tell. Where is your Emperor Napoleon?" I asked. The French did not like my question and another officer asked me, "What does the white armband on your left arm signify?" – "It is the sign of the Allied forces fighting against the French but it is also the colour of the French [Bourbon] fleur-de-lis, right?"… [By now] the French began to surround me so I became concerned that I might fall in captivity and quickly bid them adieu and galloped back to my company. Our troops were already preoccupied setting up bivouacs wherever they stood. I led my company down the hill, almost to the bottom, and was rather annoyed seeing Colonel

Magdenko's battery guns on top of the hill. This was supposed to be my spot, for I was always with the jägers in the front, but now he had pilfered this honour from me.

The French, seeing that it was impossible to hold their positions against the entire Allied army and concerned that after capturing Belleville and Montmartre we might bombard Paris with explosive shells, asked our Sovereign for an armistice and terms of truce. In consequence, all military operations were halted. The following day Marshals Mortier and Marmont, and their troops, were allowed to leave Paris that was now at the mercy of the victors.

By nightfall, we lit bivouac fires. Since we have been long procuring supplies through foraging only, we dispatched our foragers to find some bread and wine in the suburb of Montmartre but the Prussian dragoons and our jägers had already rummaged through nook and cranny. Driven by curiosity, I went inside the nearest home. There was no one there, except for a dog and a [hunting] gun in an open room. The dog, of the large Danish Bullenbeisser breed, was so docile and intelligent that it allowed me to pet. It then let me tie a bridle-rein around its neck and followed me, guiding my horse back to the bivouac, where I returned like a hunter, with a gun on my shoulder and a dog behind me, but without any game.

On 19 [31] March, at seven o'clock in the morning, the Allied Sovereigns entered Paris through the suburb of San Martin. The Guard Cossacks and the rest of the cavalry cleared the path, and were followed by the infantry of the Guard and then the Liberator of Europe and the Vanquisher of Napoleon – Emperor Alexander, who was accompanied by the Prussian king, Grand Duke Constantine, Prince Schwarzenberg, the English envoy, and all the other generals. The Austrian emperor was not present and the Austrian troops did not participate in the battle at Paris. Our Sovereign was the subject of wonderment for all Parisians. All of them, whether rich or poor, spilled out into the streets to get closer to him, desiring to see and hear the ruler who was truly blessed by Providence. In their eager gratefulness to [Alexander] for his mercifulness and liberation, the Parisians all but forgot about Napoleon and acclaimed our Emperor as the saviour of France. Indeed, the destiny of this country had changed at that moment.

Emperor [Alexander] was so touched by the Parisian exaltation that he flattered them with these words, "We did not conquer you, we are

59

your allies! The French are our friends!" Shouts of "Vive Alexandre! Vive [Frédéric-]Guillaume![9] Long Live Our Liberators!" could be heard from every direction. In the streets, where our Emperor and troops passed, windows and balconies were full of the Parisian high society; to express their joy, women applauded and waved handkerchiefs while those who stood on sidewalks were so endearing that they approached officers of the Imperial suite and asked them to lend them horses so they could see the great Russian emperor better! This was a touching and exceptional sight for the glory of Russia and her Emperor! Only the Guard received the honour of the triumphant entry into Paris, and it was quartered in the barracks inside the city. The rest of the army remained in bivouacs in the city environs.

Thus was Moscow avenged! Its ashes redeemed the Bourbon throne and freed Europe. The weight of Moscow's ashes crushed the mighty empire of Napoleon! Eternal glory to Russia!

In the afternoon, I decided to explore Montmartre. From the top of the hill, I could see the entirety of Paris, as if laid out in the palm of my hand. In a misty valley, about seven *verstas* long and surrounded by various elevations, I could make out a vast mass of buildings, though only their rooftops were visible to me. My eyes were drawn to the large, gilded dome of Les Invalides and the two tall bell towers of Notre Dame Cathedral; to the right, the Seine River shimmered, while all other buildings and palaces remained shrouded in mist; our Moscow, equally large,[10] is more beautiful than Paris because it boasts not one but numerous gilded domes and cupolas, not to mention the walls and towers of the Kremlin. At the top of Montmartre, amidst ordinary buildings, there were three or four windmills and a telegraph tower. The entire mountaintop was dotted with our cannons, which could wipe out the entire city in just a few minutes. Our jägers were bivouacked next to the artillery batteries. Further away, at some distance, was the headquarters of Count Langeron. Generals and colonels from our corps occupied all other houses. The French wandered among our batteries, examining the cannons, listening to our music, and puzzling over the Russians. Some were carrying or transporting their remaining belongings into the city.

---

9 King Frederick William III of Prussia.

10 In terms of population, Paris was more than twice the size of Moscow.

On 20 March [April 1], after making an agreement with a friend of mine, I went to Paris. Travelling from the Porte de Clichy, along the Rue Montblanc, we crossed the entire suburb of Montmartre, where we saw ordinary buildings. Only at the boulevard that runs across the city and separates it from the suburbs did we finally see a beautiful home of a new architectural style. Beautiful small Rue Napoléon led us to the Place Vendôme. In the middle of this square there is a bronze column, about 15 *sazhens* [32m/105 feet] tall, which is hollow, with a staircase leading up to the top. At the top of the column one can find a colossal statue of Napoleon, in uniform, wearing a hat and holding an orb in his right hand. This entire column, we were told, was styled after Trajan's column that stands in Rome, and was cast from the bronze of cannon that the French had captured from their defeated opponents. It is covered with spiralling bas-relief bronze plates from the bottom to the top. The base is decorated with contemporary military armament: uniforms with epaulettes, shako of the Pavlovskii Grenadier Regiment, Russian flags, cannon; French imperial eagles are in each corner of the base. The column was constructed in 1805 and is a rare work, very notable for the quality of the craftsmanship.[11]

We found multitudes of people at the square. I asked the closest Frenchmen, "Is that Napoleon on top?" – "Yes, that's him" – "He has risen too high; it is time for him to come down!" – "Sure, right this moment," said the Frenchman sneeringly. The crowd soon gathered to bring down the idol. One rogue even climbed up the shoulder of the bronze Napoleon and began wrapping around his neck a thick rope whose both ends hung all the way to the ground. Many among this lowly rabble [*chern'*], including women, held the rope intending to drag down their former idol. Such are the vicissitudes of life! This very rabble, whom Napoleon never deigned to look at while he was preoccupied with his conquests and deciding the fate of Europe, was now mocking him and dragging him down from the heights of his victories. He stood firmly at first and I did not wait to see how it ended and went on, dismayed by the flippant character of the French. Amidst the crowd we could see sullen looking men, on horseback and wearing black coats and white cocardes in round hats: these were the intrepid

---

11 The construction of the original Vendôme Column was started in 1806 and completed in 1810. It was modelled after Trajan's Column, to celebrate the victory of Austerlitz.

royalists, supporters of the Bourbon dynasty. Until now they were, of course, hiding in obscurity, but the arrival of the Russians had changed the appearance of not only Paris but its inhabitants as well! Whenever we stopped to query the Frenchmen, they anticipated each other in responding to our questions, surrounded us, looked enquiringly at us and could hardly believe that the Russians could speak so fluently their very own language. Good-looking French girls, looking out of windows, nodded our way and smiled. The Parisians, believing the descriptions of their patriots, imagined Russians as the barbarians who ate human flesh while the Cossacks were seen as the bearded cyclops; thus, they were very surprised to see the Russian Guard and its handsome officers, who were true dandies, as well-educated and as versatile and dexterous in their conversations as the foremost Parisian fops.

Leaving the Place Vendôme, we turned left onto the wide and crowded Rue Saint-Honoré, with its tall three- and four-storey homes and various fashionable stores. We soon stopped at the enormous portico of the Palais Royal. In front of the entrance, on the stairway, there was a large crowd of people. We gave our horses to boys who eagerly grabbed the reins and bragged about the honour of leading the horses of the Russian officers. Following the crowd through the lower gallery, we walked to the long courtyard that is surrounded by several-storey-tall buildings. The lower gallery had various stalls, similar to the merchant's court [gostinnyi dvor] in St. Petersburg. Throngs of people walked about and, amidst this commotion and noise, it was impossible to see what was sold in the stalls. Next to us, surrounded by men, jostled unashamedly smartly dressed French women who lured our youngsters with their eyes and pinched painfully those who did not understand their intentions...

We were told that in all of Paris, the galleries of Palais Royal showcase the best and most precious commodities, but because the glass doors of the stalls were closed and we, not intending to buy anything, did not enter them, we could not explore anything through the glass. Wax bust figures with wigs that were displayed behind the glass seemed as white and alive as the coiffeurs themselves. On the middle level of this vast building, which could accommodate up to 5,000 people at once, there are only restaurants that offer anything and everything luxurious to lure the spend-alls seeking to satisfy their every whim and desire. One glorious restaurant is *Aux Mille Colonnes*, where the hostess, dressed as the queen,[12] sits from dawn to dusk on the throne and sends out her servants bearing gifts for the customers while collecting their tribute in gold and silver. Yet as our wallets were already empty, we did not venture to enter any of these restaurants, though our Guard officers did, fully tasting the heedless pleasures of Palais Royal and leaving behind piles of monies. The top floors of this edifice are occupied by the priestesses of salacity... We heard that on the lowest or underground level, there are *auberges* [inns] for the poor where for a few sous one can eat a soup made from bones, a sauce made with mice and a roasted cat. The large inner yard, decorated with trees, offers a wonderful place to stroll and there is always a multitude of people here. Palais Royal seems a city all to itself. It does not look like a former royal palace but rather like a marketplace. Before the Revolution, it belonged to the Duc d'Orléans who, in order to sway the rabble [*chern'*] in his favour, set up inns and organized celebrations here, allowing riffraff to enter for free. Henceforth the Parisians got used to gathering here for political debates as well as for prodigality, luxury, and various types of debauchery.

From the Palais Royal we went across the street to the Imperial Square by the Tuileries chateau. This palace, the customary seat of the former Kings and of Napoleon, seems to be much less spacious than the Mikhailovskii Castle in St. Petersburg. The facade facing the square is topped by a dome and stretches 70 *sazhens* [490 feet] in length; the building, blackened with age and surrounded by a balustrade, has nothing majestic about it. The Winter Palace of our Emperors in the northern capital [St. Petersburg] is a most excellent building, far ahead of the Tuileries. Having said that, the triumphal gate in front of this palace is its best feature.[13] On the left side is an inscription in gold letters: *the Victory of Austerlitz*, and below, in bas-relief, a hussar presenting Russian prisoners to Napoleon; on the right side is a similar inscription: *the Capitulation at Ulm*, with a similar bas-relief of Austrian prisoners. On the gate there are four figures depicting Napoleonic warriors in the

---

12 Madame Romain, also known as la Belle Limonadière, renowned for her beauty. After her husband's premature death in a horse accident in 1826, she abandoned her business, entered the convent in 1828 and ended her life as a nun. Her fame endured, however, and she was mentioned in various literary works, including Honoré de Balzac's novel *César Birotteau*.

13 The Arc de Triomphe du Carrousel, built between 1806 and 1808 to commemorate Napoleon's military victories in the Wars of the Third and Fourth Coalitions.

uniforms of various guard regiments, excellently sculpted. At the very top of the gate is an empty chariot with four gilded horses taken, it is said, from Venice.[14] If Napoleon had succeeded in defeating the Russian Monarchy in 1812, then, of course, he would have put himself inside this chariot.

From the Imperial Square we entered the Louvre Gallery, or the Napoleonic Museum. As we dismounted, local boys tussled with each other to grab the reins of our horses. The lower floor, which is dedicated to sculpture, and is very spacious, is only for statues of the finest work. In front of the entrance, books are sold, with detailed descriptions of each of the statues. A lack of time prevented us from examining their silent elegance, and we went upstairs to the art gallery. Here light came in from the windows above, from which it was impossible to view a painting hanging under a window. The best paintings appear to have been hidden away because there were many abandoned empty frames. In the first hall, one's eyes are struck by a large painting, depicting the victories of Alexander the Great: it is surprisingly lifelike, and the colours in it are bright, as if only recently painted. Many other historical paintings were very entertaining, but the lack of time did not allow us to admire them for a lengthy period: it appears that a whole week would not have been enough to examine everything with the proper attention. However, of all the paintings one halted me: the Descent of the Saviour from the cross. It appeared the finest to me: the naturalness, detail and vividness of colour are amazing; the dead body of Jesus Christ inspires dread. Mary's face is emaciated with sorrow; the tears in her eyes have run dry. Magdalene's face evokes pity; one tear has stopped on her cheek, another has been wiped away and left a mark. Joseph inspires awe... But can any description portray the elegance of this painting! This was the first time that I had seen nature so faithfully depicted on canvas. In addition to historical paintings, there were many portraits and landscapes; very many... but I couldn't even take a glance at everything and must be satisfied that I got some impression of this glorious Museum. We hurried out, worrying about our horses; but the boys had the patience

---

14 The quadriga atop the arch was indeed from Venice, the famed set of bronze statues of four horses that the Venetians seized during the Sack of Constantinople in 1204. In 1797, Napoleon removed the statues from St Mark's Basilica in Venice and transported them to Paris where they remained until 1815 when they were returned to Venice. Nowadays, the Arc de Triomphe du Carrousel features a copy of the Horses of Saint Mark.

to hold them; for ten sous they were very grateful to us, surprising us with their honesty. I don't know how possible it was, anywhere in the city, to risk giving some unknown boy a horse to mind.

From the Louvre gallery we proceeded to the banks of the Seine. Its embankment is not even half of the Neva's. The river itself is slightly wider than the Fontanka, but there are fifteen bridges in Paris alone. In the middle of the river there are three islands between the Pont des Arts and Pont d'Austerlitz. The largest, la Cité, contains the oldest part of the city, Lutetia, as it was known during the time of Julius Caesar. Three bridges lead to this island: Pont Neuf, Pont au Change and Pont Notre-Dame. The island is especially notable for the huge ancient Cathedral of Notre Dame with its Gothic architecture. The next island, much smaller than the first, is St. Louis; there is one bridge to it, Pont Marie. The third island, near Pont d'Austerlitz, is small and unremarkable. However, the Pont Neuf (New Bridge), on the site of the former Pont Royal, built under Louis XIV on five large arches, seems to be the strongest of all. It is especially remarkable in that there are always crowds of people, various tradeswomen and mountebanks who trade for their daily bread in front of it. I prefer the Imperial Bridge [Pont de la Concorde], opposite the Louvre gallery, constructed like perches and only for pedestrians. The entire embankment is full of people. There are no fine buildings on the other side of the Seine; the gilded dome of Les Invalides alone rises majestically above all the buildings.

It was a shame that my visit to Paris was so brief, undertaken stealthily and without money. Paris truly embodies the capital of luxury, a centre of all sciences, arts, and pleasures; yet it is also a city of little virtue, a labyrinth of indulgence and greatest debauchery. This grand metropolis of 800,000 people seems filled with frivolous, capricious souls, of whom perhaps only a small fraction is genuinely decent, and even fewer are truly wise, learned, and virtuous. The guards were fortunate! Those with means could escape their barracks to roam freely across Paris, exploring its wonders, tasting its delights, expanding their minds with new ideas, and indulging in newfound pleasures. But alas, that was not me, and I had never felt the lack of money more keenly than then! Army officers were forbidden to travel into the city; it was only by chance that we managed to avoid the watchful eyes of our commanders.

On the way back, I was struck by the simplicity and charm of the French women. Many were quite pretty, dressed uniformly yet elegantly – simple, neat, and graceful. Most had round faces, pale complexions, fair or dark hair, lively, quick eyes, and a perpetual smile. Their figures were slender and flexible, with thin waists; they wore short dresses that left their legs visible, and they tucked their hands into the pockets of their aprons. Their hair was neatly gathered under nets or caps, and they walked with a light, careful step. They seemed unfazed by the weather, braving the cold without heavy coats.

Now, with peace between nations, trade flows freely; merchants sell everything, even the helmets and caps of the French cavalry – though who would need such things? At the Palais Royal, one can already find the uniforms, shakos, swords, epaulettes, and sashes of the Russian, Prussian, and Austrian regiments. The Parisian artisans, ever skillful and quick-witted, have capitalized on the bounty. The cart horses in Paris are massive, towering at nearly five *vershoks* [about 8¾']. They haul enormous two-wheeled carts, loaded so heavily that even our troikas would struggle to pull them. These carts have wheels four *arshins* [9'4"] in diameter, with rims nearly half an *arshin* (14") wide. The collars are so large that a person could fit inside, and the horses' hooves are as big as human heads. With thick, untrimmed manes and fetlocks, they appear as shaggy as bears, as hefty and awkward as buffaloes. These draft horses are a distinct breed. They also use donkeys and dogs for transport here. Paris is full of curiosities! They say you can find here trained mice dancing on tightropes, birds that can read and write, and fleas pulling miniature carriages...

But where was Napoleon? Rushing to the rear of the Allies, he thought to draw them onto himself and pull them away from Paris, drawing closer in the meantime to General Augereau's 40,000-man corps, which was in Lyon; but it did not work out as he had thought. Mistaking the cavalry of General NN***[15] for the vanguard of the allied army, he swiftly attacked them [leading to the battle of St Dizier]. They could not, of course, resist. He took the ground from them but lost Paris. On 18th [30th] March, on the very day of the assault on Troyes, he raced to Paris alone, but, seeing it already in the hands of the Allies, he was forced to stop at Fontainebleau,

---

15 The author likely refers to the detachment commanded by Ferdinand Wintzingerode, though it is unclear why his name was deliberately omitted.

where his 70,000-man army soon arrived, and thereafter the fate of the conqueror of Europe was sealed.

On March 21st [April 2nd], Count Langeron's corps marched ceremoniously through Paris to the far bank of the Seine, as the war with Napoleon was not yet concluded. The rain had drenched us before we entered the city, but the old soldiers saw it as a good omen. We marched through the Montmartre suburb, then along a grand boulevard reminiscent of the Nevsky Prospekt,[16] until we reached the magnificent Place de la Concorde, formerly known as Place de la Révolution, where Louis XVI had been executed. From the edges of the square extended the gardens of the Tuileries and the Champs-Élysées, inviting us for leisurely strolls. To the left, a wide avenue led to the Palais des Tuileries; to the right, the Champs-Élysées stretched toward the Arc de Triomphe,[17] standing in a field. From the square, we proceeded straight across the Royal Bridge.[18] On the far side of the bridge stood the grand Palais du Corps Législatif, its imposing portico adorned with a beautiful colonnade and four seated statues representing ancient sages. The pediment above the portico depicted the *Victoire d'Austerlitz* in bas-relief: Napoleon, astride a horse, receiving prisoners. In one corner, Neptune bowed his head in sorrow, while in another, Peace, personified as a woman with a horn of plenty, regarded the victor with a smile. The design was a striking tribute to Napoleon's vanity. Beneath the pediment, the inscription read: *À Napoléon le grand*. These monuments, built during Napoleon's lifetime, reflected both his extraordinary popularity and its inherent fragility. He sought worship for his image as the ancient Romans did for

---

16 One of the main streets in the Russian imperial capital, St. Petersburg, built by Peter the Great and named after medieval prince Alexander Nevsky.

17 Napoleon commissioned the Arc in 1806, after the victory at Austerlitz. Laying the foundations took two years; in 1810, when Napoleon entered the capital with his new bride, Archduchess Marie-Louise of Austria, he had a wooden mock-up of the completed arch constructed. The construction was halted in 1814 and was not completed until 1836.

18 Commissioned in 1787, the present-day Pont de la Concorde is an arch bridge across the Seine in Paris connecting the Quai des Tuileries at the Place de la Concorde (on the Rive Droite) and the Quai d'Orsay (on the Rive Gauche). Before the revolution it was colloquially referred to as the Royal Bridge or Pont Louis XVI. During the Revolution, it was referred to as Pont de la Révolution or Pont de la Concorde.

their emperors, perhaps sensing that all physical marks of his greatness might one day vanish but his name would resonate forever in history.[19]

From the Palais du Corps Législatif, we marched along the Rue de Bourgogne to the boulevard leading to Les Invalides. The building, vast and imposing, stood apart from others. Behind it, and slightly to the side, lay the École Militaire, or Cadet Corps, and in front, the sprawling Champ de Mars. Along the way we encountered numerous limbless veterans and elderly invalids in blue uniforms, men who had earned the comfort provided by their beneficent homeland. It seemed fitting that the Cadet Corps [École Militaire] was built so close to Les Invalides. There, youthful soldiers prepared for greatness, while here, greatness was rewarded with charity. What Frenchman would not be stirred with patriotism at the sight of this? Who among them would hesitate to sacrifice against an enemy, assured that their grateful nation would honour them in life and provide for their peace of mind should they be wounded or incapacitated? The idea of a refuge for old soldiers was first conceived by King Henry IV. Initially, the disabled were placed in the l'Hôpital d'Oursine monastery. Under Louis XIII, as the number of veterans grew, they were relocated to the larger Bicêtre castle. Finally, in 1670, Louis XIV established the Hôtel Royal des Invalides. Five years later, a church with a magnificent dome was constructed, now a landmark that not only enhances Les Invalides but also graces all of Paris. The four-storey building features a vaulted gate at the centre of its façade,

---

19 The original palace was constructed between 1722 and 1728 for Louise Françoise de Bourbon, Duchess of Bourbon, the legitimized daughter of Louis XIV and the Marquise de Montespan. During the French Revolution, the palace was nationalized and served as the meeting place of the Council of Five Hundred from 1795 to 1799. Later, Napoleon designated it as the home of the new legislature, the Corps Législatif, which proposed the construction of a new façade facing the Seine. This façade was to align with and match the design of the Temple of Glory (now the Church of the Madeleine), which Napoleon was constructing at the northern end of Rue Royale, near Place de la Concorde. The new neoclassical façade, designed by architect Bernard Poyet, featured twelve Corinthian columns, built high enough to be visible from Place de la Concorde and aligned to match the perspective of the Madeleine. The original pediment of the façade, adorned with bas-reliefs by sculptor Antoine-Denis Chaudet, depicted scenes from the opening of the Corps Législatif in 1806. It featured Napoleon on horseback, presenting captured Austrian flags from the Battle of Austerlitz to the Legislature. In 1810, additional statues were added to the façade overlooking the Seine. These included representations of the goddess Themis, holding scales in her left hand, and Athena, symbolizing wisdom, as well as statues of notable French royal ministers.

leading into a vast courtyard surrounded by splendid architecture. The first two floors open onto arcades facing the courtyard, allowing the disabled residents to enjoy fresh air even on rainy days. The facility can accommodate up to 7,000 veterans. The open esplanade in front of the building, stretching to the Seine, provides a clear view of its magnificent façade, a structure that brings honour and glory to France.

Once again, the rain began to pour as we stood opposite Les Invalides, waiting for three long hours while a bedraggled procession of ten thousand Prussians marched past. During this dreary interlude, a lively crowd of merchants appeared, calling out, *"Messieurs! La goutte! La goutte!"* ("Gentlemen! A shot of vodka!").[20] Among them were charming women whose sweet eyes and enchanting smiles gave an irresistible allure to their offerings. Their presence brought a spark of warmth to the gloomy moment, and our soldiers, at least those fortunate enough to have a coin to spare, eagerly partook, savouring not just the drink but also the delightful attention of these captivating vendors.

From Les Invalides, we proceeded along the boulevard, leaving the city behind on the Orléans road. Along the way, we encountered numerous cabs, numbered coaches, carriages, and *charabancs*[21] returning to Paris, laden with all manner of goods. The French passengers seemed cheerful and amicable, their earlier grief now lifted. Many had tied handkerchiefs around their arms as a symbol of alliance with us, greeting us warmly as we passed. It was heartening to see a semblance of peace reflected in their gestures.

By evening, an order came from the Commander-in-Chief forbidding the use of donkeys in our Corps. These animals, numerous in the regiments as pack animals, had become a nuisance during the march, worsening congestion in the columns. We made camp at Longjumeau, setting up in an open field. A strict directive was issued: no fatigue details were to be sent for straw or firewood without an officer present. These supplies, it was emphasized, were supposed to be prepared in advance by the local *Maire*, whose negligence had already caused a severe shortage of rations for the troops. Those who had managed to forage earlier still had some flour and meat to sustain them. Others, with money, bought bread from

---

20 The Germans call a sip of vodka Schnaps, while the French say la goutte.

21 A type of horse-drawn vehicle, with benched seats arranged in rows, looking forward, commonly used for large parties, whether as public conveyances or for excursions.

the locals. But those who had neither food nor funds sat idly in their bivouacs, whistling in frustration. The commissariat, meanwhile, was preoccupied with politics, leaving the army to fend for itself.

The following day, we received an order announcing that peace had been concluded with the French nation, but that the war continued against Napoleon and his army. The Bourbons, aided by their sympathizers, seized the opportunity to regain influence. Under the guidance of their shrewd leader, Talleyrand – Minister of Foreign Affairs, whose adaptable cunning had served France during the Revolution, Napoleon, and now the Bourbons – the Allies declared their refusal to engage with Napoleon or his family. They proclaimed that they would recognize any government the French people chose for themselves, provided it restored the borders of France to their pre-Revolutionary monarchy. In response, the Senate convened and declared Napoleon and his heirs deposed. They released the people and the army from their oaths of loyalty to him, citing accusations of repeated constitutional violations, exorbitant taxes, relentless wars, rejection of favourable peace terms, and the destruction of cities. Yet, these Senators, who now denounced him with such fervour, had never dared to voice such criticisms to Napoleon's face; they seemed to embody the fable of the aged lion, turning on him only when his strength had waned.

The civilian population believed the Senators, but the army did not. To Napoleon's troops, he remained the great leader who had inspired awe across Europe with his victories, faltering only in the flames of Moscow. In their eyes, he was still the figure of greatness, and they were prepared to march on Paris with him. With 70,000 soldiers, 100,000 armed Parisians, the genius of Napoleon, and the skill of his Generals, they might have delivered a devastating blow to the Allies. The outcome could have reduced Paris to ashes, just as Moscow had burned. Yet, the Parisians lacked the spirit for such a fight. Ordinary citizens, prioritizing their own happiness over a distant illusion of glory, were unwilling to sacrifice themselves for the Emperor who had so long demanded such a heavy price for his victories.

It was our Emperor Alexander's magnanimity that disarmed Napoleon, but betrayal from within his own circle sealed his fate. Those closest to Napoleon – comrades elevated by his patronage to the heights of power and prosperity – turned against him. Seduced by promises of a better future for France or for personal gain, marshals and generals betrayed him. Marmont surrendered an entire army corps to the Allies, while Ney and Lefebvre openly declared their allegiance to the Senate's ruling, not to the Emperor. In this moment, Napoleon – our adversary, but undoubtedly a great man – was worthy of compassion!

And so Louis XVIII ascended to the throne of France. The Prussians returned to Berlin with Blücher, the Austrians took their separate path, while we were promised a respite in cantonment quarters. Our Commander-in-Chief, Barclay de Tolly, conducted an inspection of Count Langeron's Corps, though the success of that parade came at a great expense of effort and preparation.

Meanwhile, we remained bivouacked in one spot, casting a glance back at Paris and savouring our simple Russian porridge. Spring had arrived; fields turned green, the fresh air softened, and after the bloodshed, nature seemed to renew itself.

Today, March 25 (April 6), an armistice was declared for 48 hours, allowing foragers to venture further with an officer, permitted to requisition necessities – bread, oats, and other supplies – by simply obtaining the local *Maire's* signature; those with money could buy additional goods. We welcomed this relief and were ready to endure more if it meant that peace was within reach. Napoleon, meanwhile, had retreated to Fontainebleau, concealed within its dense forests, negotiating with the Allies like a cornered cat. His once-loyal comrades had abandoned him; only the old guardsmen remained, vowing to stand by him to the end. Our final trophies from this campaign came with Count Chernyshev's capture of 22 cannons and 400 gunners at Fontainebleau, soldiers making their way up from the depot at Orléans.

All French prisoners were dismissed to their homes, and I witnessed a touching scene amidst the chaos of war. Three French soldiers were seated in a long wagon from Paris. Beside one of them sat a woman with a young boy, while on his lap he cradled another child. This sprawling infant, wide-eyed with wonder, never looked away from his father, nor did the mother. The father's gaze shifted tenderly between his children, his wife, and his comrades, each look heavy with unspoken emotion... The French soldiers seemed reluctant to converse with ours, as though ashamed to face the magnanimity of their victors. Our men approached them with gestures of goodwill, offering tobacco and initiating conversation through nods and hand signs. Among the dismissed soldiers were mere boys, barely eighteen years old, frail and ill-suited for the burdens of musket and knapsack; they were pitifully unworthy targets for our guns, mere fodder for cannon (*chair à canon*). It was equally poignant to observe the locals in the town. They sat quietly in the streets, on doorsteps, or at their gates, watching our soldiers with wide-eyed curiosity, as if peering into another world. Their expressions betrayed an air of detachment from the past, as though Napoleon's shadow had already faded from their memories. The fickleness of the French! Though much is made of their courtesy, one cannot help but condemn their inconsistency. They are like children, strutting cockerels with no steadfastness. The fable of the frogs petitioning the king could scarcely be more aptly applied to any other nation.[22]

29th March [10th April]. Christ is risen! By divine providence, we found ourselves near Paris on Easter Sunday, a day made more profound by the crushing of humanity's enemy. Mercy had triumphed, the bloodshed was over, and the laurels of peace now fluttered in the breeze. Our Emperor fasted, and the entire army fasted alongside him. Despite the solemnity of the day, the circumstances did not allow for a full celebration of the holiday. It was strictly ordered that no one should leave the bivouacs to enter Paris, and officers diligently ensured that no soldiers went absent. Yet we observed the feast as best we could. Matins was held in the Catholic Church of Longjumeau, attended only by Count Langeron and the General Staff. Regiments that had salvaged field chapels held their own services, and in all ranks, prayers were offered for peace. The lower ranks were granted a special ration of meat to break their fast. As for myself, I ordered a ham and a pie from Paris to mark the occasion, though red-dyed eggs[23] were nowhere to be found. Without them, the customary triple kisses were also absent. There were no swings or festivities, and the soldiers spent the holy day in their bunks, reminiscing about Mother Russia, where joyful celebrations and crimson eggs would surely abound.

---

22 In one of Aesop's fables, the frogs, dissatisfied with having no ruler, asked Zeus for a king. In response, Zeus sent them a log, which initially frightened them but soon became a source of mockery due to its inactivity. Feeling emboldened, they petitioned Zeus for a more fitting ruler. Annoyed by their complaints, Zeus sent them a stork, who promptly began devouring the frogs.

23 The traditional symbol of Easter in Russia.

Meanwhile, astonishing changes swept through Paris. Napoleon's name was erased from public view, as the French proclaimed Louis XVIII their King and pledged allegiance to him. A new constitution was drafted, and Napoleon was compelled to abdicate the throne and disband his loyal army. The victors stripped him of all territories and titles of power, granting him and his wife only the honorific Imperial title. The island of Elba was designated as his refuge, and he was granted a pension of two million francs a year from France's income, though he was required to return all valuables taken from the state treasury, making it unlikely he'd see much of that sum. Half of this pension was to go to his wife, who was given full ownership of three minor duchies in Italy, while his family members were allowed to retain the property they had accumulated. Accompanied by an escort of 1,500 guards, Napoleon was permitted to select only 400 soldiers to follow him to Elba, choosing primarily Polish loyalists. Such are the sudden reversals of fate for a once-mighty figure! The Emperor of the French, conqueror of half of Europe, terror of monarchs, and scourge of the human race was brought down from the lofty height – disarmed, stripped of power, reduced to an ordinary man. Only his name, etched in glory and infamy, would remain in the annals of history and pass into posterity.

Our troops began to cultivate their cantonment quarters. French soldiers from Napoleon's army marched past us in droves towards Paris, with passes for home leave.

At dawn on 31st March [12th April], Count Langeron's troops, consisting of 8th, 9th and 10th Corps and General Korf's cavalry, a total of twenty thousand men, set off from the bivouacs at Longjumeau towards Paris. We were expecting a review from the Emperor, and therefore marched in parade order, in strict smartness. The merchants had learned about our departure, and from the bivouacs to Paris they saw off the soldiers with their cognac, which they plied diligently, as if it were free. We entered Paris via the Boulevard de l'Hôpital. On the left were the little houses of the suburb of Saint Marcel, while to the right was a wall. Approaching the Austerlitz bridge, there was a huge building to the right: *Hôpital de la Salpetrière*. Facing the bridge itself, to the left of the boulevard, is the Botanical Gardens (*Jardin des plantes*). While the artillery was crossing the bridge, I decided to ride into the gardens. In front of the iron latticed gate sat tradeswomen with sweets, lemonade and oranges. It was warm spring weather. At the entrance to the gardens, on the right side, various animals were presented in iron cages: a lion, lioness, lion cubs, a leopard, hyena, black wolves, porcupine, beaver, and others. I liked the old lion most of all; his sullen, intelligent and regal face expressed strength and power; I regarded the king of beasts with a glow of respect. The lioness with a dog surprised me; it is said that they were fed together and got so used to one another that they cannot be parted; when they are given a piece of meat, the dog is the first to rush and eat, even daring to growl at his generous mistress if she so much as moves her paw towards the food; but for all that after dinner this faithful comrade looks for fleas and smooths the golden fur of the lioness. Two lion cubs were lying very nicely, their paws on each other. The hyena, with its fur on end and its head bowed, walked up and down in its cramped confinement, and no one dared to go near its cage. The porcupine, like a hedgehog, only seven times its size, sat motionless, raising its long and prickly needles, which, it is said, it launches at its enemies like arrows. Further into the gardens were a white elephant and monkeys; but I valued my time, concerned about lagging behind the troops and catching the eye of strict commanders, and therefore I was content with what I had seen. I glanced at the long avenue leading to the pavilion that housed the Natural History exhibit. It is a pity that now was not the time for an education on the beauty of nature. In the spring, when all the plants collected from various countries of the world bloom here, you can delight your eyes; at the moment everything is still dark, excluding the evergreen cypress trees. The banks of the Seine are quite beautiful: it is sloped on the left, upstream of the bridge, and there are many boats on the water, and on the right is a steep bank, dressed with stone. The Austerlitz Bridge is a masterpiece; it is entirely constructed from iron girders; only the railings are thin.

From the bridge we went along the Boulevard St. Antoine; the suburb of the same name remained to our right. Thus, the city is currently separated from the suburbs by boulevards. There are six suburbs on the right bank of the Seine: Saint Antoine is the largest; du Temple, Saint Martin and Saint Denis, are smaller; the suburb of Montmartre is decent, and Saint Honoré, adjacent to the Seine, is quite large. The area between the Austerlitz and King Louis XVI bridges, no more than four *verstas* [2⅔ miles], contains the best part of the city; to walk along the boulevards from one bridge to the other, it seems, should not be more than six *verstas* [four miles]. The main street to the west is Saint

74

Honoré, running three and a half *verstas* [2⅓ miles] from Pont Neuf. Another street, Saint Denis goes across the city directly to the same bridge, almost three *verstas* [two miles] distant; a street like this goes to the Notre Dame Bridge from the suburb of Saint Martin. Napoleon had planned to build a new street for another four *verstas* [2⅔ miles] from the Tuileries chateau, across the suburb of Saint Antoine; he certainly would not have regretted the many houses that would have to have been demolished for this. And so Paris, on the right bank of the Seine, would be about 7½ *verstas* [five miles] in length and up to four *verstas* [2⅔ miles] in width. There are three suburbs on the left bank of the river: Saint Marcel, Saint Jacques and Saint Germain, two of which are very large. This half of the city is almost surrounded by boulevards, in an area of about eight *verstas* [5⅓ miles] from the Austerlitz Bridge to the Louis XVI Bridge. There are still some huge buildings outside this area: Les Invalides, the University, the Cadet Corps. Moreover, the ancient Luxembourg Palace is on the outskirts of Saint Jacques, the Mint on the outskirts of Saint Germain, and on the edge of the suburb of Saint Marcel is the Astronomical Observatory. The most important street in this half of the city is rue Saint Jacques, which cuts across, from the Obervatory to the Notre Dame Bridge, almost three *verstas* [two miles] away. It can be deduced from this that if one were to enter Paris from the suburb of Saint Martin, then one could walk along the eponymous street to the Pont Notre Dame, and then along the Rue Saint Jacques to the Observatory, to cut right across the city, seven *verstas* [4⅔ miles] across. The river Seine flows eight *verstas* [5⅓ miles] through Paris, starting one *verst* [⅔ mile] from the Austerlitz Bridge, and a *verst* [⅔ mile] beyond the last, Jena Bridge, in front of which, on the right bank of the river, is the palace of the King of Rome. The river at the Austerlitz Bridge is no more than 60 *sazhens* [420'] wide, not particularly swift, and not very deep. Paris is open on all sides, and has 40 gates; on the right bank it is dominated by the high ground at Montmartre and Belleville; therefore, without fortifications or a citadel, it could always be captured by a small body of troops, if the strength of the people and the resources of the Kingdom were not enough to provide a good army to prevent an enemy from reaching the city.

From the Boulevard Saint Antoine we entered another, du Temple. Our gaze did not know where to rest, for there was so much to see! Beautiful buildings, shops with goods, dazzling crowds of people of all classes, presented various vistas on both sides of the beautiful street. We passed two theatres, the Turkish Gardens, and a magnificent fountain. The signs of the restaurants were very attractively painted and tempted us, but time and circumstances did not allow us to feast on. From the crowd of spectators, most of the ladies stopped to look at us; French women rushing to the fountain pool, brought water and very eagerly watered our soldiers. As we neared the outskirts of Saint Martin, crowds were gathering, and at last we saw a series of ceremonial carriages in a white and blue livery, leaving the Rue du Temple in the suburb of this name with theatrical spendour, towards Belleville Gate. The troops halted. Sitting in the gilded carriages, the elderly Peers, covered in powder and in their uniforms embroidered with gold, evidently fatigued, were dozing sweetly. From all floors, men and women, ugly and beautiful faces peeped out of the windows. The ladies' dress was simple. I noticed many black, velvet caps, like grenadier caps, decorated with three lilies: these had become fashionable at the time, and they were mourning for Napoleon. A passing Bashkir, in a red caftan and a yellow fox cap with earflaps, with a quiver and arrows behind his back, caused a lot of laughter in the middle of this parade. The French shouted after him: "*Voilà un amour de Sibérie!*" ("Look, a Siberian Cupid"). The National Guard were lining the sides of the street. The French soldiers, merchants, and artisans, were smartly dressed, in blue uniforms and bicorns with white cockades, in white short breeches, in stockings and shoes. Many of the ordinary soldiers were handsome youths, with spectacles on their faces and curls, carrying muskets in their right shoulders. A beautiful lady in a white dress was speaking in a friendly manner with one of these dandies. We halted and the procession of court carriages stopped; then we were ordered to wheel to the left as soon as possible, into the suburb of Saint Martin, while the procession of Lords, Dukes, Senators and very important persons continued their slow progress to meet the King's brother, Count d'Artois.

Finally, having crossed the suburb of Saint Martin, along the street, past the hospital of St. Louis, we went eight *verstas* [5⅓ miles] out of town, and stopped for the night at the village of Bondy. There were fewer people here, and the locals were rarely to be seen; only boys, with sacks around their necks, moving along the ditches, waist-deep in water, and catching green frogs to be made into sumptuous meals in restaurants. I wanted to take the risk of going to Paris to visit the theatre le Grand Opera, in addition to my thoughts about this glorious capital; but hesitated in my reasoning. Having no money but half a franc, I was ashamed to borrow some from anyone, and consoled myself with the proverb of Doctor Panglos[24] that everything will work out for the best. Maybe, I thought, troubles would have arisen for me. Then, lying on the straw, in vexation, I continued this argument as follows: Many admire Paris, but for me, is it possible to exchange St. Petersburg and its surroundings for that? No, our city is more beautiful and splendid. And that's without saying anything about the morality of the Parisians. The luxury and refinement of all the pleasures in life have been elevated here to the highest degree. Every artisan is a master of their art: blacksmith, cobbler, tailor, confectioner and baker exhibit their *chefs d'oeuvre* under excellent advertisements. But all the pleasures captivate no more than a superficial celebration; sight, taste, and smell are enslaved by artistry. The more refined the sensory pleasures are, the more one's health could be damaged.

So, farewell Paris! Now I have known you, and, having returned to Russia, I shall cross out a lot in those books where biased travellers have exalted you beyond measure. We have seen the goods in the flesh. True, there are many things in Paris worthy of curiosity and surprise; but it was a wonder for the fortunate conqueror, who had seized the throne of revolutionary France and robbed the capitals of the European States, to collect all that was best in his nest! If we have something that is good in Russia, then it is ours and was born with us; that we can brag about. If Paris is decorated with many excellent buildings, if France is provided with excellent roads, canals, and enriched in communications routes, then this is all at the expense of the countries conquered by Napoleon, at the expense of the indemnities collected by him. In Paris, one might say, is the essence of everything elegant that Napoleon could squeeze out of the fruits of industry, the arts and knowledge from the whole world. But as for morality, there is none, for this city is the true school of debauchery. Let our young travellers marvel at the exquisiteness of the free arts in the Museum, or the works of nature in the Botanical Gardens; let them learn morality in the theatres and the Palais Royal, even if they are attending the Academy and the University out of vanity; finally, satiated with all the pleasures of refined luxury, let them return

---

24 A character from Voltaire's Candide.

to their homeland, where at every step they will feel ignorance, where they will be in eternal grief from their minds, and where, bored with everyone, they themselves will be useless creatures for themselves, and harmful to the State. Such is Paris! But to conclude – I went deep into an angry judgement about it, because I myself could not take advantage of any of its gifts. One must be able to enjoy everything in moderation and to find goodness among the depravity of others without damaging one's heart. In the hands of a wise man, both the lamp of life and venom could be beneficial. So, farewell glorious, dear, sweet Paris! I shall not see you again!

Chapter V

From Paris to Sainte Menehould

On April 4th [16th], we halted for a bivouac near the town of Meaux. The weather was beautiful; fresh green shoots were sprouting from the soil, and the trees were beginning to bloom. Nature was reviving with the end of the war. Guided by a magnanimous Monarch who bestowed peace upon Europe, the Russians removed the foreign yoke from people and had given new life to France. The world rejoiced as we returned from Paris – not like the French had from Moscow, carrying with them the contagion of death and calamities – but with laurels of victory and honour, and accompanied by the people's blessings.

Passing through Meaux and Lizy [*Lizy-sur-Ourcq*], we stopped for the night at Dhuisy. It was much more pleasant in the field than in the stuffy, devastated French huts, which resembled prison cells. Nature was unfolding its spring charms; the nightingales were singing, and squirrels were jumping in the trees. This was hardly marching but a pleasant stroll for us.

I had expected the town of Château-Thierry to resemble the bustling towns near Paris, but it turned out to be a modest settlement along the River Marne. Its stone bridge had been blown up, and the town's charm lay in a single street running parallel to the riverbank, bordered by a boulevard where the finest three-storey buildings stood. Nearby, atop a hill, were the ruins of an ancient castle with crumbling walls and towers, adding a touch of history to the landscape. The town bore visible scars of destruction inflicted by the Prussians under Yorck's command.

Outside Château-Thierry, we halted at the village of Dormans, where my artillery was stationed in a picturesque spot on the Marne's left bank. I found a secluded house perched above the river, hidden from the commotion of the bivouac. There, surrounded by the serenity of spring, I gazed upon the river's glistening streams and the verdant banks, savouring a rare sense of peace and detachment from the world. In moments like these, amidst tranquil daydreams, I felt truly happy.

Our journey continued through Épernay, situated on the left bank of the Marne. Larger and more significant than Château-Thierry, Épernay marked the gateway to Champagne, the famed wine region. The town was lively and encircled by gardens, its cheerful atmosphere contrasting with the devastation we had encountered earlier. From Épernay, we proceeded through Châlons-en-Champagne without incident. The French, relieved by the lifting of war's burdens, greeted us with growing warmth, though a lingering fear still shadowed their faces. In every village, as in Châlons, crowds gathered to watch us pass.

We were eventually assigned quarters in Sainte-Menehould, or Sankt-Mathilde, located halfway between Châlons and Verdun, near the vast Bois d'Argonne forest. This town, part of the Marne district of Champagne, sits at the boundary where the chalky downs of Champagne give way to the rich black soil stretching toward Verdun. The locals make their living through timber and livestock trade. Sainte-Menehould is also steeped in history, remembered as the place where the ill-fated King Louis XVI was apprehended by the postmaster during his flight from revolutionary France and returned to Paris, sealing his tragic fate.

Our quarters were excellent. I lodged in the home of Monsieur Forten, the *Ober-Forstmeister* [Chief Forester], a modest and venerable French naturalist. His house was a treasure trove, with a library of the finest authors and a cabinet filled with meticulously preserved stuffed birds. Thrilled by this haven, I settled in to enjoy a life among the Muses, accompanied by books, a guitar, a poodle, and a red-haired Westphalian jockey. What more could one desire while on the march? Here, we found respite after so many gruelling trials, but only briefly, as rumours soon began to circulate that we would be sent to Moldavia, where it was said that the Turks, emboldened by Napoleon's propaganda, believed us defeated and were advancing boldly toward Kamenets-Podolsky (Kamianets-Podilskyi). Meanwhile, newspapers announced that Louis XVIII was on the verge of arriving in Paris to assume the throne. Napoleon, now divested of his empire, had supposedly embraced the life of a philosopher. He packed up his library – requiring 160 carts! -and was being escorted to the island of Elba by our Provost General Oertel.[1]

---

1 Fyodor Fyodorovich Oertel (1768-1825)

Out of the habit of attending church on Sundays, I agreed to accompany another officer to Sunday service at a church perched on a hillside outside the town. The senior cleric, who had visited us earlier with an invitation, personally escorted us to the chapel, leading us through a side entrance to seats near the altar. We were placed behind a balustrade, in a cramped space on a narrow pew. The service began with as much pomp as one could expect from a modest church. Two canons, clad in colourful vestments and wearing peculiar black caps resembling *shishaks* [conical Asiatic helmets], moved solemnly before the altar, alternately singing and wailing cantatas. The Prior, wearing a leather yarmulke [skull cap], performed the rituals with exaggerated expressions, though his voice was notably excellent. Meanwhile, a boys' choir provided pleasant, if occasionally unruly, accompaniment, their antics often disrupting the solemnity. Napoleon's influence had extended even to church governance, evidenced by a gendarme overseeing the service. Clad in full uniform with a hat, halberd, and sword, he maintained order and imposed reverence on the congregation. The worshippers, predominantly women seated quietly on the benches, behaved impeccably under his watchful eye. At the service's end, the gendarme accompanied a charming young woman who circulated the congregation with silver offertories, her pleasant demeanour and smiles encouraging donations. We offered half a franc and then quietly returned to our seats.

Instead of a sermon, the Prior recounted the adventures of St. Martin and the story of a pestilence that swept through Rome during the early days of Christianity. His narration, however, failed to captivate the congregation. Most of the women dozed under their bonnets or let their gazes wander, their expressions devoid of piety. A few elderly men, their spectacles perched on their noses and wigs slick with grease, occasionally sighed or raised their eyes heavenward, but they were exceptions. It seemed the church required the presence of police not just for order, but perhaps as a safeguard against the lax morals of the French. For many, the service appeared to be a social gathering rather than a spiritual experience. While the devout few focused on collecting donations, the majority came to see friends, grin at the canons' exaggerated gestures, or even wink at acquaintances. The more irreverent plugged their ears to escape the wailing and singing, making it clear that genuine piety was in short supply.

In the evening, the boulevard came alive with a leisurely promenade of townsfolk – mostly women, children, and the elderly – enjoying the music played by the 7th Jäger Regiment. Among the crowd, some strikingly pretty faces stood out, particularly those of the maids, who were often more attractive than their mistresses – a phenomenon familiar from Russia.

The town revealed much of its character through its bustling activity: shops brimming with goods, skilled artisans of every trade, two squares, and the lively boulevard. The buildings were respectable, with the *Rathaus* (town hall) standing out as the most distinguished of them. I developed a close friendship with my host during my stay, which deepened when I gifted him a copy of *Don Quixote*. In return, he presented me with two pistols. One I used to test the quality of gunpowder, while the other became a convenient tool for lighting candles at night when I lacked flint and steel.

On April 13th [25th], we attended a hunt in the Argonne Forest, which was under the jurisdiction of my forester host. Around thirty hunters assembled, giving the impression we intended to clear out all the game in the forest. We rode out about three *verstas* [two miles], then dismounted and entered the woods, each of us armed. The forest was bare of leaves, with ponds and swamps near the entrance. Our first stalking attempt was unsuccessful. Hounds were released on one side, while we lined up facing them in the centre, spread thirty paces apart. My plump host, dressed in light green, blended with the bushes, though his bright red boots stood out like roots, making him look almost like an odd forest creature that could charm any bird or animal of the Argonne Forest. Our self-appointed commander-in-chief was Monsieur Chamisseau, an old royalist on a grey horse, with his cap jauntily askew. He led with noisy enthusiasm, barking orders, which my host, the actual head of the foresters, tolerated with amusement, calling him a *tête exaltée* (hothead). I hadn't handled a gun in some time and, left on guard alone in the forest, grew a bit apprehensive, especially at the thought of encountering a wild boar. Not overly confident in my aim but armed with a good double-barrelled gun, I tried to steady myself against a sturdy tree for safety. Others without guns had prudently perched in the trees.

Just then the dogs started barking, and the beaters' shouts drew nearer, sending my heart racing. I steadied my gun, ready for the approaching quarry. Suddenly, two shots rang out to my right, and a whistle summoned us back. Our enthusiastic Monsieur Chamisseau had been the first to miss a deer, though he insisted he'd wounded it, appealing to the dogs as witnesses. We moved on to another spot, and this time, they positioned me on a slope along an actual boar's path. Bracing for an inevitable encounter with the tusked beast, I focused as the hounds' barking drew nearer. Suddenly, something black darted toward me through the trees. Bam! I fired, convinced it was a boar, only to find it was a thrush, which dropped down, while a wild goat bolted past, crashing into another officer standing sixty paces away. The goat ran to the left, along the entire line, and survived several near misses from skillful marksmen; by the time we gathered on the sound of the whistle, it had disappeared into its original lair.

Determined not to return empty-handed, we pressed on to new spots, where tracks suggested a herd of about ten boars. This time, I was placed in such dense underbrush that I could only spot game within ten paces. The boars indeed charged one of the hunters, who scrambled up a tree in panic, while another missed a shot at a wild goat. Our efforts, thus, remained fruitless. The damp weather and occasional rain added to our discouragement, and though we paused for a hunter's lunch after two attempts, most of us had lost enthusiasm. Defeated by both weather and misfortune, we abandoned the hunt and made our way back to town, chased by the rain.

In the evening, an actor who had come from Vitry with his wife decided to entertain the audience with a performance at the theatre. On the posters, he promised two operas and a comedy. We assembled at the theatre out of philanthropy. The stage and circle at first glance seemed similar to the fairground and popular theatres in Russia. The assembled audience of some 30, included six ladies and four maids. There was no music, although according to the posters for the opera there should have been nothing but music. The black curtain was raised, and what? A stereotypical, filthy old woman began to distort her face to represent a miser; she hugged her money box, talked to herself about money, and made various grimaces at the chorus. This concluded the first opera: *l'Avare*. We laughed, clapped, stomped, whistled; but the miser continued her capering without a pause. The second opera was *Défiance et Malice*, which we had seen in Châlons; there it had been played badly, but here it was even worse. The third play was the comedy, *Matilda*. Its premise was simple: a playwright wanted to write a drama, and his mistress presented various roles for him to try. Thus, two operas and a comedy had been performed without music, by one actor with his wife. With this extraordinary talent, they are now able to travel all over France, where foreign troops are quartered, and, despite the stomping and whistling of the audience, on the first night they could collect at least 30 francs, which will amount to a hefty income for one month, especially if they are travelling by donkey. How resourceful are the French!

The members of the *Municipalité*, or the Town Council, and other honourable residents decided among themselves, I don't know for what occasion, to offer dinner and supper for our General Veselitsky and for all the Russian officers. I was invited late. I was very angry with the tailor, who did not have time to make me a new outfit either for dinner or for the evening, and forced me to go to the ball in an old uniform. Many Frenchmen complained about me that I had not come to dinner, which was very plentiful, but without any order: whatever food was in front of them, they grabbed, according to the custom of the French. One needs to know one's temperament well to be able to choose a dish to one's taste and health. In the evening the officers danced until about three o'clock in the morning, and with such enthusiasm that at last everyone sat down in the corners of the hall and breathed like greyhounds after a good chase of the hare. The ladies were detained and were not let past the doors; some of them, fearing that it could not be worse, left through the windows. Punch, or *Horchata*, sweets and preserves were not served, but whoever wanted refreshments could get puff pastries at the buffet and ordinary wine only. The music came from our 7th Jäger Regiment. The dancers were very pleased. Some of them had pleasant faces, but I did not notice any beautiful ones. Their dress was very modest: only muslin, from neck to feet; even the arms were not bared: everything was under a veil, and breasts fluttered under the muslin in tight lacing and broke free. The dresses were loose, not revealing any attractive figures, but for all that they were short enough to reveal beautiful legs. It seems that the French women here did not dress according to the fashion magazines. Their hair was trimmed with flowers, ribbons, and mother-of-pearl combs; others had belts with coloured stones, in antique fashion. All the ladies were cheerful and lively. The most beautiful of them, in our judgement, was Mademoiselle Emilia, a dear coquette: her beautiful eyes, liveliness in her expression, smile, gracefulness, were attractive; some sentimental officers were already sighing after her.

For the first time, French women turned out to be well disposed towards Russian officers, and were grateful for their courtesy and finesse, which revealed quite a degree of education, which they did not expect from us at all. Despite the plain faces of the *mademoiselles* who were at the ball, I noticed in general that women, often very unattractive, seemed beautiful to us, precisely because they were women, not men, and they were dressed differently from us. For example, at the last ball there were many more good-looking officers, and if you could have dressed them in women's clothing, then all these Frenchwomen, after whom our brothers were chasing with such ardour, would not have stood a chance alongside them. The female face and their clothing alone deliver a greater impression upon us, with the help of imagination, than their intrinsic beauty. The passionate feelings of youth seek sustenance for the fiery heart; it often thinks to find charm in an object much inferior to its worth. But where passions dominate, proud reason is dumbfounded. The beauty, who tempted the young ensign so much today, if she were dressed in his clothing and in his place would certainly not have attracted the fiery gaze of a young man, while through her appearance she becomes an object of adoration. There was Emilia: take a look at her after the ball in the morning, in the kitchen, when she, in wooden clogs, trims the beef and, in the place of a maid, cooks a soup for herself that would seem tastier than manna to a man, had he only not seen with his own eyes whose hands were preparing it. Here is the beauty of one's dreams! A Chinese shadow play! They say a man is happy if he does not recognize his delusion; but it seems we would be happier if we were never deluded!

The main instigators of the ball and dinner were Monsieur Chamisseau, the hot head, and my host Monsieur Forten, both ultra royalists. During the Revolution, the former, a long-time supporter of the Bourbons, had been constantly persecuted by the governing party, which is why he lived in solitude on the interest from his savings, having been forced to sell his entire estate. The latter, also a supporter of the old dynasty, knew how to choose the middle ground without siding with one or the other party, and did well during the Napoleonic governance. During the Allied invasion of France, the *Forstmeister General* in Troyes ordered him to join Napoleon's army with a company of his forest rangers, some sixty men in all; however, Monsieur Forten did not do this using various pretexts, and therefore earned the gratitude of the new [Bourbon] Government for preserving the Argonne forest (stretching for ten [Russian] miles [46⅔ statute miles]) and for sparing the men. Both these gentlemen, much to the fury of the Bonapartists, were the first to manifest openly their commitment to the Bourbon cause through expressions of joy every day: the dinner and ball had been funded by subscription, and all Russian officers had been invited to them, as the first participants in the change of Government in France.

19th April [1st May] was a Sunday and May Day for the French. At midnight, the French youths, according to the established custom, walked around the town playing music, and in front of the doors of those houses where one or several girls lived, they played serenades, congratulating the beauties with the coming of spring. For young girls, who themselves were likened to spring, such a greeting was pleasant; but for those who, having passed through their summer and were closer to autumn, any congratulations of this kind added frown lines to their foreheads. For May Day, the French did not have any festivities, no ball, not even music on the boulevards. Some girls, dressed up, promenaded along the empty streets, while others, outside their houses, played shuttlecocks on the street, and often, following the flight of the feathery ball with their eyes, bumped into passing gentlemen... In Russia, on the contrary, on 1st May, even in the rain, there is fun and dancing.

The more my Ober-Forstmeister host learned about the character and education of Russian artillery officers, the more astonished he became. His wife, a respectable lady, mentioned that some French who had not yet encountered Russian prisoners believed that Russians walked on all fours. Monsieur Forten himself asked, "Do Russians still have harems, and how many wives do they keep?" I replied that, on the contrary, we respect women deeply, and we follow no Asiatic customs. If there were moral failings among the Russian nobility, I explained, they come largely from the tutors and governesses who fled France during the Revolution, bringing with them certain vices along with the French language. Horrified, my venerable Monsieur Forten exclaimed, "*Est-il possible*! That revolutionary corruption, which destroyed so much of France, even tried to reach you!" His astonishment only grew as I described how our nobility, entranced by anything French, had hired even the lowliest Frenchmen, like coachmen and shoemakers, to tutor

Emperor Alexander of Russia

АЛЕКСАНДРЪ ПЕРВЫЙ
ИМПЕРАТОРЪ и САМОДЕРЖЕЦЪ ВСЕРОССІЙСКІ
Его ИМПЕРАТОРСКОМУ ВЕЛИЧЕСТВУ

ALEXANDER the FIRST
EMPEROR and AUTOCRATER of all the RUSSIAS.
Dedicated to his IMPERIAL MAJESTY.

"The Three Pacifiers of Europe" – Emperor Alexander of Russia, Frederick William of Prussia and Austrian Emperor Francis. (French print, circa 1814)

THE IGNOMINIOUS *Escape of the Corsican Tyrant* FROM THE *Just Vengeance* OF THE RUSSIANS.
Bonaparte who advanced into Russia at the head of at least 300,000 Men. Elated, Confident, & loud in his Predictions of Success in 2 Months from the date of his Vaunting Proclamation that he was about to Seal the Fate of Russia, he was Outmanoeuvred as a General, Outwitted as a Politician, & compelled to devolve his Army as the head of which Conspicuous which he had led them to first departed at the Servant of Vatilecourt in a Sledge into the Villages of Smorgonie, &c. in the dusitions He read was Loosely seated with his dead Father Mehlum a Snail in the wind that is the Insignificance of its Character.

Above: *Napoleon's invasion of Russia in 1812 marked a turning point for his empire. Within six months, the French army was destroyed and Napoleon was compelled for fight for his survival in Germany. Countless prints illustrated the momentous events of 1812, including this aquatint by John Massey Wright and John Hassell, published in 1813.*

Below: *Napoleon was defeated in the epic "Battle of the Nations" at Leipzig in October 1813, paving the way for the Allied invasion of France in 1814. James Atkinson's drawing shows the meeting of the Emperor Alexander of Russia, King Frederick William III of Prussia and the Crown Prince of Sweden in the Great Square of Leipzig after the memorable battle.*

MEETING OF THE EMPEROR OF RUSSIA, KING OF PRUSSIA & THE CROWN PRINCE OF SWEDEN, *ACCIDENTALLY in the great Square of LEIPSIC, after the MEMORABLE BATTLE of the 18th of October 1813.*

In this Battle Bonaparte & his Grand Armies were completely overthrown, with the loss of 70,000 men, 150 pieces of cannon, all the magazines & stores at Leipsic, The King of Saxony, all his court, 12 French Generals, 300 staff officers, besides the rear guard of the French Army, at least 30,000 men, were made Prisoners.

Above: *Russian Artillery during the 1813–1814 Campaigns, as seen by Georg Adam (1784–1823).*

Below: *Soldiers of the Russian Imperial Guard during the 1814 Campaign, as seen by Georg Adam (1784–1823).*

Russian artillery in action during the Battle of Montmirail on 11 February 1814. (By Mikhail Mikeshin)

The Allied armies during the Battle of Paris on 31 March 1814. (By Bogdan Willewalde)

"They were captured in 1814". (By Bogdan Willewalde)

The French cavalry overrunning Russian artillery at Champaubert on 10 February 1814. (By Jean-Charles Langlois)

Panoramic view of the battle between Napoleon and the Russo-Prussian corps at Château-Thierry on 12 February 1814. (By Simeon Fort)

Сраженіе при Бріеннѣ.
Января 20 дня 1814 года

The Battle of Brienne on 29 January 1814. (A Russian lithograph, mid-19th century)

Above: *The Battle at Arcis sur Aube on 20 March 1814.* (By Friedrich-Antoine von Kleist)

Right: *"Public Singers," a scene from Parisian life in February 1814.* (By Georg-Emmanuel Opitz)

Le Mardi-gras

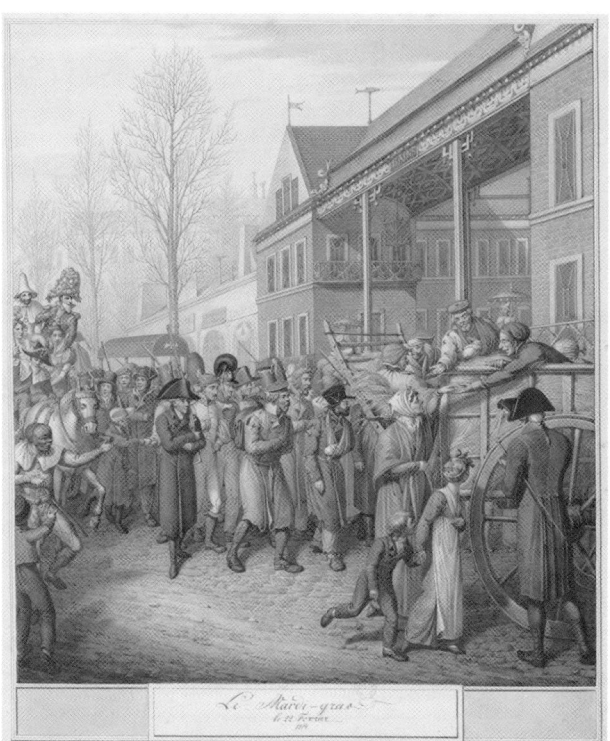

Left: *"Celebrating the Mardi Gras on 22 February 1814," with captured Russian soldiers visible in the crowd.* (By Georg-Emmanuel Opitz)

Below: *A scene from the Battle of Arcis sur Aube.* (A contemporary German print)

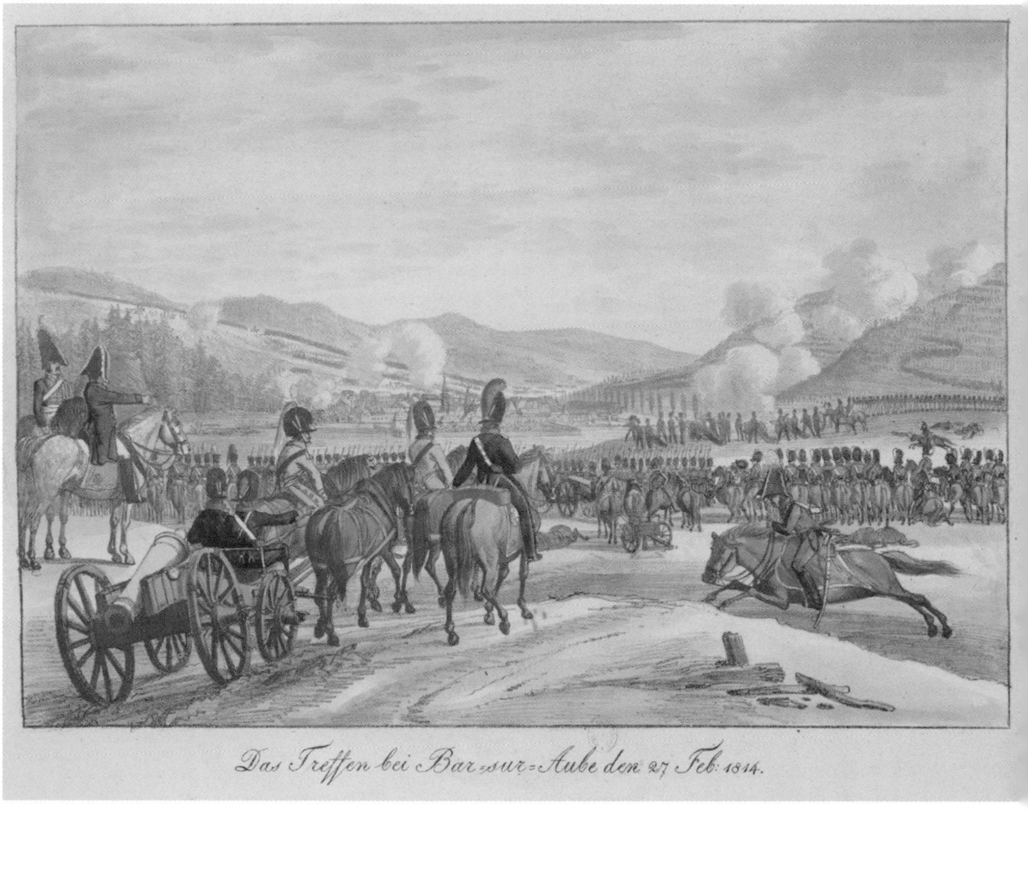
Das Treffen bei Bar-sur-Aube den 27 Feb: 1814.

Right: *"Arrival of the Good News in February 1814"*. (By Georg-Emmanuel Opitz)

Below: *A contemporary French print showing Cossacks looting and beating a French peasant in a barn; next to the Cossack lays an Allied proclamation promising personal safety and respect for private property.*

Left: *Emperor Napoleon of the French.*

Below: *Napoleon and his marshals during the campaign.*

Right: *Johann David Ludwig Graf Yorck von Wartenburg.*

Below: *Gebhard Leberecht von Blücher during the battle of Laon in March 1814.*

Барклай де Толли
Генералъ отъ Инфантеріи

Barclay de Tolly
Général d'Infanterie

Austrian Field Marshal Karl Philipp Fürst
zu Schwarzenberg.

Mikhail Barclay de Tolly

Fedor Korff

Dmitry Dokhturov

Peter Wittgenstein

Mikhail Miloradovich

Fabian von Osten-Sacken

Alexander Ostermann-Tolstoy

Aleksey Scherbatov

Ferdinand von Wintzingerode

Adam Bistrom

George Emmanuel

Fedor Oertel (Ertel)

Peter Kaptsevich

Ivan Panchulidzev

Ivan Paskevich

George Ludwig Pilar von Pilchau

Nikolai Rayevskii

Emmanuel Saint Priest

Mikhail Vorontsov

their children simply for their ability to speak French. To this day, I explained, some Frenchwomen of humble trades serve as governesses in Russia, transforming from tradeswomen to educators and becoming arbiters of taste and fashion. Shaking his head, Monsieur Forten remarked, "Your family patriarchs are terribly naive, though I see you still have many natural virtues. But as for us, alas! Nothing is as it was before the Revolution, and all this talk of equality has been misguided. But I must confess that we imagined you to be utterly wild. We were told that Cossacks ate human flesh. Now we see otherwise! You have brought with you such a standard of morality and education that one can only marvel. It is clear that Napoleon intended to depict you as savages, yet you defeated even the most cunning of enlightened conquerors, made allies of your former enemies, destroyed the common enemy of all nations, and returned peace and the good Bourbons to Europe." I explained that this was indeed the mission of our Emperor; we were but his executors. "But the glory of these deeds belongs to the entire Russian nation!" Monsieur Forten acknowledged. Such was our triumph.

According to the newspapers, Prince Electors, Dukes, Princes great and small, and all kinds of noble persons were constantly coming to Paris. The Russians had paved the way for them from all nations.

On 24th April [6th May], our General Veselitsky[2] held a Russian ball for the town in the great hall of the *Rathaus*, which was attended by Generals Rudzevich, Gurielov, and others; some 150 persons attended it. All the ladies made sure to appear in their best attire, but there was no richness in their dress, no sense of good taste or flair. Most of the girls were adorned with flowers, but their dancing was mediocre, marked by artifice and awkwardness. By way of apology, the French explained that they had rarely had the opportunity for enjoyment under Napoleon, and as a result, the ladies had neglected their dancing. The men, meanwhile, behaved like coarse republicans and Napoleonic bullies who were discourteous in their treatment of both the ladies and each other. It seemed that in his desire to transform France into a militaristic power, Napoleon had also undermined refined manners. The French were now nothing like they had been under Louis XIV: once gentle admirers and captive lovers of beauty, they had turned into brash brutes who no longer kissed ladies' hands. Meanwhile, the ladies conducted themselves like

---

2   General Gavriil Petrovich Veselitsky (1774-1829).

Amazons, drinking punch and wine, and eating with voracious appetites even at a ball. There was no sense of respect among them; their maids would sit by the doors of the hall, even if they did not participate in the dances, and remained seated even when their mistresses were standing nearby. The men only removed their hats in the presence of our Generals in the ballroom, but otherwise, they seemed glued to their heads. Apart from the French quadrille and waltz, they seemed unable to dance to anything else.

The Russians appeared most opulent at their ball, [serving] punch, lemonade, horchata, and whatever else one could wish to drink. The supper, in true French fashion, was chaotic, though delicious and abundant. The enormous, lengthy table was laden with all kinds of food, and people ate only whatever happened to be steaming directly in front of them. Our officers, attempting to display some decorum, passed dishes to the ladies, but in their clumsiness, navigating between hats and salvers, they ended up dropping asparagus or sauce onto others. French women seemed to have little taste for desserts; they were far more inclined to eat ham, crayfish, and meat than cakes, puddings, or blancmange. Monsieur Maire, the leader of the town, spared no expense in repeatedly proposing toasts with champagne to the health of our Emperor, shouting, "Vive Alexandre le Grand!" He then toasted the health of their King, the Russian Generals, and so on. At the end of the dinner, two ladies sang a verse from a popular song: *"Vive Alexandre! vive ce roi vaillant..."* Two young Frenchmen began another song, with the ladies joining in as the chorus. We applauded with cries of "Hurrah!" and kept our friends supplied with champagne. After supper, we danced for a long time.

During the final *matradura* dance, the daylight had grown so bright that candles were no longer needed, revealing the ladies in a completely different light. Some turned out to be paler, while others appeared with freckles, red faces, and wrinkles; in short, everything that had been hidden by the candlelight was now visible. The flowers on their bodices had wilted, dresses looked crumpled, and hats dishevelled; their languid eyes drooped, and their arms and legs moved lazily, all signs of sleepiness and exhaustion. Phoebus, the god of light, having touched the night's enchanting delights with his rays, had burned away all the deceptive embellishments and stripped the beauties of their polish. At five o'clock the next morning, this joyful yet exhausting ball finally came to an end.

This was a night that will remain memorable in the annals of the town of Sainte-Menehould. We stepped out onto the streets to be greeted by a bright new day. The artisans had already begun their work while we, as if drained from some official duty, were just heading off to sleep.

According to the newspapers, Louis XVIII had entered Paris on 21st April [3rd May], with all pomp and was greeted by the joyful exclamations of the people. The Duchess of Angoulême, the Prince of Condé and the Duke of Berry rode in with him. In the market square, a boy brought a basket of flowers to the Duchess, from which, at her touch, two doves flew out. Upon entering the Tuileries chateau, she was so moved by the memories of the past that she fainted. They gave speeches everywhere and everywhere welcomed them; some of the French, most of them the elderly, wept with joy, while others hid their malice under deceptive sincerity. Any perpetrators of some such lucky coup had been bundled off home. Long live Emperor Alexander! Let the laurel wreaths we pressed upon him intertwine.

On 26th April [8th May], I mounted my horse and set off with my *Ober-Forstmeister*, at about five o'clock, into the depths of the forest. The title of forest ranger was important in France. Mr. Forten was in charge of a forest 40 *verstas* [26⅔ miles] in length, containing countless trees suitable for construction. He made 40,000 francs profit for the Government annually. All trees over 40 years old may be felled; a good oak fetched 300 francs while a beech – 150 francs. The prices were shocking indeed! Mr. Forten had 60 foresters in his team, and was himself subordinated to the *Forstmeister General*, who lived in Troyes. These rangers always lived in the forest and continually patrolled their plots. Outsiders were allowed to take only dead trees or dead wood; otherwise, the perpetrators must pay a heavy fine for logging. Mr. Forten had marked all his trees, and trouble arose if he encountered someone with a branded tree.

We found cattle in the forest, which were picking leaves from the bushes. Mr. Forten wanted to get to the bottom of this with the owner of the cattle, which would cost the unfortunate man more than 800 francs for the leaves eaten by the cows, such that, according to the forester himself, his property would not be enough to pay. "But for all that, the law must be strict," he added, "it must be complied with." This is how enlightened people bring each other down, I thought. Mr. Forten was holding several villagers, forestry thieves, under arrest. Moreover, no Frenchman in his own garden dared to cut down trees without the permission of *Herr Ober-Forstmeister*. He looked after the trees as he looked after livestock; it was one of the most important streams of government revenue in France.

Within the forest, roads had been deliberately constructed, which in many places had been littered with abatis, to obstruct our troops. At the entrance of this forest, a tall, thin elm had been planted in the hedge in memory of the birth of Napoleon's son, the King of Rome. Napoleon had also left monuments to his rule inside the forest. Field hunting was also subject to the *Ober-Forstmeister*. Without his permission, no one would dare to shoot the game, even if it was sitting under his nose. When, at a certain time, that is, in the fall, in accordance with a licence, someone killed a goat, a deer or a wild boar, then the best parts had to be sent to Paris to the Court, such as a boar's head, which was valued at 40 francs; a whole wild boar cost 80, while a wild goat cost 50 francs. In one village, two *verstas* [1⅓ miles] from the town, we rested and drank apple wine called cider. It bubbles like champagne, and the taste is very pleasant. This village was surrounded by apple and cherry orchards for several *verstas*; they sold their fruit annually for 100,000 francs; moreover, they made 40,000 barrels of apple wine. Mr. Forten showed me one vast apple tree that yielded some 100 francs a year; from this tree alone they could produce two to three barrels of cider; while to make one barrel of this drink, one needed to harvest three barrels of apples. With such high prices for the products of fruit trees, they have, of necessity, become an object of special care, since a tree that does not require anything more than good husbandry is much more profitable than keeping any type of cattle. In the forest, I saw a telegraph erected on a platform, which, when needed, signals between a similar pair, each six *verstas* [four miles] apart.

The next morning, I attended church. The young preacher had a distinctly good voice and gestures. He preached on the spirit of truth and often said: "My brothers!" but he did not address the sisters, in spite of the fact that there were no decent men among their brothers, apart from a few 60-year-olds with glasses, and boys; even so, the space inside the church, on the pews, was filled with sisters who, grinning from under their high hats, were casting glances at us, while the elderly, relaxed by the voice and spirit of truth, slept. The confessor himself, who was reading the sermon, apparently not his own composition, dissembled the manuscript poorly, often stumbling over it, although he gazed beautifully at the heavens and charmingly laid his hand upon his chest. "My brothers! Endure sorrow and be comforted by the truth that dwells within you!" If Napoleon had seen him, he would have certainly taken him to the grenadiers, or to the trumpeters, he had been raised so far but was incapable of the priestly calling.

In the evening several women strolled along the boulevard and near the artillery park, while most of the maids played in the streets, until nightfall, with a shuttlecock. In the best houses here, as in Russia, acquaintances went to play cards and talk about politics, without any entertainment from their hosts.

When I read Kotzebue's memoirs about Paris and the French during the time of the Consuls,[3] I thought that he had judged France harshly, but now I see even worse in everything, which I would not have expected. Having got acquainted closer with the French, I saw the people without character, headstrong, disorderly, even rude; what could not be expected at all from the descriptions by travellers, who had judged the whole of France from Paris alone as wrongly as if foreigners had begun to judge Russia from Petersburg alone, or Moscow. My scale also, perhaps, was too small, and from the society of people in the town of Sainte Menehould alone, one cannot draw conclusions about a whole nation. However, anyone may judge without presenting their judgement as truth, because anyone may be mistaken.

Finally, everything was in motion. The artillery of 9th Corps located in our town was on the march. Count Langeron's headquarters was to arrive here tomorrow. We were leaving for Russia. The French tried to persuade our soldiers to stay with them, promising mountains of gold, and already 32 men had deserted from 9th Corps over two nights; but a good soldier would never desert, while a bad one is no loss.

Sub Lieutenant Baron Ungern-Sternberg arrived from Laon, having been recovering there from an illness, he brought the news of the death of our company commander, Lieutenant Colonel Timotheev. We had not expected this at all. His wound was curable, but the phlegmatic constitution of his body, alternating doctors, concerns about moving and other circumstances made him feverish, St Anthony's fire [ergot

---

3 August Friedrich Ferdinand von Kotzebue's two-volume *Erinnerungen aus Paris im Jahre 1804*, published in Berlin in 1804.

poisoning] in the wound had finally brought him to death's door. For now, I remain the commander of the company, or the Caliph of us.

To those who were in love, the farewells were dear. Today (30th April [12th May]), we had to part with all the beauties of the town of Sainte Menehould. The general forced us to leave before dawn to spare the inhabitants from parting and farewells, to spare a few plump cheeks, which, perhaps, would have been wet with tears; but mademoiselle Emilia already in all the splendour of her morning glory, stood like a pearl at the window, and saw us off with languid eyes. Opposite her house, a crooked beauty, also looking at us, wiped her eyes either from tears or from waking. The town was just beginning to stir; many of the shutters were still closed, the streets were deserted, and the deep silence was interrupted only by the thud of wheels on the pavement and the clinking of the traces of our artillery. Unhappy Emilia certainly hoped to see one of the company commanders, who was head over heels in love with her. Cruelty! he had not even come to say goodbye to her; he did not seem to know that she had not slept all night thinking about him, and purposely stood at the open window, before anyone else, to allow herself to be carried off, under whatever pretext. What will her rivals say now? They will smile maliciously, rejoice in the misfortunes of Emilia, who mocked them with her beauty, and finally await the fading of her beauty in sorrow...

From Sainte Menehould we passed through the town of Clermont-en-Argonne, which seemed full of promise, passing Massillon's chateau on the hill; but it was little more than a village in the hills surrounded by forest. We stopped for the night in the little village of Vrencourt.

Chapter VI

From Sainte Menehould to Nuremberg

On 1ˢᵗ [13ᵗʰ] May, the troops of the 10ᵗʰ Corps approached the fortress of Verdun, and settled in quarters in the surrounding villages that formed the suburbs of this city. The French Commandant did not want to let a single Russian into the fortress or the city itself, and kept his guard. The city stands on the river Meuse, on a plain, and is surrounded by high ground at extreme cannon range. It was no bigger than Vitry, but the fortress and buildings within the city were incomparably better. Verdun is an ancient and wealthy city: there was a lot of silver and fancy goods in the shops. It was especially famous for its boxed confectionery; however, Kiev's [*Kyiv*] candied fruits are no worse than those here. Walking through the city, I saw very few residents; the large stone houses were for the most part locked up. Everything was quiet, as if in the depths of peace.

I was quartered in an old chateau, on the outskirts of the city. All the furniture was very dilapidated: mahogany armchairs upholstered in crimson velvet collapsed at the slightest touch. One could judge the mistress from her furniture and the antiquity of the chateau. It appears avarice had established its reign here, amidst the ruins of dilapidated luxury. There were only five souls in the chateau: an old Countess, an old wench cook, an old caretaker, an old horse, and an old *spitz* [pointer dog]. I never saw the old cat, of course, because there were no mice there due to a lack of bread crumbs.

The next day we marched in parade order through Verdun. The commandant did not want to let our troops pass through the fortress and argued for a long time with the generals. But when he was threatened with sending a courier to Paris, he allowed us to pass, still complaining that it was a violation. Soon thereafter, he received a reprimand from the new [French] Government, and all our troops, much to his annoyance, passed through the fortress unhindered and festively. The inhabitants of the city were very badly disposed towards us, and displayed discourtesy everywhere.

Towards evening we came to the village of Étain, where we had good quarters and fodder. I stayed with a royalist, an old servant of the King, who, being filled with hatred for Napoleon, greeted me as best he could, proclaiming the Russians to be the saviours of France; moreover, from time to time, compelled by his enthusiasm, he quoted impromptu verse, which he had composed sitting by the fireplace. His daughter and a young neighbour, very kind girls, were very pleasant company for me.

The local actors, wishing to entertain the three Russian Generals, gave a performance, but so inappropriately and badly that their whole performance was no better than a comic puppet show. In the first play some sort of Prince fell in love with an innkeeper's daughter and did various inane things; in the second, at the feast of the innocent, three brothers with their sisters distinguished themselves through their talent for tomfoolery; in the third play a shocking ballet was presented, with vile contortions and capering by half-naked, shameless actresses. The audience had the patience to sit through the entire performance, while some whistled and others clapped their hands with loud laughter.

We were champing at the bit[1] for Metz, a vast, wealthy, populous city and fortress, hoping to have fun there; but it was not to be. The commandant resolutely refused us entry, and forced us to go across the river Moselle via a pontoon bridge downstream of the fortress. The French sentries there did not even want to let the mounted men across, so as not to damage the bridge; but I told them: "If my guns are to cross, then I have to show them the way!" and, in spite of their intransigence, having drawn his sabre, the former led the way on horseback; all the others, whom they had previously detained, followed after me. During the passage of our troops past the fortress, towards the river, many French officers, in short blue frock coats, and soldiers in uniform but unarmed, came out and regarded us with curiosity. Their faces showed that they were Bonapartists, our enemies. The city was crowded: in addition to 40,000 regular residents, half as many again had gathered who had property in the surrounding towns and villages and were mostly devotees of Napoleon, and therefore were so boldly showing hatred and disdain for their new Government.

---

1 *Ostrili my zuby*, literally, 'sharpening our teeth'

Meanwhile, according to the newspapers, during his journey through some French cities, Napoleon had been forced to shout: *Vive le Roi!* and rocks had been thrown at him in his carriage. The wonderful French populace!

The fortifications surrounding the city of Metz are as extensive as those at Mainz; it would have been costly to capture. The Prussians had not dared to approach it. The city, very ancient and wealthy, stands at the confluence of the Seille with the Moselle. It was once the capital of the [Merovingian] Kingdom of Austrasia and was now the main city of the Moselle Department; it had significant manufacturing industries. It was the seat of a Bishopric. The drawbridges were raised when I rode up to the fortress; as a result, not honouring the city with an attentive glance, I had galloped away from it.

We went to Flanville [*Ogy-Montoy-Flanville*] to spend the night. I stayed in Count Fouquet's ruined manor. He lived in Metz himself, while here everything had been turned upside down, just as in the entire village. Everything in the rooms had been smashed, broken and stained; apparently, it had served as quarters for a gang of barbarians. But on the walls there were still some quite old portraits from the Count's dynasty, and one very good painting representing four musicians: *Accord*.

Thereafter we passed through the neat towns of Fouligny and Saint Avold, and bivouacked in the hills, excluding the officers who occupied huts in a devastated village. Here again there was a shortage of food. The locals spoke a mixed dialect, most closely resembling German. There were lead bearing ore deposits near the town. We passed through the city and the fortress of Saarbrücken. Spring was in full bloom; during the entire march there were beautiful vistas to admire; however, the dry weather forced the dust down one's throat.

We halted in the town of Sankt Ingbert. Seeing Germans again, we noticed a clear distinction from everything French. Industry was found at every step, although the land, due to the mountains, could not be richly fertile. There were iron and steel works by every stream. Each of the inhabitants was engaged in some kind of business, while in France, many idlers simply gawped at passers-by, or engaged in swindles. To tell the truth, the state of France in which we had seen it shattered our high opinions of the place. The French did not commend themselves to us in their own country. The Germans were superior to them in many respects, both in morality, as in diligence and order. We were very pleased to be going back to Germany. After France, German women greeted us for the first time at Sankt Ingbert.

The corps headquarters was located in the town of Homburg [in Saarland]. This is where the Montonner Mountains [*Pfälzerwald*] begin, and the province of that name. The inhabitants are poor.

Lieutenant Katomin was returned to our company from captivity. He said that all Russian prisoners of war had been released from France back to the army; that he, along with others taken at Reims, had suffered greatly; that in France they had been held in Limoges, in mountainous country, where the locals walk on stilts during the muddy weather.

In the preceding days we had passed over the mountains through the towns of Landstuhl and Kaiserslautern. On 15th [27th] May we spent the night in the small town of Dürkheim [*Bad Dürkheim*], at the foot of the Montonner Mountains. An even plain stretches from here all the way to the Rhine.

Taking advantage of a rest day, three of us (17th [29th] May) rode from Dürkheim on horseback to seek distraction in Mannheim, which lies on the right bank of the Rhine. For dinner we stopped at a tavern, where we were served a thirty-year-old Rhine wine (1783 vintage), a Nirensteiner, and it cost six chervonets [3½ gram gold coin] for dinner, with five bottles of wine. In the evening we saw a magical opera at the theatre: *The Devil's Rock*. The local actors are incomparably better than those in Frankfurt. The red hussar, Mr. Keibel, and little Pippi, Mademoiselle Miller, were so popular with the audience that they made a curtain call to hear the festive applause.

Today the troops formally entered the city via the bridge over the Rhine, which does not have the same grandeur as that at Mainz. A crowd of dapper Germans flocked to watch us. The quarters were good.

Mannheim is a small city but pleasant; it was rebuilt in 1700 and therefore looks very new; the streets in it are straight, wide and have avenues down the middle. The residence of the Duke of Baden used to be here. The palace in which he used to live is now empty, because all the treasures from it have been transported to Karlsruhe, where the Duke himself has relocated, and where our Empress now resides. The buildings in the city are clean and of the latest architecture. The cathedral church and two squares are not inconsiderable embellishments to the city.

The theatre presented the opera *Don Juan*; it was performed perfectly. Mr. Keibel was especially engaging in the role of Don Juan: his noble figure, appropriate gestures and skillful acting revealed a fine man and a good actor. I do not think that the sentimental Germans were uninterested in admiring Keibel, and that many of them would dream of him in the most pleasant manner. The scenery, costumes and music were superior to those in Frankfurt. The fairest of the actresses was Ms. Vernet, with a clear, pure voice; the main quality of her singing was that she did not change the expression on her face in hitting the high notes and roulade. I will never forget her charming figure, in a white satin dress, under a black robe, with chestnut hair flowing over her shoulders, who raised her eyes to the sky and folded her hands over her chest as she sang like a bird of paradise! Hell was presented very naturally, although no one has ever seen it in reality. There were so many fires and demons everywhere that it seemed that the whole stage was on fire; the cinders flew out of hell even onto the sinful spectators in the stalls. It was a great pity to see such a fine man in the clutches of the demons and in the flames, the lovable rogue that was Don Juan, or Keibel!

The next day, whoever wanted could stay in Mannheim, where the residents held a ball for our Generals.

Heidelberg stands on the river Neckar, at the foot of a mountain, and over a plain stretching to Mannheim, or to the Rhine. On the mountain is the old, dilapidated castle of the former Elector. The premier rarity in this castle, attracting all travellers, is an amazing, huge barrel, five *sazhens* [35'] in length and three *sazhens* [21'] wide; the upper end of the barrel is surrounded by a platform which is ascended by a staircase with 50 steps. To this day, the coat of arms of the Elector is visible, and Bacchus, in honour of his own; also, bunches of grapes and leaves in relief add appropriate decoration to the barrel, which can hold 236,000 bottles of wine. When the Elector lived in the castle, there were often dances on this barrel. It held the oldest wine, which, before the French Revolution, never diminished, because whatever had been drunk was immediately topped up with the best fresh wine. This whole country was often ravaged by warring forces, from which the inhabitants had been impoverished; having said that, the surroundings are picturesque. Looking at the castle, with antlers on the walls and high towers; looking at the ruins of all the castles in the mountains, among the forests, in gloomy seclusion, one must conclude that the customs of the previous Germans had been rugged, as much as the wild nature surrounding them. But how everything changed with the spread of the sciences and education! Maybe our offspring will wait for this golden age in our dear fatherland, in our bellicose Russia!

Fifteen *verstas* [ten miles] from Heidelberg is the small town of Schwetzingen, and in it the summer palace of the Grand Duke of Baden, brother of our Empress. The palace itself was not large and was dilapidated, but its best feature was the gardens, about five *verstas* [3⅓ miles] in circumference.

The first captivating view in front of the palace gardens was a pool with fountains and a parterre with flowers around it. We dragged the gardener out of the old theatre to guide us and he took us to the best places in the gardens. In addition to the avenue, the vistas of the orangery, ponds, canals and pavilions were located throughout the garden with a pleasant diversity, we saw an outcrop in a gloomy thicket of trees, and on it a marble Pan with his pipes. Within this cliff was a hidden water source, from which the rock seemed to be incessantly doused with water flowing down into a channel; the clarity of the water and the water meadow attracted many birds, which were bathing immediately in front of us. Thereafter we came to a temple of Apollo, above a grotto, from where water flowed down the steps from a jug held by a Naiad; to the sides of the temple there were latticed pavilions with griffons at the entrance. Only Apollo himself, standing inside the temple, appeared rather awkward. Further on, a simple, but beautiful temple dedicated to botany, or the goddess of flowers, was visible.

The ruins were most skillfully made of yellow, porous stone: dilapidated walls, arches, steps, overgrown with moss and turf; the pool and the weeping willow, above the water, between the ruins, represented a living painting of some ancient temple, crushed by the hands of time. Here one can forget for a while, by delving into nostalgic memories of the past. Then we came to a large pool surrounded by a high wall, or to the baths in which the Duke bathed. It was there that royal luxury greeted us. The three front rooms were decorated with Chinese, French and Italian wallpaper; moreover, there were many excellently executed paintings of landscapes on the walls. In the pool room, along the walls, in bas-relief were nudes of Nymphs presented in full height in a very lively and captivating manner, especially for the bather. Descent into the bathtub was via steps of grey marble; over the bath, golden snakes let in fragrant, cold and warm water when needed; there were mirrors in the walls, around the bath; on the ceiling, the Aurora was beautifully portrayed. The place was enchanting! Right there, in this room alone, there is a corded book in which visitors enter their names, with a *kreutzer* (coin) attachment. From there we came upon a pool, in the middle of which a large eagle owl held a turkey in its claws, surrounded by various birds. When the fountain is started up, water shoots up at the owl from the turkey, and from the birds. Then we entered one avenue, which, lost in the distance, was bounded by water; this surprised us: were the gardens endless? We came to a wall. Although, according to the gardener, this painting was over twenty years old, the painting still deceived the eyes; the pigment of the paints was no different to the natural colours of wood, earth, and air. On the other side of the garden, a Turkish mosque affected Asiatic tastes through its strange architecture and patterned decoration outside and inside: the variety of colours, blue and crimson with gold, in arabesques, was very pleasing to the eye. From here the ruins of a temple to Mercury could be seen in the distance. Thence an avenue led to the temple of Minerva, with statues of Juno, Apollo and others, missing arms and noses. In front of it, a beautiful pool was surrounded by four statues representing trapped deer. The figures of these animals, in white alabaster, formed a captivating vision among the greenery. This part of the gardens was the most popular for everyone because there were many well-dressed ladies walking around there.

Once we had emerged from the gardens as if from an enchanted labyrinth, in which there were so many wonders of fine art in such a small space, our imaginations had been seduced by pleasant visions. Feeling fatigued, we went into a tavern, where a pretty girl served us. Here we drank to the health of the Duke, the brother of our Empress, with champagne and for seven francs we hired a post carriage to Heidelberg.

From Schwetzingen to the city, the road runs along a plain and stretched out like a ribbon. The mountains, at the feet of which Heidelberg stands, at first appeared blue, then, as we approached them, turned purple and, finally, by the city, represented a picturesque landscape. It was apparent that the Duke loved to live like a king. His gardens have existed for 400 years. How much work, skill, and expense had been required to produce all the ornamentation in it, which was really worthy of the attention of travellers, as a memorable curiosity!

On 20th May [1st June], we marched. From Heidelberg, our route followed the banks of the river Neckar. I have never noticed such a lovely location as here, anywhere else: on the right bank, above the road, there were steep purple cliffs, decorated in places with greenery, or gilded by the rays of the sun, while across the river, to the left, there were blue mountains in the distance and a scattering of huts along the green banks; meanwhile, sailing boats, on the dark and calm waters, completed the charm of the views, which changed with every step. I could not stop gazing at them, and I shall always remember them vividly. The march was about 30 *verstas* [20 miles] to Ambach [*Eberbach*?]. The mountains were not very steep there. The weather was fine, the road was paved or highway.

Halfway through the march the next day we crossed over the Neckar. Mosbach is an unenviable town. A colleague and I stayed in a tavern at the entrance, where General Udom, the Army Major [Chief of Staff], and his Aide de Camp were also quartered; in addition to a crowd of people and horses; however, the landlord was very nimble everywhere, from the upper floor to the lower, from there to the attic, from the attic to the cellar, from the cellar to the kitchen, from the kitchen to the wood shed; he managed to raise some noise with the hostess, scold the servants, talk to us about the news, and exchange courtesies with the General on the top floor. This man, like a spinning top, moved all over with his arms, legs, head and tongue; it was *perpetuum mobile* made real. After that we had a Russian dinner: cabbage soup with pie and even a good chunk of roast meat with cucumbers, which had not been expected from a German. For all that, he confessed to us that he would rather have ten officers in the vacant rooms, rather than six servants, because the officers hardly ate supper, or ate little, while the servants or drivers were constantly demanding food and drink, having the stomachs of gannets.

Our troops paraded through the cities and towns, and the further they went, the more they strengthened, picking up groups from hospitals, or back from captivity; only these unfortunates appeared to be in a miserable state: being covered in rags, exhausted by shortages and disease, having completely lost their military bearing. But they were immediately supplied with decent clothing and placed in the ranks, or sent to the wagon lines.

For several days we marched through the mountains of the Duchy of Baden; the rain and stony roads made our trip unpleasant. We changed our daily routine: we got up at 2 o'clock in the morning, set off at 4 o'clock, had a halt at 7 o'clock to have breakfast, and slept until noon; then arrived at our new location quite early. The inhabitants of the village of Schweigern, where we were staying that day, were poor; we had seen this poverty since Mosbach itself, although it was greater here in the villages. Some of them were towns in name only – there was no wine and no beer to be found in them, and we were fed very poorly. The Grand Duchy of Baden belonged to the German Confederation; it had no more than a million inhabitants, and they had been quite ruined by taxes levied by the Duke and by war indemnities.

The stage to Igersheim was ten *verstas* [6⅔ miles], all of it up hill and down dale, in cloudy weather. The frontier where the Kingdom of Württemberg begins is four *verstas* [2⅔ miles] short of Mergentheim [*Bad Mergentheim*]. From the last mountain, the whole Kingdom was in full view in front of us: such was the range of the visibility. The sun, illuminating the mountains in patches through the rain clouds, presented pleasant vistas. These mountains, covered with pine and spruce, were named Schwarzwald (Forêt Noire).[2] We all went down the mountain, and suddenly, to the left, we saw the town of Mergentheim, and behind it many villages in a beautiful perspective. I admired this view for a long time, without moving from my place, and involuntarily exclaimed: "How rich the nature of the earth is in diverse views! Lucky locals!" The country here was more fertile than the one we had travelled through, and the land was highly cultivated: every patch of turf on the hills had been seeded or ploughed; grapevines planted everywhere. All the bad things finally came to an end here; the shortages, poverty, and devastation that we had encountered in the Duchy of Baden had disappeared. The people of Württemberg led incomparably better lives; it was apparent that they had been spared the destructive sword of Mars. Their clothing was old-fashioned, very similar to that of the Altenburgers.

Mergentheim lies on the banks of the River Tauber and was once the residence of the Grand Master of the Teutonic Order. We were quartered in the village of Igersheim, a sizeable settlement where the inhabitants seemed to keep to themselves. Even as we departed the area, we encountered very few people; perhaps they were hiding from us, or simply stayed preoccupied with their domestic and agricultural tasks.

The weather was pleasant, making the day's march enjoyable. The route through the hills, though challenging, was manageable. Evidence of industriousness was everywhere – no corner of the land was

---

2 Not to be confused with the Black Forest on the Franco-German border.

neglected. Despite the stony ground, the terrain had been painstakingly cleared. Stones were gathered into neat heaps, and even the crests of the hills were cultivated with care. Along the way, we passed through two towns: Weikersheim and Röttingen. In the former stands the ancient, uninhabited castle of Prince Hohenlohe. Though in ruins, its statuary and monuments offered a glimpse into the grandeur it must have once possessed.

We halted in the affluent village of Riedenheim, which surpassed many towns in Baden in charm and prosperity. Surrounded by expansive grain fields, the area radiated abundance, filling the heart with joy at such a sight. The villagers appeared prosperous, their well-fed figures as robust as their oxen. The women, however, lacked beauty, resembling stout Russian barmaids. Their attire was equally unappealing: scarves tied over their heads flared at the back, with flaps covering their ears. They wore thick, multi-coloured, knee-length skirts, heavily pleated as if supported by a bustle. Corsets compressed their chests, while a belt cinched their waists. Their bare legs, with ruddy, chunky calves, resembled those of geese. The men's clothing was equally distinctive, featuring skullcaps and knee-length leather trousers reminiscent of the Chumaks.[3] The houses were decorated with intricate red patterns against a white background, and some displayed painted images of saints.

On 28th May [9th June], we marched about twenty *verstas* [13⅓ miles] across a beautiful plain of grain fields. Tall rye swayed in front of us, and the ears rippled across the field. How nice it was to see valleys and hills after high mountains! It seemed relaxing to the eye. Halfway along the route was the town of Aub, located on a big hill; it had once been a fortress. To one side, in front of the town, the ruins of an ancient castle with towers were revealed through a dense forest.

Our journey from the Rhine had been picturesque, with the season enhancing the natural beauty, save for a few rainy and overcast days that briefly dulled the splendour of the landscape. The border of Württemberg lay four *verstas* [2⅔ miles] from the Bavarian town of Uffenheim. Although small, this kingdom was comparable in size to some of the larger Russian provinces, showcasing the results of efficient governance at every turn. With a population of roughly 1.4 million, Württemberg provided its king with an income of 20 million [roubles], sufficient to maintain an army of

---

3 The Ukrainian oxcart drivers

10,000 men. Napoleon had elevated the duke to kingship when forming the Confederation of the Rhine, further cementing its stature.[4]

While Württemberg had seemed pleasant, entering Bavaria brought a striking change. In the village of Rudolzshofen, we encountered robust, healthy Germans, stouter and ruddier than their leaner Prussian, Saxon, Badenese, or Westphalian counterparts. The women, with features reminiscent of Tatars or Kalmyks, could not be considered beautiful. Fashion appeared to have bypassed these people entirely; their clothing and customs were quaintly archaic. Both men and women wore peculiar, old-fashioned attire that added to their unpolished appearance. The men, in particular, sported loose, dubbin-saturated trousers, leather caps, and short jackets fastened with large copper buttons resembling coins. Yet, despite their unconventional dress and lack of refinement, their homes were impeccably clean, their economy flourishing, and abundance was evident even in the humblest households. The food, however, left much to be desired – they seemed unfamiliar with seasoning, offering us watery soups and boiled beef sprinkled with various herbs. As night fell, watchmen patrolled the crossroads, calling out the hours and singing hymns. Their voices lent an almost medieval charm to the village atmosphere, a quaint reminder of the olden days.

Bavaria was a land of remarkable beauty, its valleys and hills dotted with sprawling villages, lush meadows, and vast grain fields. The natural abundance captivated the eye and offered a serene comfort to any peaceful observer. Nature had been especially generous here, blessing the land with fertile, dark soil, interrupted only by occasional streams and patches of forest.

We soon passed through the small town of Windsheim and lodged in Lenkersheim, where we stayed in the workshop of a master cobbler. These towns lay within the province of Ansbach, which had previously been under Prussian control. In an interesting turn of events, we discovered that the pastor of Lenkersheim, a man named Oertel, was a relative of our Provost General.[5] Coincidentally, Artillery Captain Pavlov happened to stay in the very house where [our General] Oertel himself had been born. From the pastor, we learned the detailed history

---

4   Frederick III, the Duke of Württemberg (1754–1816), assumed the title of King Frederick I of Württemberg on 1 January 1806.

5   Fyodor Fyodorovich Oertel (1768-1825)

of his nephew, a revelation that added a deeply personal and unexpected connection to our journey.

On May 31st [June 12th], we fell short of completing the 15 *verstas* [10 miles] to Nuremberg [Nürnberg] and were forced to halt for the day in Langenzenn, a rather unimpressive locale. While the weather was pleasant and the scenery picturesque, the absence of vineyards was a disappointment, as we had not encountered any for quite some time. Instead of fine wine, we were served bitter beer. The hillsides were covered in hops, whose leaves, deceptively similar to those of grapevines, briefly offered the illusion of vineyards, but, alas, without any of their promise.

Chapter VII

From Nuremberg to Dresden

Nuremberg lies on a plain near the river Pegnitz, close to a prominent hill crowned by an ancient castle. On June 1st [13th], just under seven *verstas* [4⅔ miles] from this town, we passed through the bustling town of Fürth, where it seemed the entire population had turned out to watch us march by. The troops then entered Nuremberg in parade formation, surrounded on all sides by curious onlookers.

The city itself presented a mix of grandeur and decay. Its houses, built in a range of ancient architectural styles and painted in various colours, displayed an extreme diversity of appearance but were generally dilapidated. Notable among the buildings were the immense yet crumbling *Rathaus* [town hall] and the Church of St. Lorenz. The streets were uneven and narrow in places, with numerous bridges crossing the Pegnitz. Shops, located in a central area much like the *Gostinyi Dvor* in St. Petersburg, were surprisingly sparse in their offerings. Having heard of the famed Nuremberg goods in Russia, I expected to find lavishly stocked shops similar to Dresden or Frankfurt; instead, they were disappointingly poor. Though Nuremberg was once counted among the leading trading cities, and its population was largely composed of merchants, trade had greatly declined due to the war. A few shops still sold fine goods, but they were rare. Only the children's toys lived up to their reputation, crafted so well that they were exported to St. Petersburg and even America. The local theatre was reputed to be slightly better than that in Châlons, but I missed the performance of "Cossacks of the Don" while lingering in a shop selling caricatures. The Nuremberg residents, assuming that we had become wealthy after exacting a heavy indemnity from the Parisians, charged us triple the usual prices for everything, making our stay here an expensive one.

I was assigned quarters with a wealthy but astonishingly miserly merchant. His hospitality left much to be desired: he served me watery soup so unappealing that even my poodle refused to eat it, and offered vinegar in place of wine. At first, I avoided direct confrontation, instead sending a messenger to offer payment for better food. However, his callous refusal forced me to take matters into my own hands. I demanded to take charge of my own provisions and went to the *Rathaus*, where I promptly exchanged my voucher. My boldness enraged the proud miser. He claimed that for twenty years he had hosted soldiers, all of whom had been satisfied with his hospitality. I remained unmoved by his protests and ordered my batman to gather my things and move to new quarters. This prompted the merchant to summon a police officer, complaining bitterly that I had insulted him by giving his 'fine soup, flavoured with cinnamon', to my poodle. The officer, however, had witnessed my poodle's disdainful rejection of the meal and was unconvinced. My host, growing more indignant, demanded that the officer take an official statement. He thumped his chest, swore on his honour as a Lieutenant in the National Guard, and declared that he would not allow foreigners to insult him in such a manner. His fervour struck me as utterly absurd, and I could not help but laugh. My poodle barked in agreement, the officer chuckled, and the merchant, overwhelmed by the scene, cried out in frustration. Though my new quarters were humbler, my new host was kind and straightforward, offering me whatever he could.

At my new quarters, I was intrigued by a striking depiction painted on the wall of the house. It portrayed a giant named Jakob Domann, known as the "Wild Man of Lüneburg". Born in 1612, Domann was said to have reached the astonishing height of 96 inches or 8 feet by the age of 21 years and 6 months. According to the inscription, he had once lived in this very house. His olive complexion and love of the forest added to his mystique. Renowned as an excellent marksman, the painting depicted him wearing a coat and holding a gun.[1]

Nuremberg is particularly notable for its strict enforcement of public morality, especially regarding the absence of *nymphs of joy*. The city police diligently monitor such matters, and if any *nymphs* are discovered, they face a fine of 25 guilders or a jail sentence until relatives or

---

1 The Wilder Mann (comparable to the north American Bigfoot) was a popular mythical figure in the Duchy of Braunschweig-Lüneburg, especially in the Harz mountains, and often appeared in the heraldry of the region. It would appear that Radozhitskii was told a fairy tale by his host. Jakob Domann might well have been the name of the painter of the mural.

benefactors can secure their release. As a result of these measures, some forty of these unfortunate yet charming women were then housed in the ancient castle on the hill.

Nuremberg holds the distinction of being the birthplace of the pocket watch, originally known as *Nürenbergische Eierlein* (Nuremberg eggs) due to their spherical shape. Over time, these watches were made flatter, evolving into the familiar form. The residents of Nuremberg have long been skilled in crafting miniature items, particularly children's toys, for which the city is still renowned. However, Nuremberg's former splendour faded after the French Revolution. Both French and Austrian troops, upon attacking this merchant city, imposed exorbitant indemnities, bankrupting many merchants and depleting the wealth of its citizens. The city's once-thriving trade collapsed entirely, and without trade, merchant cities – in fact, entire nations – cannot sustain themselves. It struck me that the six Nuremberg shops in St. Petersburg seemed wealthier than this entire city. Even basic items such as a violin bow, books, a camera obscura, paints, or mathematical instruments were nowhere to be found. The merchant Bestelmeier,[2] reputed to be the wealthiest in Nuremberg, was the only one with a somewhat extensive collection of dazzling trinkets and fancy goods.

The following afternoon, my comrades and I visited Rosa's Tavern to see an exhibition of natural curiosities presented by a certain Mr. Brunner who was staying there. Although the display was modest in size, it featured a fascinating array of exhibits. Among them were a Chinese bell, shoes, and umbrellas; a crocodile; various lizards, dragons, and salamanders; a collection of saltwater shellfish; different coral and polyp specimens; and a remarkable turtle shell measuring nearly an *arshin* [28 inches] in length and three-quarters of an *arshin* [21 inches] in width. Particularly striking were the exquisite shells, including Mother of Pearl and Venus varieties. The exhibit also showcased a variety of bird species – parrots and birds of paradise among them – alongside bird and fish skeletons, stuffed animals, flying and thorny fish, and samples of different woods, seeds, ores, minerals, and rocks. Among the highlights were beautiful mosaics depicting a dog and a cat, rendered so precisely that their intricate stone patterns could only be discerned

---

2 Georg Hieronimus Bestelmeier, famous German merchant and wholesaler, who made his fortune starting the first mail order catalogue in 1793.

through a microscope. A basket with a cherry-stone handle represented the pinnacle of delicate craftsmanship.

All of this was displayed in one room. In another room, an assortment of butterflies was arranged in perfect symmetry, alongside silkworms in pouches and an astonishing display of silvery silk spun from spiders' webs. Mr. Brunner claimed that fabrics made from spider silk were far stronger, lighter, and cheaper than ordinary silk, requiring only the scattering of spiders in a room coated with fly bait to harvest it. Additional displays included scorpions, tarantulas, centipedes, enormous beetles, and sea lice. A separate room contained a more anatomical collection, including wax models detailing the gestation of a baby from the first to the ninth month. One model, a woman's interior, showed the heart, lungs, liver, intestines, and fetus in realistic detail, so lifelike it was almost repulsive. Another wax figure displayed an exposed hermaphrodite, which seemed utterly incredible. Yet, Mr. Brunner assured us it was based on an actual specimen preserved in alcohol by a Professor in Halle.

The highlight of Mr. Brunner's exhibition was a remarkable trained canary, a ten-year-old bird with a broken leg, which he claimed was intelligent and highly skilled. We gathered around a table where small cards, about two inches square, each printed with a large letter from the French alphabet, were spread in order, with the canary jumping on the table. Mr. Brunner invited us to request a name for the canary to spell out. We chose "Aleksandr". The trainer repeated the name and asked the bird to identify the first letter. The canary immediately hopped to the card with the letter A, picked it up in its beak, and handed it to him. *"Gut!"* he praised, then asked for the next letter. The bird dutifully brought the L and E. However, when it reached the double letters KS, the canary hesitated, unsure whether to choose Q or X. It jumped indecisively between the two before returning to the trainer empty beaked. To our dismay, the trainer scolded the bird, tweaking its head, causing it to chirp in protest. He repeated the name firmly and ordered the bird to fetch the next letter without naming it. Seemingly recalling a previous lesson, the canary correctly brought the X. The trainer then stroked it gently, and the bird quickly fetched the remaining letters, ending with the R. When the name was complete, the trainer praised the canary, which proudly hopped around the table, chirping with the final card in its beak and showing us the letter.

The performance wasn't over yet! Mr. Brunner claimed the bird could also solve mathematical problems using cards marked with numbers. To demonstrate, he asked, "How much is two times two?" The canary brought the card with the number 4. Then he asked, "How much is three times six?" This time, it fetched two cards in sequence: 1 and 8. Finally, Mr. Brunner asked one of us to show the canary a watch. "What time is it?" he asked the bird. The watch read 12 minutes past five. After studying the watch carefully, the canary first brought the Roman numeral V, then, with equal precision, fetched the Arabic numerals 1 and 2. We were astounded. How could such a small bird learn skills that many of the so-called intelligent creatures struggle to master? The canary, clearly no automaton, was later placed in a cage where it happily pecked at seeds. Beneath the table stood two more cages: one holding a goldfinch, the other a siskin. Mr. Brunner referred to these as his "students" and claimed that the goldfinch was even cleverer than the siskin. Impressed by the spectacle, we willingly paid him a *Thaler* [silver Dollar] for the experience. Reflecting on this display, we were struck by the extraordinary patience and effort Mr. Brunner must have invested in teaching the canary to respond so precisely to his voice. Surely, this is evidence that animals possess varying degrees of consciousness, understanding, and judgement, qualities intrinsic to all living beings.

After visiting the trained canary exhibition, we attended the theatre. Its state was a profound disappointment. Once a proud establishment, it had fallen into decay: faded scenery, worn-out costumes, and actors whose performances had dulled over time. The standout was Mr. Gnaut, who played Rochus Pumpernickel.[3] His antics were reminiscent of Châlons' Dumas, full of trickery and exaggerated gestures, and he managed to amuse the audience the most with his clowning. The play itself was insipid, featuring suggestive scenes and indecent arias that undermined morality, yet Gnaut's tomfoolery drew raucous cheers from the crowd, to which he responded with a grand, comical bow. The orchestra, despite its pretensions, was mediocre. The conductor, gesturing like a frustrated artist, flailed his hands, head, and legs to keep harmony and tempo.

After the theatre, we left the city to watch fireworks from a wooden platform. The crowd was immense – residents claimed it rivalled even the reception of the King of Bavaria. The fireworks were spectacular,

---

3   A Viennese folk comedy by Matthäus Stegmayer (1771-1820).

with features like cascades, a grand sun, bouquets, Chinese wheels, and a simulated bombardment of the city. The illusion was remarkable: walls and towers outlined with candles became the target of Mars's fire, while star shells [*Lichtkugeln*] were launched back at the fortress. It was a magnificent, harmless recreation of the war, a testament to the artists who had transformed scenes of destruction into an artful spectacle.

Regretfully, time did not allow us to visit the ancient Royal Castle in the mountains, with its art gallery and famed well with a 33-second drop.

In the city, balls were held nightly for our generals, and one could have made pleasant acquaintances given more time, especially since beautiful faces with languid eyes often peeked out of windows. Even in its diminished state, Nuremberg had offered us a surprising amount of enjoyment in just two days. One could only imagine what it was like when trade flourished and its artists were celebrated. But war, as always, consumes and destroys everything.

There was a tavern in the city, under the deceptive name of the Museum, which was the gathering place of all the spendthrifts with money to lose or to spend on drink.

We left Nuremberg with some regret on June 3rd [15th]. The route was hilly, skirting the edge of the Bohemian mountains, and we stopped in the impoverished village of Kappel. Here, nature's vistas turned grim: wild cliffs, sandy expanses, jagged rocks, and endless pines and firs dotted with burial mounds created a sombre atmosphere. The next day, we reached Hiltpoltstein, a village dramatically perched atop cliffs. Its church, built on the highest rock, offered a panoramic view of the surrounding countryside. We met the Pastor, a man with six daughters, each lovelier than the last and all charming us with their lively conversation.

Afterwards, we undertook a long march of over 30 *verstas* [20 miles] through the mountains, stopping in Creußen, a wild and desolate village. Here, the contrast between the beauty of the landscape and the hardships of its residents was stark. The rugged cliffs and dramatic scenery might inspire admiration in a painting, but living among them was another matter entirely, as we learned during our rest day. In every village we passed, beggars crowded the roads. Many claimed to be wounded soldiers, praising Christ as they held out their hands. Even women showed their scars, a stark reminder of the suffering left in the wake of war.

On June 7th [19th], we passed through the city of Bayreuth, but were unable to enjoy it, as we were quartered three *verstas* [two miles] beyond it in the village of Bindlach. Curious about its peculiar name, I asked about its origin and was told this story: during the Thirty Years War, the village had not yet acquired a definitive name. After a battle was fought nearby, a wounded Prussian officer, shot through the arm and in agony, repeatedly cried out, "*Bind Loch!*" [bind the hole]. It took a long time to find a physician, but the residents, passing by the house, heard his frequent shouts and so *Bind Loch* stuck around, giving the village its name.[4]

Unfortunately, we couldn't admire Bayreuth or visit the ancient castle of the Margrave with its renowned gardens. Our village quarters were dull, and incessant rain soaked us thoroughly, both outdoors and inside the huts. The next four days of marching took us through remote, impoverished, mountainous regions. Our worst stop was in the town of Gefrees, where the gunners were quartered in huts scattered across the mountains, thirty men to a hut over a span of three *verstas* [two miles]. These wild places were covered in forests, with dramatic cliffs and castle ruins offering unmatched views, but poverty and misery dominated the landscape. To our dismay, we had to spend a rest day in Gefrees.

Passing through Münchberg and reaching the village of Schlegel, I stayed alone in a peasant's hut that reminded me of those in Belorussia. The locals here were extremely poor. Villages were isolated, with huts tucked among rocks, and only occasionally gathered in clusters.

Hof, the last city in the Kingdom of Bavaria, offered little to regret upon our departure from this barren, impoverished region. Since Nuremberg, the land had been increasingly mountainous and infertile, its people ravaged by war, and coarse in manner and speech. By contrast, the earlier parts of Bavaria and the Kingdom of Württemberg had been far better. There, the fertile soil, industriousness of the people, and the paternal care of the King of Württemberg were evident in the prosperity of the residents, even though their way of life seemed old-fashioned.

---

4 Once more, Radozhitskii has been told a fairy tale. The first mention of the town (as Bintlvke) dates from 1178. The name Bindlach may be derived from the Old Saxon word Binutlaka meaning "Small, standing lake overgrown with juncus". Bindlach was home to part of the US 2nd Armored Cavalry Regiment during the Cold War.

Hof itself was modest, with no central square. The houses and residents appeared thoroughly provincial, and the shops were unimpressive. At the *Rathaus* guardhouse, ten Bavarian soldiers stood watch. The sentry kept shouting "Heraus!" each time he spotted someone passing in fringed epaulettes, prompting the guard to stand to arms. They even fired a two-shot salute for two military ladies passing by in a carriage on their way to a promenade. Under the windows of my quarters traders sold green groceries, drawing many pretty girls, their Saxon-style clothing lending a touch of charm.

Crossing into Saxony marked a stark contrast. Though the landscape remained mountainous, sandy, and forested with pines like in Bavaria, the condition of the people was far superior. Villages were clean, houses whitewashed, and the hard work and diligence of the residents were apparent everywhere. Each villager had something to trade, reflecting the care of a benevolent sovereign. The Saxons loved their King, a victim of political machinations, and greeted us with warmth and anticipation of our needs, a refreshing change from the gruff, indifferent Bavarians.

We found ourselves in the village of Fochsberg [possibly Fuchspöhl], nestled on rocky slopes with a view of Oelsnitz nearby. Towering above the village on a high cliff stood the ruins of an ancient castle, overgrown with trees, exuding a silent reverence for its antiquity.

The relentless rain continued to torment us as we marched near the town of Reichenbach [Reichenbach im Vogtland], passing the highest hills with their alum works. To our right lay the town of Plauen. The countryside in this region was dreary, though the scenery had a certain charm: dark pines, sandy stretches, rocky formations, and overcast skies offered a picturesque quality that might have been admired in a painting, but certainly not by those trudging through it on a wet march. Beyond Reichenbach, the landscape transitioned to a plain with fertile fields, yet we were stationed in a poor village at the foot of the mountains.

A Saxon officer, accompanied by three Landwehr privates, took it upon himself to guide us to a place suitable for our artillery and quarters. He was meticulous in ensuring that neither our cannons nor our horses damaged the crops, particularly the plentiful potato fields that stretched close to the village. The town itself had a textile factory, and I noticed that nearly every household seemed connected to its production. In one house, they wove; in another, they spun; elsewhere, they carded or combed the wool, pounded it, or worked the shuttle.

Adjutant General Prince Repnin-Volkonsky[5] had been appointed governor of Saxony. It was said that he shortened our stages so that we could do without rest days. However, our troops were fed better here than in Bavaria.

We soon came to the village of Eckersbach, near the town of Zwickau. Our artillery was staying in villages more and more often; but it made little difference: sometimes a village was better than a town, especially for the horses. The inhabitants of Zwickau greeted Count Langeron with music and flags flying.

Thereafter we marched more than 30 *verstas* [20 miles] from Zwickau to Chemnitz. Approaching Chemnitz from Lichtenstein, there were extensive villages along the streams: Longwitz [*Oberlungwitz*] alone extended more than seven *verstas* [4⅔ miles]. It was delightful to revisit the places where we had been quartered a year earlier during Easter week. The owner of the cotton mill and his daughter recognized me immediately and greeted me warmly. The city itself remained unchanged, with everything much as I had left it. However, instead of the former dandies in French uniforms, young Landwehr soldiers now stood guard, their hats adorned with brass crosses and green ones stitched onto their coats. I was assigned quarters in the Neustadt suburb with a wealthy merchant. His home was tastefully decorated, though the handiwork of a coach painter was evident in the murals: deer, hares, dogs, foxes, squirrels, and ducks all looked strikingly similar, as if siblings of the same parent. In contrast, the painted oaks, firs, willows, and lindens had leaves meticulously shaded with care. The furniture was of polished mahogany, and muslin curtains, trimmed with wide fringes, hung elegantly over the windows on gilded rods. The hospitality was exceptional. I was fed generously, in true merchant fashion, to my heart's content.

As I walked around the city, I couldn't help but admire the Saxons. While some were not particularly attractive, their tasteful and elegant dress gave them a certain charm. Those who were naturally good-looking, enhanced by their fine attire, were even more captivating. The musicians of the Olonetskii Regiment played lively tunes in the square to entertain the public. However, their performance faced stiff competition from the city musicians, who paraded through the streets

---

5 Nikolay Grigorevich Repnin-Volkonsky (1778-1845).

with drums and blaring trumpets, drowning out our regiment's efforts. The city itself boasted factories producing wool, cambric, and cotton prints, a testament to the industriousness of its people.

On June 17th [29th], we marched over 30 *verstas* (20 miles) to Freiberg. No sooner had I arrived at my quarters than I was dispatched to Dresden to arrange accommodations for the company, leaving me no time to explore Freiberg's renowned mines. These mines, stretching beneath the entire city and extending four miles beyond it, were a marvel. The miners formed a distinct class, with some six thousand of them living and working underground. I caught a glimpse of young miners dressed in the same red leather outfits as their adult counterparts, a striking sight. The mines produced mostly silver, with some gold as well. A quarter of the mining operations belonged to the King, while the remainder were developed by private individuals who paid for permits. Though the mines were lucrative, the work was perilous; it was said that around twelve miners lost their lives there each year.

Taking a dilapidated post-carriage drawn by two bony nags, three of us set off from Freiberg to Dresden. However, as the saying goes, the work is not so quickly done. Halfway along the road, in the village of Herzogswalde, our postman halted, demanded Trinkgeld (a gratuity), and ushered us to a country tavern. There, we discovered from the newspapers that our Tsar and the King of Prussia were visiting London. Meanwhile, Napoleon, exiled on the island of Elba, was reportedly toying with the idea of designing medals bearing the inscription: "God is in heaven, while Napoleon is on earth", to commemorate his stay in Moscow. While we absorbed this news, the postman drank a glass of vodka, lit his pipe, and allowed his horses to nibble on a scrap of hay. Once suitably recovered, he finally resumed the journey, and we reached Dresden late at night. Fortunately, we managed to secure sleeping quarters with the artillerymen.

In Dresden, all the 8th Corps infantry were housed within the city, while the artillery, including us, were sent to nearby villages. Count Langeron formally presented the troops to Prince Repnin during a ceremonial entrance into the city. Dresden itself was still reeling from a recent disaster. A spark from the discharge of a shell had ignited a powder magazine in the Neustadt, causing a devastating explosion. Besides severe damage to the buildings, the tragedy claimed the lives of around 200 residents and soldiers. Adding to the city's unrest, Saxon soldiers had recently clashed with ours, resulting in about 20 fatalities on both sides. We frequently encountered the Saxon red grenadiers in their tall bearskins – the same troops who had defected to us at Leipzig.[6] Still infused with Napoleonic fervour, they often quarrelled with our 'moustaches' [grenadiers], their disputes echoing the lingering tensions of the war.

Our artillery quarters were assigned in the village of Pesterwitz, located in the direction from which the Austrians had previously approached Dresden with a force of 30,000 [in August 1813]. Their advance, however, had been marred by poor conditions; for three days, they stood in mud under relentless rain, without rations. Napoleon, returning from Silesia, seized the opportunity to send his cavalry against them, capturing an entire division along with 20 cannons. On this side, Dresden itself had suffered relatively little. While most areas had been broken into and plundered, there was minimal damage from fires. The city's entire perimeter had been reinforced with redoubts and double entrenchments.

On June 18th [30th], Italian actors performed the opera *Don Juan* at the Dresden theatre, but it was a disappointment, far worse than expected. None of the actors had the vocal range needed for the arias. The sole exception was the actress playing Donna Elvira. Despite her crooked leg, reminiscent of the Nuremberg canary's, she sang with a natural, gentle voice, though not a girlish one. In the second act, she delivered the best aria admirably, though she could not match the charm of Mannheim's Madame Vernet. Overall, these Italians could not hold a candle to Mannheim's performers. Don Juan himself lacked any presence; he was like a cold idol. His wooden performance made me think longingly of the incomparable Keibel, whose portrayal of the character had been so masterful that, despite not being a woman, I had been nearly in love with him. This version of the opera missed or altered many elements. The actors sang mechanically, devoid of feeling or finesse. The sets and costumes were infinitely inferior to those of Mannheim, though the orchestra was passable.

---

6 The Saxon Leib Grenadier Guard Regiment wore red uniforms; Saxon line infantry regiments wore white with regimental facing colours and buttons

Mozart had poured all of his genius into this opera. I marvelled at his ability to weave such charm into the music. The melodies, with their seamless transitions into different keys, the harmony, and the interplay of instruments were mesmerizing.

Even Frankfurt's theatre surpasses Dresden's, which reflects poorly on the Saxon King's apparent indifference to theatrical arts. As for the Italian language, it proved far more suited to opera than German. Its musicality, soft consonants, and abundance of vowels make it ideal for love declarations, while French lends itself to flattery, German to cursing, and… Russian? Russian is the language of empathy.

I visited an art gallery that had once been celebrated but now bore the scars of the clutching hands[7] of war. Many frames hung empty, the paintings they once held having been taken, though the curator was too ashamed to admit it and claimed they were "being copied". In their place were portraits of French Generals, Mamelukes, and formidable Saxons, which felt out of place. The arrangement of the remaining works lacked logic; some paintings were hung too high to be seen properly, while others suffered from poor lighting and glare. By contrast, the Paris Museum had displayed its paintings more thoughtfully, each in a suitable position, making the experience far more coherent.

In the first hall, paintings of various sizes and styles covered every available space, including the floor where many paintings were resting. Large antique works hung at the top, reminiscent of the St. Petersburg Academy of Arts, but poor lighting rendered them nearly invisible. Rubens' painting of a hunt,[8] for example, was positioned so awkwardly that visitors failed to appreciate its detail. However, there were some exceptional works. Dutch painter Dujardin[9] impressed me with his meticulous realism, evident in a self-portrait of him in his study, sitting among books, a globe and papers, and a moving depiction of a monk praying before a crucifix. The precision of his brushwork captured every hair and vein with lifelike accuracy; the facial features were very lively and expressive

---

7 *Kosmatye lapy*, literally shaggy paws.

8 Probably Peter Paul Rubens' 1615 work 'Diana Returning from the Hunt'

9 Karel Dujardin (1626-1678) was a Dutch Golden Age painter, known for his small Italianate landscape scenes.

Two small paintings by Mr. Dietrich[10] also caught my attention: they depicted beautiful women bathing. Beyond their harmonious colours and subtle interplay of light and shadow, the figures and landscapes were rendered with captivating skill. Rubens, as always, astonished with his depictions of fruit, game, and cooking utensils, each object so lifelike that one could almost feel their textures: every shrimp, fly, seed, or needle was shown, and nothing was missing anywhere.

The gallery's collection also included compelling landscapes, historical works, and portraits. One painting of Venus receiving the apple from Paris stood out, with the figures of Juno and Minerva, and the half-hidden shepherd in a thicket, stepping back to highlight Venus's beauty. There were many paintings of historical figures or famous people, including Charlemagne, Maria de' Medici, and Henry IV, adorning the walls, their historical accuracy secondary to the remarkable skill of their creators.

The central room housed Italian masterpieces, though I found them uneven whether due to their age or my lack of taste. Raphael's Madonna with a crucifix, accompanied by St. Paul and Magdalene, along with two cherubs, struck me as too simple despite the beauty of the faces. On the other hand, Correggio's[11] works captivated me. His bold use of colour, the boldness of the brushwork, masterful musculature of figures, and interplay of light and shadow gave his paintings a freshness as if they had just been completed. His Magdalene, reclining in a cave beside a skull and engrossed in a book, was particularly moving.

The gallery curator praised a painting of the Burgomaster of Basel's family before the Madonna, but I found it unremarkable, its style reminiscent of images seen in old Russian churches; I kept quiet and did not want to laugh out loud at him or at his ignorance. Meanwhile, a corpulent General T*** and his entourage wandered the gallery, marvelling at the paintings and calculating their monetary value in *chervonets* [gold coins], missing their artistic merit entirely. He estimated new paintings were worth 17,365 chervonets, and praised very enthusiastically the faded paint of the caricatures.

---

10 Christian Wilhelm Ernst Dietrich (1712–1774) was a German painter and art administrator who served as inspector of galleries in Saxony.

11 Antonio Allegri da Correggio (1489–1534) was an Italian Renaissance painter, considered the foremost painter of the Parma school of the High Renaissance.

There was one big painting under a muslin curtain but the ladies did not look at it, only reading the explanation above it. Yet this curtain was not natural, but painted, and so skillfully that it deceived everyone.[12] Two landscapes by Vernet amazed me with their vibrant colours and lifelike depictions. Rubens' dramatic painting of hell depicted his first wife ascending to heaven while demons dragged his second wife into the flames, with Rubens himself caught in between, trying to grab hold of both.

The third room was filled with portraits, mostly of women, though none particularly stood out to me. Oddly, among these feminine figures, our hero Suvorov appeared as if among the enemies. But he was always known for politeness and here too he had given up a place on the walls to the ladies and instead rested on the floor, wearing an Austrian uniform. Another portrait showed him full-length, in [Emperor] Paul's period uniform, with sword in hand and no hat, as though charging into battle. Nearby, Cupid sharpened an arrow with a mischievous smile, suggesting his weapon was deadlier than all of Suvorov's assaults. The ladies in attendance, ever drawn to fashion, carefully studied the headdresses in the portraits, seemingly searching for their own likenesses. Throughout the gallery, art students and academics busily copied old paintings. Some worked modestly, while others showed off their questionable skills. The most notable copier was an elderly lady behind a screen, reproducing Correggio's Magdalene. She did not appear to seek fame but instead seemed driven by pride, as nearly every visitor paused to ask, "Where is the beautiful lady copying Correggio's Magdalene?"

Walking across the Augustus Bridge, I was struck by the unparalleled views of both sides of the river. They looked just like the scenic paintings sold in the city for eight Groschen. Near the spot of the recent explosion on the bridge[13] stood a crucifix, beneath which a Latin inscription in gold lettering paid tribute to Emperor Alexander. The bridge itself was bustling with people, a constant crowd crossing from the old city to the

---

12 Radozhitskii is describing a technique known as Trompe-l'œil in which the artist creates an optical illusion so that the painting (or parts of it) appear to be three-dimensional objects

13 In March 1813, Marshal Davout had ordered the bridge to be destroyed as the French were retreating and, on 19th March 1813 the fourth pillar from the left bank was blown up, causing the collapse of the arches on either side. The crucifix dates from 1670

new one. In the old city, in front of the cathedral, a magnificent ascent of wide steps had been constructed, leading up to a boulevard along the embankment. This new promenade, lined with chestnut trees and still fenced off, offered a novel and pleasant addition to the cityscape. Prince Repnin, desiring to leave a lasting legacy in Dresden, planned to dedicate this walk to the residents, ensuring his memory would endure.

A curious trend had emerged among the military stationed in Dresden: walking out in tailcoats. This fashion arose to ease tensions, as confrontations frequently occurred between those in brightly coloured uniforms. The modest, dark tailcoats provided a neutral, unifying alternative. It was particularly amusing to see a military dandy sporting a German frock coat, complete with a moustache and spurs, a peculiar mix of formality and flair.

Rumours were circulating that war might resume with the Austrians. I noticed our Quartermaster General purchasing a map of Galicia while I, coincidentally, was browsing views of Switzerland in an art store.

As vice is to the city, so customs are to the village. In Dresden, the government trustee took a pragmatic approach to the "nymphs of joy," opting to regulate them, rather than persecuting, by imposing an excise duty. Unlike in Nuremberg, where such activities were strictly suppressed, Dresden's policy seemed to have helped avoid family strife and incidents involving respectable women, a peculiar example of finding a blessing in disguise.

At three o'clock in the morning, on June 20th [July 2nd], we departed from the village of Pesterwitz with the artillery. Passing through Dresden in the rain, we moved quietly while the city still slept. Neustadt, however, bore visible scars from the recent explosion of the powder magazine, despite its distance from the centre. We passed by the charred and crumbling ruins of buildings, their desolation a grim reminder of the city's recent suffering.

From Neustadt along the road, the gardens had not been damaged, but the surrounding pine forests, along the banks, had been felled to the range of a cannon shot, through which the French had obtained new views of Dresden from this direction, which had been obscured by the forest. It was all to the good. This naked appearance had now been masterfully fortified with entrenchments; isolated buildings had been enclosed with palisades; every hill top had been furnished with redoubts and communications trenches. Although Dresden had never been a fortress, but fortified from all sides, in the best possible way, it now represented a stronghold, which would cost a lot of effort and casualties to take by armed force. Saint-Cyr,[14] abandoned here with a 30,000 man garrison, made frequent forays against General Markov,[15] who had blockaded the city with 15,000, mostly militia. The French cut off a small group of ours, and once, they say, captured six guns. Saint-Cyr could have marched freely to Teplitz [*Teplice*], or to Prague, but perhaps he did not dare to deviate from the instructions given to him by Napoleon, or, considering himself remote from the main forces, believed such an enterprise to be pointless. When Klenau's[16] Austrian Corps was brought up, Saint-Cyr shut himself up in his entrenchments and even dug up the streets, with the firm intention of defending himself; but hunger and disease shook his resolve. For a whole week the French ate horses in the city and the inhabitants suffered; finally they were offered honourable terms of capitulation; once they heard about this, they gladly agreed, and were thinking of returning to their homeland, when suddenly they were directed to Bohemia from Alpenburg, leaving only Saint-Cyr to return to Paris; but he, fearing reproaches from Napoleon, went to Switzerland. Thus, the Austrians avenged their Mack,[17] who had surrendered to the French at Ulm.[18]

We stopped in a village, not far short of the town of Stolpen, from where we could see the plain where, last year, we had manoeuvred from Neustadt, against the Poles.

Finally, something more must be said about the unforgettable partisan Figner, who, with the enthusiasm of love for Russia, so skillfully took revenge on our enemies, and rendered important services, was useful to the Tsar, glorified his name, and finally disappeared without a trace. Following his Danzig [*Gdańsk*] expedition,[19] he had conceived

---

14 Laurent de Gouvion Saint-Cyr

15 Evgeny Ivanovich Markov

16 Johann Joseph Cajetan Graf von Klenau und Janowitz

17 Karl Freiherr Mack von Leiberich

18 The battle of Ulm, 16th – 19th October 1805, in which Mack surrendered 27,000 men to Napoleon's Grande Armee

19 During the siege of Danzig in 1813, Figner is alleged to have entered the fortress posing as an Italian. It is claimed that he was able to obtain copies of the French commandant's (General Jean Rapp) dispatches as a result of his espionage

something extraordinary: to form the 'vengeful legions' from fugitive French deserters. Although most of his men were Spaniards and Italians, they were not trustworthy. Figner, hoping to replicate the miracles he had performed in Russia to earn their loyalty and admiration, was forced to grant them a degree of independence. However, in his efforts to disrupt the enemy, he ended up ravaging Saxony, which provoked superior forces against him. His campaign came to a tragic end near Dessau, where he was lured into an ambush beyond the Elbe by the Polish cavalry under General Krasnitsky and annihilated along with his entire detachment. Only those who had remained in the city managed to survive. Among the survivors was Artillery Sub-Lieutenant Bibikov, the brother of Figner's wife, who told me that Figner might still be in captivity. However, other reports suggested a grimmer fate: that he was struck in the chest by a bullet while fleeing across the Elbe and drowned. What a pity! Figner, with his remarkable military skill and extraordinary bravery, deserved a far better fate. Rest in peace, my good old friend!

Chapter VIII

From Dresden to Białystok

On 22nd June [4th July], in the evening, we arrived in Bautzen, where we had a rest day. I was going to explore the surroundings of the town, but a severe fever forced me to stay at home. The town stands on the rocky and elevated bank of the river Spree, and from this direction it seemed impregnable. Some of the inhabitants speak a Slavic language and call themselves Wendish or Vandals.[1]

After Bautzen we passed through the field where the general battle had taken place on 9th [21st] May last year,[2] and on passing, many pointed out the places where someone had distinguished themselves. The Allied position was very advantageous, and Napoleon could overcome it only by enveloping the right flank. Despite the fact that our batteries had been protected by earthworks, now there was no visible trace left: where blood had flowed, now grows lush vegetation.

Bischofswerda was being rebuilt[3] but there were still no intact buildings in the town. They had been burned down during the war.

Several times we had passed through such ruined locations; however, the traces of the horrors of war were soon erased. In one village where we stayed for the night, Baron T***'s artillery company had been foraging the previous year. Our host recognised the foragers who had turned his home upside down and turned him over, and said that he would gladly

---

1 Radozhitskii has conflated Wends – who speak a slavic dialect known as Sorbian, with Vandals who spoke a Germanic dialect and were a distinctly different ethnic group

2 On 20th – 21st May 1813, Napoleon had attempted to fix and envelope the Russo-Prussian Army of Silesia making a stand on the banks of the Spree, but the allies were able to extricate themselves and Napoleon, lacking good cavalry, had been unable to mount an effective pursuit

3 Bischofswerda had been largely destroyed when a fire broke out among the medieval timber buildings on 12th May 1813

identify the men who had once honoured him with their visit: even then everything in his rooms was still broken, scattered and torn apart.

Passing through Görlitz, we remembered only that the French here, on the Neisse River, had sunk our *cantinièrs*. Near Lauban [*Lubań*], we were escorted from Saxony by the same blind clarinettist who had met us the first time we entered here. Farewell Saxony! A beautiful country, in which the good King had wanted to build heaven, and Napoleon had turned it into hell. Saxony also faded; we were entering Silesia.

On the border of Silesia, we were greeted by a triumphal arch constructed, instead of laurels, of spiny evergreen branches of spruce and pine. The monogram of Alexander I hung in the middle, and either side of his monogram were Francis' and Frederick's; on the top there was a Russian inscription on a black board: "Long live the saviours of Germany!" We passed through similar gates in every village. At Löwenberg [*Lwówek Śląski*], one had been built with particular skill, decorated with monograms, armatures, and pyramids. Through the streets, on the buildings, even on a lowly cobbler's, there were garlands, wreaths, and everywhere the inscription: "Long live the victors!" The monogram of our Tsar was everywhere with the inscription: "*Vivat Aleksandr*, and his victorious troops!" The residents welcomed us with great joy, but saw us off with greater pleasure wishing us a safe journey to Russia, that is, such that we might never return to them.

The Prussians seemed to have awakened after the painful yoke of the French. Indeed, if they felt a change in their situation, they owed this to the alliance with the Russians, and partly to their own enthusiasm for the restoration of national liberty. Frederick the Great had evoked a warlike spirit in them, and the Prussians had proved that, of all the Germanic tribes, their nation was the most valiant; maybe only the Bavarians would keep up with them in this. However, whether out of sheer diligence, or as a matter of policy alone, they displayed honours to us, proclaiming us victors and saviours everywhere, however, it was pleasant to see the signs of friendliness and cheerful faces, especially the cute little German girls, carefully noticing those fortunate ones who passed under the wreaths woven through their generosity.

Why had there been no triumphal arches in Saxony? Of course, due to the fact that the Saxons, facing the unknown with regard to their true fate, had not known whether to rejoice or to grieve; they had seemed gloomier than ever. This meant that their love for the King, considering that he had been in alliance with Napoleon, had become the cause of all their misfortunes. Such gloom or sorrow among the people was commendable; it had revealed their true character. The commitment of the people cannot be defeated with weapons, but must be won through the establishment of prosperity.

The traces of the past war had not yet been erased, but it was surprising how quickly they managed to recover here: cattle appeared again, bread, and even new dishes. The entire local peasant economy had been resumed, as if during a resettlement. Moreover, the Prussians must have loved their King, who cared about their welfare, like a good father.

After Löwenberg, I looked with pleasure at the places where our feet had so often wandered, and where terrible events had happened. There was the hillock where the skirmishers of the 7th Jäger Regiment had been overwhelmed by French lancers; here was the steep bank, from where the troops of General Puthod's [*Jacques-Pierre-Louis-Marie-Joseph Puthod*] Division had been forced either to throw themselves into the river, to seek a watery death or salvation, or to surrender to the victors.[4] I took a look at the opposite bank, from where an enemy shell, in front of my eyes, had suddenly struck down two jäger officers in one blast; Finally I looked at that big rock, upon which I had rested my sword, where a wounded Frenchman was aiming to fire at us, and where my comrade, Baron Sh***, had been sitting, picking up his long legs so that they would not be torn off by round shot. I recalled all this so vividly then, as if it had been the present; but the barren, stony ground, soaked with the blood of our enemies, was already overgrown with rye and flax. I wanted to sketch the location where our regiments had been escorting entire French columns into captivity, and where General Puthod had stood in respectful anticipation of his fate, in front of Count Langeron; I wanted to draw the French drowning and swept away by the flooding waters; but so many subjects accumulated then in my head that I stood still for half an hour, deep in thoughts of the past, and completely forgot that the artillery was waiting for me at the foot of the mountain.

The Prussian King had sent three million *Thaler*s to Silesia to greet and treat the Russian troops as friends and allies. That is why we got

---

4 This is a reference to the battle of Katzbach on 26th August 1813, when Marshal MacDonald's French Corps was decisively beaten by the Russo-Prussian Army of Silesia

such a magnificent welcome everywhere. At Löwenberg, General Korf had been greeted by the National Guard [*Landsturm*] with a parade and cheers; girls had thrown flowers along his route. Count Langeron had departed Dresden for Berlin. At a ball, this same General had been met by twelve pretty girls, with garlands and woven wreaths; one of them was so bold that she had wanted to place a wreath on the General, and gave an eloquent greeting to him. They danced a lot, dined, and drank champagne giving toasts to the health of the victorious allies.

But in Goldberg [*Złotoryja*] there was no ball, although the inscription on the triumphal arch stated: "*Vivat* Aleksandr I, Frederick III, Francis I, Blücher and Langeron!" while for the victorious troops: "*Mit herzlichem Willkommen!*"

According to the newspapers, France now had a population of 29 million; from an Empire, it had been demoted to a Kingdom, and was to pay the Allied Sovereigns 500 million francs in war reparations. That is how Napoleon's conquests had rebounded on him.

There was also no ball at Jauer [*Jawor*] because of the cramped quartering. The town was quite formal and had some 10,000 residents. The *Rathaus* stood in the middle of a vast square. Solid benches, under a gallery with arches, surrounding the square, gave a very good view; above the benches there were large, four-storey stone houses, rather old fashioned. There were many pretty faces peeking out of the windows.

The town of Striegau [*Strzegom*] seemed to be very old; many buildings in it were derelict and had been abandoned, while others were overgrown with moss and grass; the suburbs had been reclaimed by the forest.

Passing Schweidnitz [*Świdnica*], I stopped at an inn with some officers to have breakfast. At that moment the 36th Jäger and Arkhangelogorod regiments were passing through the town; all the residents came running to meet them, with joy and curiosity, to see people who had come straight from Paris. During the passage of the regiments, the town's musicians played on the tower of the *Rathaus*, although not in unison, but enthusiastically; the soldiers marched as if they had been beaten, and did not notice the wonderment and triumph with which they had been greeted and seen off; they expressed their displeasure with angry faces, in particular the musicians, who, after each stage, had to entertain the residents.

In Jauernig [*Javorník*], on the triumphal arch, was written: "Glory to the victors!" while in Schweidnitz it had been: "Hurrah for the Russians!" From the faces of the residents it was clear that the Prussians were all for our return to Russia.

In the village of Grädinz [*Grodziszcze*], halfway from Schweidnitz to Reichenbach [*Dzierżoniów*], we were billeted in a dilapidated manor, with a Prussian official. We were received as conquerors, wreaths had been woven for us, they showered us with flowers and did not spare any commendable inscriptions; but we had to get strawberries and cherries ourselves from a huge garden. In the central avenue there was a place densely overgrown with linden trees, where our Tsar, according to the owner, during the last retreat, had his favourite resting place, while he had been quartered here. Fate had led me now to sit and write, perhaps in the same place: it was isolated from everywhere, and was open only in one direction towards the highway, along which the Tsar would have seen everyone passing by, and the bivouacs of his army, without being noticed himself.

I had noticed the most beautiful locations in Silesia from Schweidnitz beyond Reichenbach, at the foot of the Giant Mountains [*Krkonoše*]; the fertile plain between these two towns was especially pleasant: on the one side, the Giant Mountains rise, while on the other, the high mount Zobten [*Ślęża*] stands independently, like an outpost; the valley was full of villages, connected by avenues, and in between, fields with green grain were being cultivated. The beauty of nature inspired feelings of well being. The people of Reichenbach welcomed the Russians with particular friendliness, remembering their good behaviour and generosity during the truce.[5] They hosted a ball; but as our artillery had been stationed in the village of Mellendorf [*Młynica*], we could not participate in the festivities with the army officers. My quarters were in a dilapidated house on the estate of Count Schönau. Traces of its former splendour were visible on the top floor: brocade, dilapidated wallpaper, gilded fireplaces, mirrors, and Gothic ornamentation under gold leaf, from which a skilled Jew might still have scraped together one gold chervonets. I was greeted at my quarters with poetry, and all the rooms had been strewn with flowers. I would never have dreamed

---

5   The Truce of Pläswitz between Napoleon and the Coalition had lasted from 4th June to 10th August 1813

of such an honour. But glory is just a smokescreen if there is nothing to eat. It is much easier to scatter verses and flowers than to feed well. The Prussians had been cunning in this respect.

The landowners in Silesia lived as we do in Russia: the villages have good manor houses, with gardens and all the amenities for a pleasant, secluded rural life.

The residents, meeting us with pleasure, had remembered their former guests, from whom, during the continuation of the armistice, they had feathered their nests quite well, taking bribes from conscientious commanders, for medical bills, for salad and potatoes.

With each step, we were coming closer to Poland and to poverty. Our triumphal progress was ending. Already in the vicinity of Brieg [*Brzeg*], on the Oder, the places were not so charming and fruitful as those near Reichenbach; already the villages were not so clean and the huts had a Polish look; we had already begun to encounter raggedy people.

In Brieg, a ball was held for the Generals, at which there were so many guests that the ladies were fainting from the stuffiness. Count Langeron, returning from Berlin, added brilliance to the ball with his presence. The town of Brieg was similar in layout to Schweidnitz, surrounded by a stone wall with towers, over which, it seemed, one could jump; it was so low. From Brieg we marched up the Oder, which remained to our left. Blessed Silesia ended here; the inhabitants were poor, and the villages were similar to those in Poland; rags and soot were the adornment of the creatures that we would meet without exception from here on. Remarkable! The fields were abundant with grain, the land was fruitful, idleness was not evident, there had been no war here, yet the poverty was extreme. Of course, this part of Silesia was not the property of the Kingdom; it had been leased, to tenant farmers.

Near the village of Niwa, outside the town of Schurgast [*Skorogoszcz*], we lodged in a very run down house on an estate; but near the village of Goldendorf [*Golschwitz, Golczowice?*] we came across an estate, free with everything, as if bidding farewell to the abundant Silesia. Here they already spoke Polish, even though the border with Poland was still far beyond the Oder. The Germans who have populated Europe apparently had not yet managed to overpower the Slavic language here during their expansion.

The town of Oppeln [*Opole*], which lies on the right bank of the Oder, is small, old and reminiscent of Bunzlau [*Bolesławiec*]. It is remarkable only for every house gable having strange figures, and long pipes to drain off rainwater.

Grinding poverty met us beyond the Oder. The Oder seemed to constitute Germany's natural border with Poland. Although according to the geographical and political division of lands, it flows almost through the centre of Silesia, however, the difference in the tribes of peoples on the right and left banks of the river was clearly evident.

On the road to the town of Strehlitz [*Strzelce*], the terrain was sandy, although with black soil, and produced very short grain, half an *arshin* [14"] in height; but even that the passing troops thoughtlessly trampled, especially the officers' batmen with their baggage, destroying the last hope of the exhausted villagers. The dark pines and uniform emptiness were depressing; poor, lowly hovels were scattered along the road, as if ashamed of themselves. In some places there might be a tavern whitewashed in order to tempt those passing; the occasional Jew under a skull cap [*yarmulke*], with a gray beard and thick side locks, would look out of a window and, seeing the Muscovites, immediately hide. The cloudy weather completed the gloom of the picture. Two companies of our artillery were stationed in thirty farmyards, in the poor village of Ellguth [*Ligota Toszecka*]. The miserable residents gave up the latter in tears. Entering the peasant hut, I felt a certain thrill of horror. Having the excellent quarters that had recently been abandoned fresh in my memory, having gone through more than one land of plenty and the state of the inhabitants, now suddenly, as if by involuntary force, I found myself transported to a Polish hut, where I heard my native language. My room was separated from the stable only by a curtain: here people, animals and insects lived together. Flies had cruelly tormented us for several stages, and if a student of the Pythagorean sect[6] had happened to be here, he would have said that these flies were the souls of the French who had died and frozen in Russia and who now, in a new incarnation, could not pass up the opportunity to take revenge upon us. The ceiling was black, the floor was dirty... But feeling the closeness of my native land, I repeated Derzhavin's[7] verses with feeling: "Good news about

---

6 Pythagoreanism holds that every soul is immortal and, upon death, enters into a new body

7 Gavriil Romanovich Derzhavin

our land is sweet to us; fatherland and smoke is honey and pleasant to us."

We, it seemed, had deliberately begun to make longer stages, almost 40 *verstas* [26⅔ miles] each, in order to cross this poorest part of Silesia more quickly, it being so dissimilar to the preceding part. Passing the grain-planted plains, looking at the rippling greenery of the imminent harvest, one might have concluded that the villagers were hardworking; but encountering the hovels and the ugly creatures of humanity dwelling in them, exhausted by burdensome work, was to see misfortune. From where had it come? According to the custom that existed in Poland, and according to a charitable institution, it had been decreed for landlords and tenants here to take two men from each household for the Corvee [forced labour]; three days a week had been allowed for this, but the peasants were employed every day, and only managed to work for themselves at night. Furthermore, the villagers were obliged to give the landlord, or the tenant; from livestock and all living things that nature itself had produced, from each courtyard, a pair from the first-born, two hundred eggs, and 15 *Thalers*. Because of this, the unfortunate peasants, with all their hard work, were barely able to feed themselves and their families; the remainder of the wealth of the fields, with which nature had blessed them, they, having no time to harvest, gave to the Jew in the tavern. This was the reason for the poverty of most of the peasants in Poland and in the lands acquired from it by Prussia.

On 12th [24th] June, we passed through the town of Tost [*Toszek*], where the retired Prussian General, Graf von Hohenlohe, met our troops not only with a triumphal arch and music, but even with a cannon salute. On a mountain, in front of the town, the magnificent ruins of the glorious Count's castle of 50 years could be seen.[8] Other than that, there was nothing remarkable here. The officers of our two artillery companies stayed at a farm near the village of Zacharzowice, where the steward gave us our fill.

Although the town of Tarnowitz [*Tarnowskie Góry*] was as insignificant as the rest of this part of Silesia, the inhabitants here were more prosperous, because most of them were Prussians, whose employment consisted in the development of the mines in the vicinity of

---

8 In 1797, the castle was sold to Count Franciszek Adam Gaschinów. Shortly after, in 1811, the castle burned down and became a ruin.

the town. We were accommodated in the village of Bobrowniki, where all the villagers were miners. Some officers, on a rest day, travelled into the underworld, and told of the wonders they had seen there. I, who had been on duty could not satisfy my curiosity this time; however, as I had seen something similar in the Siegen mines of the Duchy of Berg, on the Rhine, I did not really regret the present omission. Between the sources of the Oder and Vistula rivers, separating the Giant Mountains from the Carpathian Mountains, there is a branch of the mountains extending to those places in which lead, silver and gold were mined. The Tarnowitz mines all belong to the Prussian Government, which pays workers one and a half zlotys per day, or 80 kopecks in our money. From 120 pounds of mined lead comes 60 pounds and 3 Lots [1⅓ oz] of pure silver. Up to 70 Poods [2,528 lb] of this metal comes out of one mine pit per year. Having said that, workers often died there from various causes: sometimes they are killed under the ground by gases, and recently six workers fell from a height of 25 *sazhens* [175'] into the depths, from which only one remained alive, and the rest died.

According to the new Order of Battle, our artillery company and Lieutenant Colonel Taube's would be going through Warsaw to permanent quarters in Białystok, in General Kaptsevich's[9] 4th Corps; Veselitsky's Battery Company was to go to Dubno.

At the time we were on our way to the town of Siewierz, 70 *verstas* [46⅔ miles] from Krakow. This was Poland proper, although a strip of land between Krakow and Tschenstochau [*Czestochowa*] still belonged to Prussia. In the village of Wojkowice, a colleague and I were given quarters with an organist, in a closet, two *sazhens* square [14' x 14'], with perforated walls, without a ceiling or floor; having said that he fed us our fill, having cooked a dozen dishes, of the same flavour, only different in appearance. Here, a company of the Nizhny Novgorod Infantry Regiment of 15th Division had taken up permanent quarters, holding the border opposite Galicia.

There were vast fertile fields around Siewierz. To look at them made the heart rejoice; what should one think, how could the local villagers not be more prosperous than the Germans, who sow much less grain. On the contrary, it all belonged to the tenant farmers.

---

9 Pyotr Mikhailovich Kaptsevich

Siewierz was nothing more than a group of small huts, in the image of all Polish townships. The headquarters of the Ladoga Regiment from Prince Lobanov Rostovsky's[10] Reserve Army was located here. Behind Siewierz were deep sands and gloomy pine forests. We stayed near the town of Koziegłówy, in the impoverished village of Gensene, in a huge barn; at least there were many comrades to have fun with, and we were fed by donations. We had now entered the Duchy of Warsaw, where our rations had changed: an officer was entitled to three pounds of bread and a pound of meat per day. Prior to Siewierz, Count Langeron's Corps had been heading towards New Galicia [*Neugalizien*]; but the Austrians had voluntarily ceded it to Russia; thereafter, from Siewierz the troops had turned sharply to the left, towards Warsaw.

Count Langeron, distributing the regiments into independent corps, sensitively said farewell to everyone, in which he announced by order that he had taken part in nine campaigns with the soldiers of the Army of Silesia, had been with them in nine general battles and in forty-five actions; that he owed all his successes to the courage of the Russian armed forces; he had ended an incredible, dangerous and memorable war with them; finally he had been with them – to Paris. Right at the very end was added: "The brightest day of my life will be the one when fate brings me to you again!"

We began to make longer stages, four Polish miles [28.6 km] a day, arriving around midnight for our overnight stay.

On 18th [30th] July, we passed through the town of Tschenstochau, famous for its ancient monastery and the miraculous icon of the Madonna. The monastery was located on a mountain [*Jasna Góra*]. The icon is still luxuriant to this day, despite the fact that the godless French had stolen it, and extorted contributions from the monks. During the French retreat from Warsaw, the previous year, Prince Poniatowski,[11] with 1,500 of his troops, settled down behind the stone walls of the town, and held out against Baron Osten-Saken[12] for six weeks,[13] because the

---

10 Dmitry Ivanovich Lobanov-Rostovsky

11 Józef Antoni Poniatowski

12 Fabian Wilhelmovich Osten-Saken

13 The fortress was occupied by the Russians on 2nd April 1813, after a siege that had lasted from 25th March

General wished to spare the inhabitants rather than the enemy. However, several Russian round shot had pierced the walls of the monastery; three well aimed shots had set fire to a ration store; hunger and lack of water finally forced the enemy to surrender, while Prince Poniatowski himself managed to escape via Galicia to Napoleon.

We had quarters with the artillery, a *Meile* [4⅔ miles] from Tschenstochau, in the village of Rędziny, in a manor house. The house looked quite promising, and inside the owner of the house greeted us with vodka, while the affectionate hostess greeted us with her eyes. From the very start she assailed us with questions, not noticing that after a tiring march, we were losing our wits and were in a sleepy reverie. Having said that, the next day we were entertained and had a pleasant time. From the look of the furniture and the hostess's businesses, one might think that she and her husband owned a large estate; on the contrary, of the fifty *dymov* they had bought three years before, they had only twenty left, and the rest had all gone, which proved their good economics. *Panya Gospodarka* complained, not without cause, about the laziness of her subjects, because they were as skinny as autumn flies... It was not new to us to see how the lords and tenants in Poland sucked the bloody sweat from the unfortunate villagers, and grew fat only because of this. Our hostess, an agile dexterous, talkative *Polka*, did not waste crumbs in vain; babbled in French, loved to speak equivocally herself, and hung around with our seniors. I showed her amusing pictures, transparencies and sketches, which I had bought in Nuremberg and in Dresden; but she, having looked at them, said to me in French: "I don't like transparencies or closed things..." Our hostess was visible all over the house; her husband was a stranger. At the table, intending to show off as a cook, she had treated us to sour and salty pork. She extolled the furniture in her rooms; showed us a cozy alcove calling for a luxurious couch for voluptuous thoughts. She had a service of Saxon porcelain and all this from twenty *dymov*! The garden was small, but full of contrivances; bosquets, swings, gazebos, pavilions, pyramids, ruins – everything had a place. She showed us two pits in which she wanted to build grottoes. The husband, following her, and not understanding the schemes of his convoluted mistress, explained it this way: "There will be different rules here." But we liked the strawberries and raspberries best of all in the garden.

The hostess' brother, who had previously been in French service, came to our room. Initially he had been with the forces under MacDonald's command, towards Riga, then in Danzig, where, being blockaded by the Russians, the French had eaten horses, cats and mice. This serviceman had considered himself fortunate that, on one occasion, during a sortie by the garrison, he had been wounded by a Russian bayonet, was captured, and then released, while most of the garrison had died from hunger. Having endured a lot of suffering, and having got to know the Russians better, he was modest, polite, and not such a braggart as the young Poles were.

The agility and courage of the Polish children, it seemed, came from the fact that they got used to men's company from a young age. The host's daughter, Josefina, a very nice girl of nine years old, behaved like a boy, constantly hanging around us, joking, walking on our straw, singing, danced a mazurka, hung on everyone's neck, and, spoke too pointedly for her age; but being still innocent or ignorant, she did not make herself blush at others.

Be that as it may, we left the house with gratitude, where we had found good quarters and a kind welcome. The hostess rightly said that her neighbours from much of the neighbourhood find enjoyment with her, often coming to parties.

From the town of Kłomnice, in the village of Lhote, where we stayed for the night, the landlord-tenant for the third day only had possession of thirteen *Dymov*, having paid 1,000 zlotys (less than a thousand rubles) to the treasury. From his physiognomy, he seemed kind, but his lady-mistress did not look like an angel. Having said that the *panna-tsurechka*, his daughter, like an early lily, had been touched by the first frosts of poverty; although the sun of joy did not shine upon her, still beauty remained – beauty even in poverty. I brought her a dish of strawberries just to see a smile of pleasure through her mist of sadness. Unhappy beauty! In the best of circumstances, she would have been the adoration of many of Fortune's favourites.

Even on that day we were satisfied with our host. The Poles, like the French, were more hospitable than the Germans. We were already getting used to the shabby appearance of the locals, and to the barren, gloomy nature of these places.

In the town of Pławno we crossed the river Warta. Poverty and tenant farmers were ubiquitous. Outside the town of Radomsko, in the village of Okrajszów, on a seemingly good estate, the tenant farmer had only lived there for a week, following the contracts of St. Jan, and therefore had not yet managed to start to farm.

The village of Barczkowice, near the town of Kamieńsk, was just six huts, and the peasants in it barely resembled human beings. The town itself was worse than the village: in it one large stone building which served as an embellishment for all, and for the wealth of the *pan* [lord]. He takes a *czynsz*, or rent, of two chervonets from each household, and has no further interest in anything else. The residents said that the war had drained them, especially with donations to restore their homeland: all the requirements from the French Marshals, for the maintenance of Napoleon's troops, had been willingly fulfilled, and then the Muscovites began to demand the same. Poland was then at a crossroads on the political map between the major powers; whoever wished could come in, have a drink and a meal without saying thank you. We collected barely enough food for ourselves paying for everything in cash.

Not quite a Meile [4⅔ miles] from the city of Petrikau [*Piotrków Trybunalski*], we stopped in the village of Krzyżanów. Accustomed to seeing poverty and a miserable population in sandy Galicia as we passed, we saw some improvement here. The village belonged to the Duchy of Warsaw; the nobleman Tokchevsky had rented it for six years, and had leased it for another twelve. Whether it was from the fact that he had been in military service (under the command of General Kosciuszko[14]), where a lot can be learned about necessities and learning to survive, only his farm was different from other tenant farmers'. Each of his peasants was like a landowner in comparison with the others; he did not burden them with *panshchina* [feudal obligations], and as a result healthy, cheerful, but weather beaten faces were encountered. In return, the kind tenant farmer Tokchevsky was rewarded with the love and zeal of his subjects. At any time of the passage of enemy and our troops, he had known how to receive whom; as a result, not a single hen was wasted; even now, although his home was outwardly poor, he had everything necessary to be a good host. Having issued rations to the passing troops, he took receipts from them, and, by settling the account at reference prices, payed almost nothing to the Duchy all year round by presenting receipts, while sparing his peasants through this. The hussars who had

---

14 Andrzej Tadeusz Bonawentura Kościuszko

stayed with him two days before us had earned him 4,000 zlotys; we had earned him 1,500 zlotys; and in total he payed 7,000 zlotys to the Duchy per month for the village, and he assured us that in the current troubled times it was much more profitable to be a tenant than an owner, because the owners were losing their properties. Thus every master craftsman was worried.

According to the newspapers, disagreements had arisen in France, and the King had been forced to expel all opponents of the new constitution. The French felt sorry for Napoleon. Therefore, one had to guess that the peace would not continue. Our troops, according to a new disposition, were to be stationed right on the border; only the reserves would go into the interior of the Empire, such as the guards to St. Petersburg, the grenadiers to Livonia and Estonia; one division would go to Finland, another to Odessa; the other reserve forces would be stationed in Lithuania and Podolia. The active corps were to occupy part of the Duchy of Warsaw, from Kovno [*Kaunas*] to Krakow.

The town of Wolbórz was a green village lined with poplars; within it, the Bishop of Kujawy's palace gave a good view of the surroundings. Along our route through the Duchy, half of the huts in every village were empty and the fields were uncultivated. The war and devastation from occupying troops, had forced many gentry and villagers to scatter to work farther away, in various directions, to wherever there were no troops.

On today's march, gunner Dergunov from our artillery company amused me with stories of his captivity. He had been abandoned, at the start of the campaign in Russia, in an ambulance cart, in Yashiny [*Jašiūnai*], near Vilna [*Vilnius*]. The French had caught them by surprise, and captured all the sick; however, the healthy ones scattered across the field, into the thick rye, where they got entangled, and also fell into the hands of the mounted unbelievers [*basurman*]. They were then taken away and locked up in Danzig. When, after the destruction of Napoleon's army in Russia, the French survivors went to Danzig, then all the Russian prisoners had suddenly been released from jail, and were led away. In Stettin [*Szczecin*], during the march of the prisoners, the Commandant had instructed them to attack their escorts; they did it and broke free. But the French soon reentered the city, and, having learned the whole story, shot the Prussian Commandant. During his march across Germany, Dergunov attempted to flee the party six times, but was always betrayed to the French by unfaithful Germans; some had given him directions, while others had led him to the enemy pickets. Dergunov said that on one occasion he had been brought to Bonaparte himself, who ordered him to be shot, but seeing that he was not intimidated, spared him. During the drive of our prisoners, the French had treated them very cruelly; if anyone had lagged behind, they shot him. In France itself, beyond Lyon, they had been kept in a dungeon, issued three pounds of bread and three sous (15 kopecks) per day. Before the invasion of France by Russian troops, the prisoners had lived in barracks and had freedom. Many French women had fallen in love with my gunner, seduced him with their wealth and freedom, took him to their houses, where he lived with them for several weeks, while they tried to persuade him to stay forever; but he, remembering his wife and two sons, left behind in Russia, immediately jumped out of the seductress' soft bed, and went to the barracks, to his comrades in bondage. "Perish the thought, Your Honour!" he said, "to be a traitor to the fatherland and Russian laws, my heart would break!" Good soldier! you are worthy of having your name passed on to posterity... "Who was the Commandant that was shot?" asked the grey-haired Colonel in Chief of the N*** Regiment, who was riding by on horseback, while the carriage with his sleeping wife was dragging along in front – and thus stopped our conversation.[15]

Outside the town of Lubochnia, we stopped in the village of Jasień. Here we had a spacious barn, in which we slept on fragrant herbs. The flies were not tyrannizing us so much as they had on previous stages. We always had campaign meals: gruel and meatballs. Each of the comrades would be busy in their own way: one would sleep, another was out walking, a third was writing, the fourth and fifth were standing picket, while the sixth, sitting with his pipe in the corner, was plunged into a sweet or bitter reverie. this is how we spent most of our time en route through the Duchy of Warsaw.

Today in the forest, crawling on all fours hunting for berries, I was like that son of nature, which the sensitive Rousseau [*Jean-Jacques Rousseau*] always wanted to see; but apparently he had not experienced such a life himself: otherwise, he would have changed his system of Philosophy.

---

15 The comment about the Stettin Commandant occurred later; but for the sake of the flow of the story we have placed it where it is.

In Poland, comic moments are not uncommon. When we paraded into the city of Rawa [*Rawa Mazowiecka*], we were met by a Jew holding a bowl of stew, which he, watching us, sipped with great appetite; then, through a window pane, we saw a lady doing her makeup in front of a mirror: looking at us, she tried on a cap with roses, which made me laugh, and her also; then a fat-bellied Pole, with a grey moustache and a bald head, who was standing in front of the open window of his house, who was eating, while looking at us, a piece of bread thickly smeared with butter, and thus whetted our appetites; then, at the bazaar, the ragged villagers appeared with geese and pigs, the beloved comrades of the farmstead economy and tenant farmers; then we saw a young, short lady, on the arm of a tall dandy: from under her hat, her face appeared, and her figure, trimmed with satin in the shape of Venus, promised something charming... These were the sights of Rawa, which, however, looked like an ordinary Jewish town.

The artillery company halted in the village of Kanonitsy [possibly Konopnica], and we took shelter on a nearby estate. The *pan* himself had gone to Warsaw, leaving his brother in charge, a young, bald, frosty man, unsteady on his legs, with shifty eyes and sluggish movements. His face bore the marks of a dissipated life and the poison of indulgence... "Ha, our brother, the reveller!" remarked our captain, glancing at him. Indeed... we each stifled an involuntary sigh, reluctant to acknowledge our own weaknesses. This Pole, prematurely aged, had served nine years in Napoleon's army for his homeland and had recently returned from Modlin. The construction of the Modlin fortress had begun at the same time as ours in Bobruisk [Babruysk].[16] The fortress housed a garrison of about 4,000 men, who entered it just two days ahead of the Austrians. On the advice of Count [Mikhail] Miloradovich, the Austrians had hoped to move their rearguard into the fortress, allowing themselves to be blockaded and thus hastening capitulation. However, the Poles refused to let them in. The fortress was vulnerable in winter, when the river froze, and General Markov could have seized it. Yet, with troops needed for field operations, Russian generals neglected this position and spared only the remaining veterans of the Patriotic War [of 1812]. After General Markov, General [Ivan] Paskevich was sent to blockade the

---

16 The construction of Bobruisk Fortress began in 1810, that of Modlin Fortress in early 1807

fortress with his division, which numbered no more than 2,000 fighting men. Initially, the besieged managed well. They had so much food that after a ten-month blockade, wheat supplies still remained. However, meat became scarce, and they resorted to eating their horses. During the truce, they sold excess salt to purchase meat, paying a month's salary for it. The commandant was the Dutchman, General [Herman Willem] Daendels. The *Platz-Commandant* was Colonel Krasnitski, and the chief of artillery, a one-legged officer, who was perpetually drunk. The fortress was equipped with one hundred cannons. The garrison could not mount a significant sortie because half of its forces were always manning the ramparts, and incessant desertions reduced their numbers further. In preparation for an assault, they stockpiled hand grenades, hot pitch, and logs.

The fortress, surrounded by dense forests, provided concealment for the blockading Russian troops. The Poles anticipated an attack, as Russian soldiers had been practicing assault drills, reportedly climbing Jewish taverns with ladders, a detail relayed by Polish scouts. The besieged maintained communication with Warsaw via the river until the Russians placed a blockhouse to sever this link.

Meanwhile, the Russian generals and officers blockading the fortress lived comfortably, enjoying cordial relations with the local landowners. During the day, the troops hid in the forests, emerging at night to advance their batteries closer to the fortress as a precaution against sorties. General Paskevich even corresponded with the Commandant, sending him newspapers and basic necessities. Shortly before the armistice, Paskevich initiated a bombardment that would have forced the garrison to surrender. However, a courier from the Allied Monarchs' headquarters ordered all batteries silenced and hostilities ceased.

The Commandant's surrender terms included allowing the garrison to march to France, fully armed, with the freedom to sell their remaining wheat and the right to reenter service against Russia after three months. These terms were sent to the Tsar for approval, but his response was decisive: *"Dismiss the Poles to their homes, take the French as prisoners, and leave the wheat for the Russian garrison. If they do not agree, let them rot in the fortress."* Upon receiving this refusal, the Commandant, having no means to sustain the siege, surrendered unconditionally. His prudence in holding the fortress to the bitter end was commendable, serving as an exemplary model of fortitude and leadership for all future Commandants.

We marched from Rawa to Warsaw over the course of three days, encountering no notable events along the way. The terrain remained sandy, dominated by plains and stretches of pine forest.

The troops stopped, 15 *verstas* [ten miles] from Warsaw, in the very place where, in 1809, Prince Poniatowski (according to the testimony of the locals) with 600 Poles defeated 40,000 Austrians,[17] having also 70 artillery pieces and the Polish-Lithuanian Commonwealth Militia. The Austrians fled, but the next day, approaching Warsaw, they demanded that it yield in capitulation. Poniatowski hesitated for some time, finally having moved to Praga, he left Warsaw to the Austrians. Meanwhile, General Dombrowski[18] marched into the rear of the Austrians via Galicia with a strong detachment after which the Austrians were forced to abandon Warsaw themselves.

Here they also told us that last year, while we were drowning the French in Silesia, in the Katzbach [*Kaczawa*] and the Bober [*Bóbr*], the flooding of the Vistula, Warta and Oder rivers had caused many disasters for the Poles, drowning their families and inundating all their property. In Posen [*Poznań*], it was as if the entire house of one landowner, with guests, had been swept off by the waters, then, hitting the bridge, had collapsed it; of the whole company, only two girls were saved, sitting on a table, from whom it was barely possible to discover their surnames. Elsewhere, a bullock was found floating in the water, and a cradle, with a baby and 200 chervonets. So, during one period of time, the French and their most faithful allies had suffered from the hostile elements of nature turned against them.

On 31st July [12th August], we made our ceremonial entrance into Warsaw, filled with Russian troops. We had changed our clothing for

---

17 The battle of Raszyn on 19th April 1809 was an indecisive engagement between Polish and Saxon forces on one side and Austrians on the other. The account given to Radozhitskii appears to be mostly local legend.

18 Jan Henryk Dąbrowski (1755-1818), was a Polish general and statesman who fought the Russians during the Polish Partitions in the 1790s and later immigrated to France, where he established the Polish Legion and distinguished himself in the Revolutionary and Napoleonic Wars. The Polish national anthem, "Poland Is Not Yet Lost", written and first sung by the Polish legionnaires in Italy, mentions Dąbrowski by name, and known as "Dąbrowski's Mazurka"

this at the Jerusalem tollgate [*Rogatki Jerozolimskie*] and entered via the Krakow suburb. Here the Inspector in Chief of Artillery, Baron Möller-Zakomelsky[19] observed us, and was pleased that we, continuing such a long march, had preserved our shakos and cap-cords, new uniforms, swords and pouches; he even said that our company was the best of those which had paraded through the city, and therefore would not let it reform in Russia, but would leave it on the border. In the city itself, in a square in front of a crowd of people, the Commander-in-Chief inspected us along with other troops. However, no matter how pleased everyone had been with us, they would not leave us in the city to have fun, but sent us beyond Praga, to the village of Białołęka.

As far as I could see when crossing Warsaw, the city seemed to be larger than Dresden; however there were excellent buildings on only two streets: Dolgoy and Medovoy. In the Krakow suburb, on a small platform, there was a tall pillar, and on it is a statue of John Sobieski, the warrior-King, the saviour of Vienna from the Turks, who was presented in a formidable pose, with a sabre in his hand.[20] The shops were very attractive; but quality goods could not be found in them, especially ornamental items. The houses were mostly blackened with age; outstanding buildings included the Royal Palace, in front of the large square, and the Cadet Corps [*Ujazdów Castle*?]; there were several excellent private residences. In general, there was a lot of uncleanness and untidiness in the city, especially where the Jews lived. The city was surrounded by a rampart, which, from the direction of Praga, had been razed, there were almost no traces of the fortifications. The Vistula river seemed to me somewhat wider here than the Elbe in Dresden; the bridge was on pontoons, because the river is navigable and the pontoons were often raised. The bare banks were littered with timber and did not give a good view. On the bridge, a toll was collected from everyone on arrival and departure. There were many taverns in Warsaw; the main ones were; Hôtel de France, Hôtel d'Allemagne, Hôtel de Hambourg, and the best, Hôtel de Wilna, where, it was said, our Inspector himself often went to dine, and all the nobility or the wealthy, because the doorman would greet them at their destination. A good dinner would cost a gold chervonets, and an ordinary one cost a silver rouble. Among the many

---

19 Peter Ivanovich Möller-Zakomelsky (1755–1823)

20 Jan III Sobieski

military men young Poles would be encountered, Napoleon's retired warriors, in tailcoats, with moustaches, muscular cockerels. In many places the city had been burnt out and neglected. It was said that Princess R*** had visited all the Russian Generals in order to collect donations in favour of those burned out; but one of them had told her that he had given all his spare cash to those who had been burned out in Moscow. For a long time Warsaw, like a stubborn beauty, would not submit to the Russian Tsar; for a long time the Poles had quarrelled and feuded with the Russians, their fellow tribesmen; now, at last, it had surrendered, and the two peoples, having ceased their mutual enmity, would form one friendly nation, invincible Slavs of the great Empire. On the other side of the Vistula, the suburb of Praga, glorious prior to Suvorov's assault,[21] was now nothing more than a ravaged, empty place.

On 2nd [14th] August, we arrived in the village of Nieporęt. Was it a large village? "Oh, it's large, *Pane*, fifty gentlemen!" And what of it? The stewards, clergy (*księża*), and postmaster were present, but the other so-called gentlemen-peasants had fled to the towns to work for the Jews, leaving their houses abandoned and reduced to firewood for the guests. Those who remained explained that the village had been ravaged by water and war. We found this situation rather unpleasant. Both we and our gunners, along with our horses, were forced onto a strict diet that day. Rations finally arrived in the evening, having been deliberately requested from a Jewish settlement 20 *verstas* [approximately 13⅓ miles] away.

Along the route from Warsaw, we had been assigned short stages, and every two days a rest day, in order to prepare for the long march; but instead, with very meagre rations, the men and horses became very emaciated and marched miserably.

Opposite the town of Serock, the river Bug flows into the Narew, across which there was a wooden bridge; the right bank, where the town is located, is high, while the left bank is low; dense forests extended for a considerable distance. The town was enclosed by a rampart, and formed a kind of bridgehead, which had now been completely demolished.

---

21 Suvorov's Russian forces stormed Praga in November 1794, during the Kosciuszko uprising. The assaulting troops, allegedly enraged by the defenders sniping from civilian homes, immediately went on an infamous rampage, increasing the mutual enmity mentioned by Radozhitskii

We found ourselves in purpose built barracks and stables. There was a pyramid in the square, built by the Poles in memory of their dreams of freedom and victory over the Austrians. The town was insignificant, but it had three taverns and beautiful women. We stayed in the best house. The year 1798 was engraved above the door in the hallway, and a fish had been drawn, an *arshin* [28"] in length, which had been caught in this place during the flooding of the Narew, that is, in the year shown, the water level here had risen by some 15 *sazhens* [105'] in height: from this the extent of the devastation and the calamities this had caused at the time could be judged.

We continued marching through forests and sandy terrain, with the River Narew flowing steadily to our right. The stages of the journey were largely uneventful. As we approached Pułtusk, I gazed with satisfaction at the fields where, on 14th [26th] December 1806, General Bennigsen thwarted the French and compelled them to withdraw.

I had imagined Pułtusk to be a respectable town, but it quickly became clear that good towns were scarce in Poland. As before, we could not secure decent quarters for ourselves until the evening. Unfortunately, a newly formed division of grenadiers, numbering around 3,000 men, was travelling with us, and their officers had already occupied all the best houses. Although the town was relatively large, much of it had been burned or destroyed during the war. The castle, church, and a few remaining houses gave some semblance of a town, but overall, it was worse than a typical German village. Without suitable lodgings, we stopped at an Austrian tavern, where the slender and charming proprietress, despite her polished manners, tried to turn us away. Undeterred, we ordered dinner, paid promptly, and engaged her in friendly conversation. Gradually, her demeanour softened, and she even began to smile. Yet, the issue of finding a place to sleep remained. I wandered from house to house in search of accommodations. At one home, I encountered a German widow, the wife of a former accountant. Hearing her speak German was a welcome relief, transporting me momentarily back to lovely Germany. I stopped for a brief but pleasant conversation with her modest, blonde-haired daughter, who exuded a quiet charm. Not wanting to impose on their kindness, I eventually resumed my search. By nightfall, I finally found an empty hut shared with a retired soldier. Exhausted, I spent the night there as I was, without even undressing.

Sometimes, during our time in France and Germany, each stage of the journey brought so many new impressions that my mind overflowed, leaving me no time to record them all in my campaign notebook. But now, everything felt monotonous: forests, sands, and in the town of Różan, the same impoverishment of the inhabitants. For several days, we encountered French prisoners who had been captured at Danzig and were now returning from Russia. They had marched all the way from Kiev [Kyiv] and Chernigov [Chernihiv], and many had been held in Bobruisk, performing forced labour. They bitterly lamented their unhappy fate, though they now found themselves unexpectedly freed.

The town of Ostrołęka was much like every other in Poland: a cluster of Jewish houses, a market square, and a church at its centre. At least here, people were present, though not a single peasant remained in the surrounding villages; they had all fled. The huts were overgrown with oats, and the streets were choked with brushwood. Only the taverns were still inhabited, sheltering the fearless tinkers. We deliberately spent a rest day in Ostrołęka to stay in step with the infantry, which remained inseparable from us. Our quarters were with the Salt Bailiff [the local police chief], reputedly the best accommodations in town, though the house was worse than that of a typical German villager. A portrait of Moses hanging above the doors lent an air of grandeur to an otherwise empty room. Our journey thus far had taken us through forests and sands, along the Narew, across the poorest part of the Duchy of Warsaw.

The town of Łomża appeared quite pleasant to us, as the weather had cleared up; when nature brightens, the spirit tends to follow suit. In the town, many French prisoners, captured at Danzig, were gathered as they prepared to return home. They were marching as soldiers, equipped with helmets, knapsacks, and swords, while the officers rode on horseback in full uniform. These men had been held in the Kursk and Orel governorates and spoke warmly of the hospitality they had received from Russian landowners. Many officers had been welcomed into noble households, where they were tasked with teaching languages, dancing, or any other skills they possessed. Some grew so close to their hosts that they married their students and chose to remain in Russia. Those returning to France carried with them a peculiar assortment of mongrels, dogs that had learned to bark in French manner. We could not help but reflect, with some justification, on the broader consequences of this dispersion. A significant number of French captives had been scattered across Russian families, where they inevitably influenced the simplicity of local morals, instilling their foreign ways and vices in the fledgling youth. These youngsters, whose innocence had been so tenderly guarded, would ultimately leave their nests bearing traces of this foreign influence.

In Łomża, the great Napoleon, driven from Russia by fate and all the horrors of the disaster, had stopped at an inn and admitted the Prefect into his presence. He had, we were told, really wanted to eat, but they couldn't find anything better for him than simple jelly, or Polish preserves, and Jewish bagels. In place of such delicacies, the Prefect offered two bottles of old French wine from his cellar, of which the Mameluke, Napoleon's constant companion, hid one for himself, saying that the Emperor was old, so let him drink new wine, while a young man must drink the old.

Furthermore, here, at the popular theatre, actors travelling from Krakow performed the opera *Don Juan*, but it was so bad that, after the Mannheim and Dresden performances, I had to close my eyes and walk out.

Łomża stands on the elevated left bank of the Narew, which, flowing from here in meanders, began to lose its bluffs; from which the views were more pleasant.

Near the village of Mężenin, we stopped in the empty manor house of the Prefect of Plotsk, Rambulski, a very wealthy nobleman who had a good house near Warsaw, and who had bought an estate near Slonim for three million zlotys. In front of the house there was a lake with the banks lined with poplars; alongside the house there was a garden with shady avenues, and many fruit trees, over which we obsessed in turn. Who would not want to live with such choice! But the circumstances at the time had forced the owner to abandon the peaceful pleasures of rural life.

The town of Tykocin was better than Łomża. In the middle of the square there was a monument to the Polish nobleman, Count Branicki [*Jan Klemens Branicki*]; the statue, made of plain stone, held a bronze mace in its hand.[22] Opposite the statue was the beautiful facade of the

---

22 The statue Radozhitskii describes matches that of the statue of Stefan Czarniecki which has stood in front of the Holy Trinity church since 1763.

church, built in an Asiatic style. There were not many good private residences.

This was the frontier of the Duchy of Warsaw, and on the bridge over the Narew was the Russian border post.

As we crossed, captured Frenchmen passed us, with music and all their baggage. Have Russian prisoners ever returned from France so well fed and in such good condition, with all their acquired property? On the contrary, it was rumoured that our soldiers returning from hospitals had been killed near Reims and throughout Champagne.

We had finally completed our expedition abroad, departing from Paris for Russia on 1st [13th] April. Over the course of four months, with only a brief respite in Saint-Menehould, we marched more than 1,700 *verstas* [1,133 miles], traversing many lands without dawdling, keeping a steady pace throughout.

Chapter IX

Permanent Quarters

"Farewell, Saxony, Silesia, Germany, France! Farewell, sweet lands! You have fed us, watered us, and cosseted us!" So spoke the Russian soldier, stepping through the border post and looking back. Then, turning his gaze forward, he would cry out: "Greetings, dear Mother Russia! May you prosper forever!"

The Russians, having returned, greeted their fatherland with much rejoicing. *The Fatherland!* This sweet-sounding word carries profound meaning. We had fought for it, shed our blood for it, and sacrificed our lives for it. Now, having been spared, we were fortunate to return and savour our homeland once more. We had preserved the glory of the [Russian] Crown, ensured the well-being of the nobility, and now hoped to enjoy the fruits of our labour. As invincible victors, we had been met in foreign lands with a range of emotions: as enemies, as friends, as allies, as liberators. Now, returning home, we were welcomed with affection and warmth. In every gaze, we saw the same sentiment: "We are so glad to see you. Our homes are open to you, take whatever you need." Yet, these triumphant soldiers, humble even in victory, chose to bivouac in open fields, drinking their *krupnik*[1] and eating hardtack biscuits. Though no triumphal arches awaited these men, they crowned themselves with simple spruce branches tucked into their caps, the evergreen myrtle of their valour.

At 3 o'clock in the morning, on 13th [25th] August, we crossed our borders, via the border post on the Narew bridge in Tykocin. None of the customs officials stopped us to search for contraband; it was clear to everyone that we had not squandered our money on such frivolities. The Narew River, divided into numerous channels at this point, required us to cross nine bridges within the span of just two

---

1 A vodka and honey based liqueur

verstas [1⅓ miles]. From the river to Białystok, we marched more than 30 *verstas* [20 miles] along the main thoroughfare. Along the way, we passed through villages bustling with residents. The grain had already been harvested from the fields, and the peasants appeared well-off, dressed in sturdy caftans and even boots, something we had not seen in the Duchy of Warsaw for quite some time. In contrast, everything in the Duchy seemed depleted and devastated; villages lay abandoned, as many of the inhabitants fled their homeland. As a result, a significant number of Poles and Jews had crossed into our borders seeking refuge.

At 2 o'clock in the afternoon, we arrived in Białystok, but were kept waiting for two hours before being granted permission to enter. When we finally entered the city, we did so in parade order, with sprigs of fir adorning our shakos, as clean and tidy as we had been in Warsaw. Our Captain received the same recognition from General Kaptsevich as before.

Białystok is larger than Grodno, but its layout is less favourable. The houses were small, and the marketplace was modest. There was only one fancy goods shop, which sold items like sashes, collars, sugar, tea, and pomade. The best houses in the city had been built by the Prussians[2] and formed a linden-lined street, though they had taken over the nearby hospital. Much of Białystok consisted of poplar-lined streets, with the castle standing as its most notable feature. Once owned by the sister of the Polish King Mniszek, the castle was now property of the state.[3] The castle had weathered the ravages of time quite well. It was surrounded by a large garden, though it lacked water features. While it boasted Italian-style avenues and English groves, these could not rival the charm and pleasantness of the Nesvizh Palace gardens, owned by the Radziwiłł Princes, as a place for strolling.

We marched from Białystok through a dark forest, covering a good five *Meilen* [approximately 23 miles], to the town of Gródek. Despite its designation as a town, it was little more than a village, with a church and a synagogue, situated on the border of the Grodno Governorate.

---

2 Białystok had been ceded to Russia by Prussia in 1807 as part of the Treaty of Tilsit

3 The castle was built for Piotr Wiesiołowski (the Younger) around 1570 on the site of an old manor house. Mniszek was the surname of a Polish noble family, but they were not royalty

Three hundred years ago, the town belonged to General Khatkovsky, who, during a war with the Turks, captured some 2,000 prisoners. He built a castle and a monastery on this site and settled the captives within an enclosed rampart, marking the origins of the town. Today, no traces of these foundations remain, except for the remnants of the collapsed rampart, now overgrown and dotted with huts. Gródek, once part of the vast holdings of the Radziwiłł Princes of Nesvizh, who had defected to Napoleon, was now under state ownership.

The town of Śvislač could be considered a city. We hadn't expected it to be so good compared to the others. It was about three *verstas* [two miles] beyond a forest, neat houses of a uniform shape, made of white trunks unenclosed on a pristine field. Moving closer, we came to an avenue; from a bridge to the right, one's gaze was pleasantly led to a rectangular lake, with an island where, under the shade of trees, there was a gazebo. The house of the landowner himself, Count Tyshkevich,[4] was wooden, simple, but in a good location, surrounded by a garden with trimmed trees. I have not seen a single provincial town that was as cleanly and regularly maintained as the town of Śvislač: it was like Mannheim in miniature. Six streets lead from the vast square; each of them ends with a stone arch; along one is the avenue to the Count's house. Around the square, to one side, there was an extensive stock exchange, where merchants were now gathered for a fair. I watched our bearded men with pleasure as if with old acquaintances, with Vyazma gingerbread cookies, with boots, and with tea. The streets were wide; the houses were uniform, and were separated from each other by wide courtyards; it was not Jewish faces that peeped out of the windows, but the pleasant faces of the Count's officials. There was a pyramid in the middle of the square for decoration.

The landowner, Count Tyshkevich, was very rich and childless. It was said that he had appointed one of the poor peasants, a good host, as his heir, because he himself had come from simple peasants.[5]

Before our arrival, General Khitrovo had been quartered in Śvislač, while reforming the cuirassiers. Some officials and the sick with the baggage still remained; and therefore, although permanent quarters

---

4 Probably Vincenty Tyszkiewicz

5 Śvislač was eventually inherited by Tadeusz Tyszkiewicz, who had fought as a General of Brigade in Poniatowski's Polish V Corps of the Grand Armee in 1812

had been assigned for our artillery here, however, we could not find premises, and the following day we would have to be dispersed to the surrounding villages.

According to the assignments by our Captain, I, with part of the company, would go to stay three *verstas* [two miles] from Śvislač, in the village of Patsui. The reception from the *pan* was rather rude. Having a large house, he showed me my quarters in a hut that looked like a chicken coop. Initially I was indignant, demanded better lodgings, but after being assured of the vastness of the landlord's family, that is, the multitude of children and nannies, I agreed that he would be cramped in six rooms himself; and I remembered that I was no longer a guest, but among my own people, where they would not allow me to be picky. If I had felt the weight of resounding virtue in my pockets for the peace granted to him through our efforts, or had in mind something better than the present, then of course I could have avoided the need to beg this nobleman for a refuge; but the present cruel circumstances forced me to take advantage of him... What to do? In the chicken coop! I had, day and night a hole in the wall, called a window, and doorways without doors always open; maybe fresh air would clear the stench and rot. Now I had to live as a host myself, and I had already bought a cup, a glass and a spoon at the fair; but my poodle was now as hungry as I.

The next day, I called a truce with my host and hostess, after which, of course, peace should soon follow; we had not yet agreed on the line of demarcation: he had given my gunners only six huts to live in, so I ordered them to take them all. Lying in my kennel, which is eight paces long and four paces wide, I learned that my neighbour, brother Ungern's, was even worse: although he had a whole farmhouse, and four rooms, they have only walls and windows. The steward would not give him a bucket or an axe, and sold him a chicken grudgingly. At least my colleague could enjoy nature through a large window, to see how the ducks waddled around the yard and talked about their guest, or how turkey cocks, puffing themselves up, trailed after apathetic turkey hens; I was even deprived of these pleasures.

I did not expect that in such a small place as Śvislač one could find so many pleasures. In the morning, a *kirmes*, or fair, had opened. The whole square was filled with carts, and at each of them were different groups; the noise of peasants, women, and the cry of geese, ascended above the pyramid. I pushed my way across the square into the church; it was not big and was filled with people. Visiting landowners and gentlewomen were sitting on the pews; several of them were pretty, but not a single one that could be called a beauty; They read very diligently in their prayer books, and often looked back at the incoming worshippers. The rural women, in grey caftans, with white headscarves, occupied all the space between the walls and pews, on their knees, or sitting on the floor. They were holding either children with bagels, or chickens and roosters in their arms, whose cries sometimes interfered with the sound of the organ and with the hymn singing.

From the church I entered the tavern: here I won five chervonets from the first card-sharp, and three from the green major (as we named him after his light green tailcoat); and so dinner, a show, and the redoubt had cost me nothing.

Count Tyshkevich, by building a stock exchange for the exchange of goods, had done a lot for himself and the visiting merchants, who conveniently laid out their goods in the stalls, without fear of damage from bad weather. However, the products were not refined: rural necessities. Most of the merchants were Jews from Berdichev [*Berdichiv*], and bearded men from Suzdal. In the gallery, between the stalls, there were many gentlewomen and young ladies walking about.

At 7 pm, after three shots from a signal gun, a performance began in the Count's theatre. The theatre was small, homely, but quite well decorated: with boxes, stalls and a gallery. The orchestra played a respectable overture; but the musicians were evidently serfs, and the instruments homemade. By all appearances, the Count had his own concept. The curtain opened, and we saw an actor who had been playing with the green major in the morning. He twisted his visage according to the sound of the words but was not feeling their meaning. The first play was a comedy in Polish: *One Must Love Women*. A certain Lord, abandoning women, was travelling and stopped at an inn. His old friend came to visit, a retired sailor, who incessantly sang, scolded women, and rejoiced that his wife was dead. Suddenly a poor girl appeared with a guitar; she captivated the Lord with her gentle, pleasant voice, her sighs and tears, her languid eyes and the story of the misfortunes common to beauties. The Englishman, despite his severity, felt something in his chest, in his heart, and consoled the beauty with a precious ring, and then married her. The actress, *panna* Kolosova, played her role perfectly. I had noticed that the Polish language is musical, especially on the lips of a pretty beauty, although it has very heavy syllables: *prshe, brzhe*, and so on. After the comedy, during the intermission, the virtuoso Reut from Vilna played polonaise-concerto on stage, in the style of the glorious Rode;[6] his play was very free and pleasant; the violin sounded like a bell, and sometimes surprised with transitions into unfamiliar tones. Thereafter two characters presented an opera in one act: The huntsman of a great *pan*, while on a hunt, got lost at night and, holding forth aloud over a bottle of wine, sang a song. An echo kept repeating the final syllable. The huntsman, called by the echo, walked on; suddenly a woman appeared with a basket, who had been foraging for mushrooms, and had also got lost at night; she sang, and they both bumped into each other in the dark. After various jokes between them, and candour, one at the expense of her husband, and the other at the expense of his wife, the huntsman finally asked the gods to bring on the day in order for him to see this amiable woman who could forge his drinking horn if he were her husband. The scene turned from night to day, the huntsman recognized the woman as his wife. The ending was quite amusing. The husband and wife fought over their poor opinion of each other, but they soon made up again, thinking that their disagreement might upset their household. Both performed decently; the actress sang loudly, fluently and stridently. In a woman's voice, there is some kind of force that affects the emotions; upon hearing a gentle, melodic voice, an angel could be imagined; but the shrill, thin voice of a screamer conjures up a witch. If, moreover, the singer is ugly with a hideous figure, then this phenomenon is worse than the devil. The opera was even enticing in its morality: seeing a night scene of a man with a woman, the female spectators, it seemed, blushed involuntarily. In general, plays in which love is an impetuous passion are harmful to innocent girls: all the secrets of love, trysts, explanations, tricks, kisses, little notes, seen at the theatre, serve as a lesson for the vestals entering the world, who themselves, by the inclination of their hearts, would soon wish to be similar actresses in the real world, especially since the actors are always in front of their eyes. That is as may be, but Count Tyshkevich's theatre, beyond expectations, turned out to be as good as we had seen in France, excluding Nancy.

An hour after the theatre, I went to the redoubt: in Poland this means a meeting of gentlemen and ladies, for dancing and gambling, where,

---

6 Jacques Pierre Joseph Rode

having paid half a dollar in silver at the entrance, everyone is good for his penny. Important people denigrate the dance, while the devout regard it as a diabolical obsession; but for me there was nothing bad there: the movements were incomparable. Spinning with a beautiful woman in a waltz, or frolicking between them in a quadrille, a man might imagine themselves to be the Sultan in a seraglio [harem]. It is very pleasant for our class, after a gloomy lesson with lead feet, to occasionally have fun with the dear ones. The green major's wife was the most attractive of all with languor in her eyes, a smile on her lips and agility in dancing. This delightful creature, wrapped in an orange shawl, flashed before everyone's eyes, like an evening butterfly. Oh, green major! Were you worthy of her as a reward for your awful skill at beating our brothers! The unfortunate woman has been with her husband for another week, yet she does not see her husband, and is always in tears about her fate. Her cruel father did not spare her, giving her to an old invalid; she was forced to hide her grief from him, and find secret pleasures for which she had been born in all perfection. Many worthy men had sought her hand, but money and thick epaulettes triumphed over everyone. Her father sold her, enjoying the profits, but making her miserable. Does this mean that it is better not to produce children at all than to be their murderers? What daughter would bless the memory of parents who had caused her such distress?

The ladies in Śvislač were pretty simple, the girls' education was not impressive. Many of them chatted in French, danced mazurkas, and sang songs with a guitar: that was the extent of their education. All of them are bold, agile, and do not panic at minor misfortunes. A boarding education for them was very different from that at home: from the start, the girls were to be improved, sentimental, and put on a strict diet, so as not to be stout, but pale and thin; for all that, they were more witty and amiable; with a home education, the *pannas* were heavy, plump, ruddy, noisy, or silent, so that at first glance one could distinguish a boarder from a farm *panna* raised with geese.

I was raised up to the light from my chicken coop, following an intimidating inspector's review from the Divisional Commander. I had raced headlong into Śvislač in full dress at dawn, and found everyone asleep. The officers, who had been writing the returns and equipment states for the document inspection until 3 o'clock in the morning, had overslept the arrival of the Brigade Commander.

I had received orders to go to Białystok, at the request of General Kaptsevich, for drafting plans, and therefore, having filled a suitcase with my worldly goods, I gladly said goodbye to the owner of the chicken coop; he was also glad that I was leaving.

Meanwhile, the fair in Śvislač had dispersed, but the actors had managed to present several plays by Moliere[7] quite successfully, such as *The Reluctant Healer* and *The School for Wives*.

On 1st [13th] September, I rode on a jolting wagon 9 *Meilen* from Śvislač to Białystok, and called on the General, and then on the Chief Quartermaster of His Majesty's Suite, Colonel [Platon] Pensky. He promptly informed me that I was being assigned to the Grodno Governorate for a military reconnaissance mission. My task was to compile a topographic, statistical, and strategic description of the Kobryn district, as well as to update and correct its map with detailed information about the locations. This was my first assignment of such a nature. However, recalling everything I had once studied, I began preparing diligently for it, organizing a number of maps, designing forms for returns, and securing the necessary instruments and supplies.

Białystok was not a city where one could afford to waste time. There were no good restaurants, though the best options were located on Warsaw Street. There, a certain Madame ran a boarding school for girls from noble families, sent by farmers for their education. With the profits from their upbringing, she had opened a tavern and hired French prisoners of war as teachers. Another restaurateur, who also doubled as a confectioner, operated almost underground on the lowest floor of a large casino building. A third establishment, run by a *panya* hunchback, housed a boarding house for the nymphs of joy. For a walk, the castle garden might have been a pleasant choice if it hadn't been left in disrepair and fallen into ruin. A theatre with decent actors offered one of the few enjoyable entertainments Białystok had to offer. Here I saw a performance of the Polish Drama: *The Selection of Recruits*, translated into Russian. The words were not distorted by the Polish accents, and the whole play was well performed. I admired seeing

---

7 Jean-Baptiste Poquelin, known as Molière (1622–1673), was a renowned French playwright, actor, and poet. A master of comedy, his works, such as *Tartuffe*, *The Misanthrope*, and *The Imaginary Invalid*, satirized social norms, hypocrisy, and human folly. Molière's legacy profoundly shaped French theatre and modern comedic tradition.

Russian nationality, albeit at the theatre. Among the actors, Mr. Gentzel, who played the role of Obiralov, was extremely characterful, and was not inferior in skill to our [Alexander] Ponomarev. The audience often applauded him. He knew how to express himself not only with language, but with facial features and his entire physiognomy. The theatre director himself, Mr. Kaminsky, portrayed the headman well, and Mr. Fischer was quite characterful in the role of Hippolyte. A new actress portrayed Anyuta poorly. The audience was very pleased with the play, and often applauded; I even saw tears in the eyes, under the glasses of one sensitive German spectator, at the farewell scene of Alexei with his family: it was a triumph for the cast. One could have called out for Gentzel, but his minor role did not allow for that; having said that he himself went out to introduce the play the next time, and was greeted and seen off with loud, general applause.

Chapter X

The Reconnaissance Mission

On 6th [18th] September, I was issued a corded notebook, a travel warrant, and an open document granting me unrestricted passage throughout the Kobryn district. On the first day, I rode as far as the village of Kopyly, a distance of about 100 *verstas* [67 miles], a feat I had not anticipated, given the condition of the emaciated peasant horses I received.

Along the way, I passed numerous carts filled with peasant women, dressed in typical village attire, hurrying to market with roosters and geese. Their destinations were the town square, the church, or the inn. I also encountered several French prisoners returning from Tambov and Saratov, being concentrated in Białystok. The county town of Belsk [Bielsk Podlaski], located five *Meilen* [23 miles] from the district centre, was impoverished. On Sundays, however, its drinking houses were lively, with Jews playing violins and cymbals to accompany the revelry. Throughout the villages, the peasants, dressed in their best caftans, sat amid the debris near their huts, basking in the sun like flies in front of a stove. It had been a long time since I had seen such a peaceful rural scene. No one seemed to think of the enemy anymore, and the traces of war were starting to vanish. The sunny day added to the scene's charm, as nature herself seemed to smile, like an elderly beauty whose charms had faded but whose grace remained.

The last 20 *verstas* [13 miles], from the town of Kleszczele to Kopyly, I travelled by night and quickly became lost. The Jews in the taverns refused to venture out to guide me, as they were all asleep. Riding alone through a forest at night was far from pleasant. Eventually, I reached Kopyly, entered a farmhouse, and rekindled a fire myself. Fortunately, I found a ready-made bed in the first room, while the sleepy steward lay sprawled in the other. Without hesitation, I followed him into Morpheus' kingdom.

They say the seventh day is unlucky, and that good people should not start anything on a Monday. Curious to test this superstition, I found myself doing nothing on that seventh day, Monday. As luck would have it, my non-commissioned officer, sent ahead the previous day, had gotten lost, leaving me to wait alone in Kopyly until ten o'clock. The steward, a kindly old man of 70, treated me to coffee and breakfast. Remarkably fresh and youthful despite his age, he bore the weight of recent tragedy: the loss of his entire family of three sons and a wife. His two daughters, however, had married dragoon officers stationed in the area to form regiments.

In the town of Kamyanyets, I paused to change horses; everyone was in a rush: now setting up for the Tsar's visit, now at the fair in Kobryn, now in the field, at work. Not wanting to waste time, I rode my old horses to the village of Glinyanki, 65 *verstas* [43 miles]. It was preferable for me to start the reconnaissance of the Kobryn district from the village of Bul'kovo, outside Brest-Litovsk; but through the diabolical delusion of the seventh day and Monday I had ridden almost as far as the Pruzhany road, to the village of Vezhki.

The next day, I was pleased with the start of my mission. From the village of Vezhki I rode to Bul'kovo, 40 *verstas* [27 miles], and described in one go what I thought would take me three days. True, there was a lot of work: to note the position of all villages, the distances between them, the directions of rivers and roads, the sizes and locations of forests, how everything should be indicated on a map; moreover, to note locations appropriate for attack or defence by troops; denote the number of households, the number of souls, the number of cattle, horses, the situation and occupation of the inhabitants of each village, so that, throughout the day, my head ached from many impressions and the exertions of attention; but I was drawing and writing until midnight. I rarely found the landowners in their villages; only in Stepanki and in Sokoli [*Sakalova*?] were they present; in Rachki lived a retired General, while Bul'kovo belonged to Marshal-of-the-Nobility Raisky's [*Stefan Rajski*] family. They were absent themselves, but the remaining *panna*-steward, with blue eyes and a hare lip, treated me to dinner, which she spiced up with her sweet glances; but I was immersed in thoughts about the statistics of the Kobryn district, more than about her hare lip.

THE RECONNAISSANCE MISSION

It was here on 14th [25th] July 1812 that General Tormasov,[1] having learned that Kobryn had been occupied by the enemy, went there with cavalry alone for a reconnaissance; the next day he linked up there with General Czaplic's[2] vanguard, and made arrangements for an attack. Bul'kovo's landowner, Marshal Raisky, having learned that during the fighting between the Russians and the Saxons, his house in Kobryn had burned down, was so distressed that he died four days later.[3]

The day before, at 9 o'clock in the morning, the Emperor had passed through Bul'kovo and drank coffee here. He had left St. Petersburg on the 2nd, with Prince Volkonsky,[4] and was riding in a simple carriage, day and night, hurrying to the Congress of Vienna. Here the district police chief and the head of the nobility had been waiting for him for two days, and they did not sleep at night, laying bonfires along the route; but on the 7th day, before their arrival, like sinners, everyone had fallen asleep. The Tsar had been cheerful; the mercy in his features was illuminated by the pleasant hope that everything would be fulfilled according to his will as the council of the Allied Monarchs determined the fate of the European Powers and confirmed their national independence.

The next day I rode through the swamps, to Brest-Litovsk. In Franopol', on an estate, I dined with the venerable *Podkomorye* [Chamberlain] Belsky, a kind old man who greatly facilitated my research by telling me about all the villages lying south to Dzivin and Mokrany, among the forests and swamps. He had a lot of children: two sons and three daughters were present, one fewer than the other. When the Russians and Austrians had alternately marched through his farm, he defended himself and his children: certainly, everyone survived, excluding food and drink, he did not lose anything except money for indemnities. That night I went to visit his brother in Atachizna, near the village of Ragozna. The estate was isolated, and it was the best of all that I had seen thus far.

---

1   Alexander Petrovich Tormasov (1752-1819)

2   Yefim (Eufemiusz) Ignatievich Czaplic (1768-1825)

3   In the attack on Kobryn on 27th July 1812, Tormasov overwhelmed Klengel's Saxon brigade, marking the first Russian victory of the campaign. Tormasov received the Order of St. George 2nd Class for this

4   Pyotr Mikhailovich Volkonsky (1776-1852) was a talented Russian staff officer, considered the founder of the Russian General Staff

He greeted me suspiciously, as passing marauders were usually greeted; but after reading the free passage document, and noticing compliance by me, because I had agreed to return to the village, to spend the night in a tavern, he called me back and led me into the living room, apologizing that he had a large family. I saw many ladies in the room; I was dazzled by the expensive furniture, the glitter of lamps and candles, and dancing in the middle of the room to the music of a piano, two girls delighted me. I imagined myself having been suddenly transported from the swamps to a Fairy's magical castle. The ballet lasted for half an hour, and I was transfixed, fixing my eyes on a sweet little girl, a beautiful girl dancing easily and very well for her age: her leaps were like the jumps of a dove when she fawns for her mate. Another girl, twice as tall as the first, was much more modest, moving her legs, which were skillfully concealed by a long dress. Looking at them, I was not without thoughts: how flattering to be called their father! Having a dozen babies of both sexes, I would have let them leap in front of him: here comes the ballet; and once they all could speak, or sing, here comes the opera. Domestic entertainment should be very joyful; I noticed that the mother was pleased with the skill of her little one, in discovering her talent; at an ideal age, she will certainly turn the heads of many sighing suitors. There were several beauties among those present: one had arrived from Kharkov [*Kharkiv*], a kind young lady; another girl, even better than her, resembling mademoiselle Emilia from Saint-Menehould; she wore coral around her neck just like that one... Oh women! How adorable you were! In your presence I was becoming more careful, more circumspect; in front of you, I pondered every word and every step, so as not to incur your ridicule, or an unfavourable impression; in your presence, I treasured each one of your approving glances. You were definitely created by nature to enlarge our hearts, to instill in us the most pleasant sensations: only with a beautiful, intelligent woman can one taste the true bliss of life!

His *Mosc*, a landowner in a *kuntush* [caftan] and with a moustache, my host's neighbour, had not ceased to be a supporter of the great Napoleon, and assigned all the wise policies of the Allies to luck, in expectation of the patriotic participation of all Poland. The host was more attentive to me and, as badly as we had met, we parted excellently.

The next day I had a lot of work on. I travelled along the river Mukhavets and had lunch with just a chicken at a *panna's*, in Sekhnovichi

[*Sukhovchitsy*]. This lively woman told me many anecdotes about the Austrians and Spaniards who had been her guests, and about the fact that she had not given the Governor money to greet the Tsar, having read in the Warsaw newspaper that our Sovereign Emperor forbade all expenses for this meeting. "Those are the benefits of newspapers", I said: "*I za pevne*" (that's it exactly), she answered.

Having learned that Artillery Captain S*** was accommodated in the village of Litvinki, with a horse company, I rode to meet him. He was an old colleague of mine, a classmate from the corps. The greeting from an old acquaintance, who had always sat in front of me in classes, was rather reserved, due to the enormous distance between us: he was already a Captain and a company commander, while I was a stray Lieutenant.

And so I travelled around the western part of the Kobryn district, for the most part. At Krupczyce [*Chyzhewshchyna*], where the hero Suvorov had won a famous battle over the Poles,[5] I noted a fighting position; although the right flank could be enveloped via the Sditovsky crossing. In the evening I arrived in Kobryn. I was shown quarters with stinking [*sic*] Jews; at least I consoled myself with the fact that it depended on me to stay here more or less on my own feet. The whole town had been burned out during the war; the many flues were the only remains showing the locations of former dwellings. In the course of two years, barely a handful of huts and the market had been rebuilt. The chief of police now had the best house.

In the morning, I captured an eye-catching image of the burned-out town and its surroundings. Lacking a horse, I walked the main streets with a measured pace, toured around the town, and drew what I saw. It's hard to be a military land surveyor: one must have a faithful eye in order not to be mistaken over distances, a sound memory and a good hand.

I was in a hurry with my work, drawing and writing from morning to evening, and still could not finish my review during the four days of my trip. The weather was fine; sunny days, and cheerful; romantic moonlit evenings. In the evenings, I would go for a walk to the bridge; I noticed the physiognomy of animals passing by; admired the small, winged

---

5 On 6/17 September 1794, during the Kościuszko Uprising, the Battle of Krupczyce occurred near the walls of a Carmelite monastery. The clash, between a Russian army commanded by A. V. Suvorov and a Polish detachment led by Karol Józef Sierakowski, resulted in a Russian victory

creatures that, in the moonlight, jumping over each other on the surface of the water, revived the still moisture. Even they have their passions: the all-embracing soul of the world revives the same water mosquito, as it does the airborne swallow and the earthly man.

Kobryn suffered greatly from the unfortunate battle with the Saxons on 15th [27th] July 1812. General Klengel,[6] commanding the Saxon forces, made the imprudent decision to position most of his cavalry in front of the town on the road to Bul'kovo, facing Count Lambert's[7] detachment, while leaving his left flank completely exposed in the direction of Antopal. Noticing this critical oversight, Commander-in-Chief General Tormasov swiftly dispatched General Czaplic to approach the town from the unprotected flank. Czaplic launched an attack with the 13th Jäger Regiment, while Count Lambert pushed back the Saxon cavalry in front of him. This forced the enemy to retreat into the outlying houses and hastily dug trenches. The arrival of General Tormasov's entire corps sealed the Saxons' fate, surrounding them on all sides. Count Lambert promptly ordered Colonel Prince Madatov,[8] with his light cavalry, to cross the Mukhavets River and cut off the enemy's retreat by taking the Pruzhany road. The Saxons held out for nine hours, fighting desperately in trenches, houses, the stone monastery, and at the bridge. However, their resistance was in vain. Reinforcements arrived for General Czaplic, including the Ryazhskii Regiment and a battalion of the Apsheronskii Regiment, which enabled him to take the bridge. The town, engulfed in flames, became untenable, and the remaining Saxon forces surrendered. General Klengel himself was captured, paying the price for attempting to hold out with just 4,000 troops against 30,000 Russians. The victory, remarkable for its scale, came at little cost to our side. From Kobryn, General Tormasov advanced with his army toward Pruzhany.

---

6 Heinrich Christian Magnus von Klengel (1761-1814) was a Saxon officer, commanding the 1st brigade of the 22nd Division in 1812

7 Karl Osipovich de Lambert (1773-1843) was a Russian general of the French descent. In 1812, he commanded cavalry in the 3rd Army of Observation

8 Valerian Grigorevich Madatov (1782-1829) was a Russian general of Armenian descent. Promoted to a lieutenant colonel in December 1810, he served with the Aleksandriiskii Hussar Regiment in the 3rd Army of Observation and distinguished himself at Kobryn and Gorodechno, for which he was promoted to a colonel in December 1812

To this day, the Poles remain very sympathetic towards the French. I witnessed this firsthand through the following anecdote. A French prisoner in a tailcoat entered the tavern while I was present. He had once served as Commandant here and was warmly greeted by many acquaintances in the room. They began drinking wine and punch together like old friends, though one man expressed dissatisfaction with him. The Frenchman, clearly offended, grew indignant and began defending himself in broken Polish, claiming he had done good for everyone and that no one had the right to judge him. He dismissed the criticism, stating that the opinion of one man meant nothing to him. Sensing his nationality, I interrupted him in French. The former Commandant eagerly switched languages, repeating his defence with the eloquence and wit characteristic of his countrymen. However, his antagonist, determined to defend his own honour, called the Frenchman a braggart and a liar. The argument escalated into the demands of satisfaction, plenty of shuffling and stomping. Not wanting to witness the foolishness of a duel, I left the scene. It was clear to me how easily this Frenchman's fiery temperament, like that of a rooster, could be provoked, always ready for a fight.

The next day I left Kobryn. The weather had suddenly changed: the wind and rain battered at me like hostile forces, making it difficult at every step for the skinny nags, dragging me in a jolting cart, huddled under a topographer's greatcoat. Along the Dzivinsky road, I drove into the so-called Shlyakhetsky and Jesuit swamps, where the people had always lived like frogs in the water. This whole country, around Kobrin, had once belonged to General Helvig, who had served under Suvorov in the Russian army. Kobryn itself, with the surrounding area, belonged to Count Suvorov. During the Patriotic War, Helvig's properties in Kobryn, to the value of 200,000 rubles, had burned down as well as his beautiful house, half a *verst* [600 yards] from the town. This unfortunate, deprived of everything in his old age, without a wife, without a family, now lived out his days in a poor hut that had survived in his farmyard; to walk wearing a bare sheepskin coat and a *colpak*, having with him at any one time no more than five paper rubles in cash, while his commissar, or gentleman-accountant, the manager of his estate, profited and grew fat, presenting to his *pan*-philosopher neat reports where the income and the outgoings were correct.

For lunch I went to Rodtsy to visit the retired and ill Ensign B***. His great-grandfather had received this estate as a gift from the hero

Suvorov, in 1794.[9] The wife of the retired Ensign was the same beautiful lady whom I had admired in Atachizna. She had been born in Kharkov, but the lot of the female had brought her with her young husband so far from her homeland. Both of them welcomed me as Russians do, with sincere cordiality. Their estate had been leased for two years by the Mayor [*Gorodnichy*] of Kobrin, an army Major, who not only did not pay them anything for this, but had also taken 500 rubles from them for the redemption of the lease; therefore they now seemed poor, and had not had the chance to start a farm. The hostess complained that she could not get used to the fake kindness and cold politeness of the Poles, who, with honey on their lips, stored bitter bile in their hearts, and started incessant litigation; the strong trying to ruin the weak. She had not yet made a sincere acquaintance with any Polish lady in the district, and therefore, not without reason, she longed for her homeland. This was precisely how Russians had to live among the Poles, because of the deep-rooted hostility of these latter to the former, meant to seek voluntarily ruin. Here almost every neighbour complains about their neighbour, and each was right in their own mind; but to unravel their truth even Shemyaka[10] himself would most likely have arrived at an impasse. However, the general voice of indignation rushed to the three most important persons in the district: the grey-haired police chief, the snub nosed Judicial Secretary and the fickle Marshal-of-Nobility.

From Rodtsy I went to Kamen Shlyakhetsky, where I found the magazine deputy, whom I had met while still in Cherevachitsy. He described to me the young landowner B *** as an officer of bad behaviour who had lost his estate at cards. Only by marrying a widow, with the help of her dowry and donations from friends, could he redeem his recklessly lost property. After that I could guess why the Mayor of Kobryn, for two years of his tenancy had paid nothing to the young landowner, and taken more from him; thus the daring Mayor could not miss an opportunity to dangle his bait. The deputy praised the wife of this landowner to me as an intelligent woman who always cared for her sick husband, and, being beautiful, always succeeded, because beauty has an irresistible power to defeat the most morose of judges. Despite

---

9　For defeating the Polish Confederates, Suvorov had received a significant estate from Empress Catherine II in the Kobryn district

10　Shemyaka's Justice is a Russian phrase meaning a hasty and unfair judgement

the fact that she had lived with her first husband for six years, she had retained all her freshness and youth.

On 20th September [2nd October], it became cold and snow fell. It was unpleasant to be a field surveyor at a time like this. That's what service means. All day I rode through the swamps in the northwestern part of the district. I spent the night in the village of Bukhovichi, in the house of the venerable grandmother N ***. I saw only one female here. I was greeted by the arranged bride of some lucky man, an aged miss, the granddaughter of the respectable grandmother, a languid, pale beauty: she had arranged with 50,000 zlotys for a singular young fellow whom she herself had chosen according to her heart. Thus, the grandmother had already accommodated two sisters of this granddaughter; now was the turn of the last one. Matchmaking is not a trifle; one needs to be able to smarten up the couple: old women understand this business better. The owner of the house himself, a noble gentleman, was in St. Petersburg under some kind of contract, in order to receive from the treasury several tens of thousands of zlotys. The commissar, or steward, for the arrival of his master, had plastered the newly built wooden rooms with clay, or covered them with colourful strips of paper. During the horrors of the last war, all the granddaughters had fled from this house; there was only the solitary fearless grandmother left to guard the property. Indeed, everything had survived with her, because she knew how to meet, treat and see off, both enemies and friends. When I entered the room upon my arrival in the evening, the old woman, seeing a military guest, was alarmed. I was told that the grandmother shuddered, sometimes even cried out if someone hit a glass, rattled a spoon, scraped a chair, stamped their feet, and so on; and therefore, in her presence, strict silence was observed: everyone walked on tiptoe and spoke in whispers. By virtue of such rules, and wishing to please the grandmother, I dined at the common table very quietly, carefully and economically. She, with her languid granddaughter, her still sedate companion, the respectful steward and I, all sat most decorously, for our conservative meal. The barefoot maids carried the food and were careful not to clatter. To please the grandmother, I had to send my non-commissioned officer at night to another village for horses, ready for the morning ride; the grandmother protects her subjects, who were not yet up to speed with horses.

I rode around Kobryn now to the right, now to the left. That day I travelled 60 *verstas* [40 miles], in the vicinity of the town, through forests and swamps. I was on the estate of General [Gregory] Engelhardt; I passed Planta, the manor house of General [Alexander] Gove [Howe]. At Zapruda, a kind steward fed me, and told me about the swamps beyond the village of Poddubno, where on 31st July [12th August], 1812, the Austrians, under the command of General [Jean] Reynier, enveloped the left flank of Tormasov's army, which was located at Gorodechno, towards which the Tyrolians and Croats had waded waist-deep through an impenetrable swamp; they carried their muskets on their heads, and, having crossed the swamp, struck at ours, opposite Poddubno.[11] This battle had almost been won by the Austrians, and only the coming night stopped their efforts, while General Tormasov was given the opportunity to hastily retreat to Kobryn, which was occupied after the Austrians on 1st [13th] August.

In the evening I arrived in Grushany [*Grushevo?*], and just in time for dinner. At the table I accidentally found three *Marszałek*, or Leaders of the Nobility, who had gathered here on the occasion of a *polevan'ya*, or a game hunt.

Between them I recognized the Governorate's, wealthy and noble *pan, Marszałek* P***, became very attentive to him, and answered his questions carefully. This important *Marszałek* had the tradition, annually, with comrades, at his invitation, and with a large retinue of dog handlers, hunters and Hortaya (greyhounds), for the whole of September to hunt through the forests of the entire Grodno Governorate, for wolves, of which many were destroyed in such *polevan'ya*, and provided security for the winter for their own and their neighbours sheepfolds. Thus far, he had already hunted 22 wolves. After supper, the *Marshalki* sat playing cards until midnight; but I, astonished at their activity, demurred, to rest myself, through the door, into a cold room, where, to my delight, I found a guitar, which I took up with no less enthusiasm than the *Marshalki* with their cards. During the supper, *Marszałek* P*** had treated me very kindly; I did not see in him the pride with which he indulged himself during the ball he gave in Slonim, before the start of the war, in 1812. He told me that he had recently been to Warsaw, to the Field Marshal's,

---

11 The battle of Gorodechno was fought between part of Tormasov's army against Schwarzenberg's Austrian Corps and Reynier's Saxons. Tormasov's left flank was turned by the Saxons supported by Austrian cavalry, forcing Tormasov to withdraw, after which Schwarzenberg advanced with his infantry

he knew all the Generals there, and the Sovereign Emperor had deigned to breakfast with him. This *Marszałek* was the richest *pan* in the whole of Lithuania, and a very good master of his vast estates.

In the morning, the *Marshalki* set off for Chomsk for the wolves, while I continued my journey to the east of Kobryn. Towards evening I arrived at the Basilian Monastery of Tarakanov. From this curious name, I really imagined that I was about to enter the kingdom of cockroaches,[12] however, to my surprise, I entered a huge, white-stone, spacious building, which from a distance looked somehow majestic. Here, among the humble brethren, removed from the mundane world, I immediately found hospitality once my written talisman revealed to them my right to statistical research of the entire Kobryn district. Due to their poverty, these brethren had a village nearby of 300 souls, belonging to them or to the monastery, for the maintenance of sixteen lay hermits. I found shelter with them in a modest cell, and tasted their repast, and, having drunk a glass of port, I fell asleep so deeply that, waking up the next day, I felt much healthier. From this sacred abode, the food and drink itself had restored the strength lost by labour.

The abbot himself was not at the monastery; he was in the town of Beden, Slonim *Powiat* [Polish term for a local government district, equivalent to a Russian *Uezd*], with the chapter at the congress, where new Abbots and treasurers were elected. The Father Vicar and *Ksenza* Professor had greeted me and hosted me. This Professor had an impressive physiognomy, a quick, penetrating gaze, and I discovered from his actions and conversations the mind of a Jesuit. From him I learned that the Tarakanov Monastery had existed for over 300 years. It was of the Basilian Order, and was founded by the *pogtsivoyu paney* (venerable lady) Pyasetskaya, who, out of zeal for the Orthodox Catholic faith and St. Basil, used her estate for the construction and maintenance of two monasteries, Tarakanov and Zhidichin, assigning 500 souls for both. The monastery had a school of *Ksenza*, or Theological Seminary, from which they graduated capable people to spread their religion. During the war, the Austrians, or the French, drove these humble brethren to Vilna, and a military hospital was established in the monastery, from which a nervous fever still raged even then. Indeed, the *Ksenza* Professor proved that with the jaundice of his long face; but the Father Vicar, with his rosy

---

12 Tarakan is Russian for cockroach

cheeks and the extensive roundness of his caftan, revealed the opposite: perhaps the Professor had been engaged in more mental, and the Vicar in more physical labour.

After two filigrees of good cava, I set off from the humble Basilians of Tarakanov for my day-long journey. The old map, according to which I had been directed to verify the Kobryn district, was so inaccurate that I was forced to draft another. At noon I arrived at the Zakozel' castle; here two young landowners, the Orzeszki brothers, greeted me as an army officer with condescending grace; as a result of this I ignored their dinner invitations, and, having asked for what I needed, set off further. For a long time I was lost in the swamps, before I arrived for the night in Osovtsy [*Vosaŭcy*]. I entered a large, cold, empty house; in the end room, in front of a fireplace, there were two gentlemen: one in a rough sheepskin coat, and the other in a dressing gown. The latter struck me with his resemblance to the hospitable Orzeszki's; were they not charming? But as I needed to stop here for the night, I handed him my written talisman, or my free passage document. These were again two Orzeszki brothers, but their welcome was very different from the first. They seemed poorer, and therefore were more amiable. Our company was strengthened with the land surveyor. It was explained that the four brothers had divided the estate after the death of their father: Zakozel', Ovzichi and Osovtsy. Their father had been the *Powiat* Judge, and had made a decent fortune; for the heirs, it was a treasure, but their creditors robbed all the cash, and therefore both houses were empty; these last two brothers had recently recovered from a fever. An epidemic of diseases was still raging in places within the district, the legacy of enemy hospitals, such that the inhabitants of entire villages had become ill, and many of them died.

Riding around the eastern part of the district, I arrived at the estate of *Marszałek* Poslavsky for the night, three *verstas* [two miles] from Chomsk, directly at his farm. In everything I saw here there was well-maintained husbandry, different from the husbandry of other landowners: even plump sheep, guarded by Siberian dogs, and grinding mills with many millstones, even cloth, even the peasants themselves were taller and healthier than in other parts of the district. This was what it meant to be a good steward: an invisible eye watched over them everywhere, and in his absence, it seemed he saw everything. The trusted steward was active, diligent. When I walked in on him, he was surrounded by the foremen and their deputies, to whom he was giving orders and details for the morning's work, with no less emphasis than a regimental commander to his sergeant major.

The town of Chomsk stood by a swamp, near the Yasel'da river, on a sandy hill and in an open space; the construction of it was of wood, because there was quite a large forest around. I did not notice any Jews here. The textile mill produced 13,000 *arshins* [10,000 yards] of cloth annually, which went to the Guard.

From Chomsk, via Goshevo, I arrived at Bezdezh for the night. "Where did the *pan* come from?" the steward asked me. – From Chomsk! – "It took you all day to go half a *meile* [2⅓ miles]!" – "No, I have ridden ten *meilen* [47 miles]." – "And why did *pan* circle like that?" – "To get to Bezdezh". – "A likely story!"

At the town of Motaĺ, standing on the banks of the Yasel'da river, I admired a lake, two *verstas* [1⅓ miles] long, four *sazhens* [28'] wide. I had not seen such a view of nature for a long time: at the end of the lake was a manor house in the middle of a yellow-green grove, the water was as smooth as a mirror, reflecting the houses, the grove and the lofty banks; fishermen, in pairs in their boats, quietly cast their nets; the day turned to evening; the setting sun gilded the landscape, and the clouds that were painted on the smooth surface of the water; the coolness and purity of the air refreshed the senses. I was delighted by the beauty of nature. It seemed that the locals themselves felt it, and, in their Sunday clothes, shared their delight with me. It was a state-owned town, and the peasants were cheerful. The women appeared in simple but pleasant attire; some showed their panache with ribbons and shawls in bright colours. They were untouched by the sting of war; the well-being of the inhabitants had been preserved from that.

On the way out of Motaĺ, I saw another, heavenly view, more magnificent than the first. The sun was leaning towards the west. The thick, leaden clouds that had accumulated from the east occupied half of the sky from the horizon, and slowly moved towards the west like a wall; the surface of the earth beneath them was clothed in darkness, while on the other side the setting sun was still gilding the landscape. Orange wisps of cloud, scattered over the clear half of the sky, patiently awaited the thunder clouds, not fearing to be swallowed up by them. Just as infants had patiently watched the enemies of the fatherland, who had come to destroy the homes of their fathers, and kidnap the little ones themselves. Still the last rays of the dying day gilded the top of a sepulchral cross among the dry pines; a huge cloud, hanging over me, startled me with a thunderclap. I felt the greatness and strength of the power of the heavens. The thought, introduced from infancy regarding the end of the world and the next life, flashed through me. I imagined seeing the heavens opening up, and there the terrible Judge, casting thunderbolts upon me... A gust of wind, the harbinger of a storm, blew in my face; the birds were in a rush to hide in the thick foliage of the trees, and I, wrapping myself in my greatcoat, directed the brown nags with a generous clap to walk on, wishing to get out from under the gloomy half of the sky and into the clear; but the speed of an arrow would be insignificant here in comparison with the apparent slowness of the advancing clouds: suddenly large drops of rain began to pelt me, and within half an hour I was soaked by the rain. Lightning and thunder burst out over me: flash after flash, strike after strike... I barely had time to shelter in the village of Vavulichi, having travelled four *verstas* [2⅔ miles] beneath the storm. Here, I found genuine hospitality albeit poor shelter. The venerable Mrs. Vishnevskaya, with only eight souls in her possession, treated me better than other landowners with 300 souls.

The next day I covered no more than ten *verstas* [6⅔ miles], to the village of Vorotsevichi. Here, on the vast manor of the *Pani* of *Marszałkova* Ordina, in her absence, I spent the rest of the day with the steward of the estate, a kind old man, *Pan Shambelian* [Lord Chamberlain]. But when in the evening the *Marszałkova* arrived herself with her two beautiful daughters, I was revived by their company, in the like of which I had not happened to be for a long time. The *Marszałkova*, a Polish lady of the highest class, a widow who was not yet elderly, with a good income, lived like a general. She had her own music orchestra and numerous servants from the gentry. With an adult son and three daughters, of whom the eldest was already married, she was still quite young. I had noticed, in the course of my travels, that Polish ladies, mainly in comparison with the ladies of other nations, were able to maintain the freshness of their beauty into old age, whether from their skill at dressing, or from moderation in the pleasures of life.

The evening was spent in the best possible way. Initially all the house guests spoke quietly among themselves, out of respect for the hostess; but soon the musicians appeared, put their music stands in the hall, tuned their instruments, and with a loud overture they resurrected those present from being put to sleep. The eldest daughter of the *Marszałkova*, a beautiful, slender girl, appeared with a palm flute, which under her lips emitted magical sounds that enchanted the heart. I shall never forget this image, the likeness of an angel, in white clothes, masking the adorable appearance of a young maiden; of this happy flute, brought to life by her lips, which made quivering sounds – an echo of heartfelt emotions! I shall never forget those quick eyes, with the fire of love looking to delight with every note! I watched, listened – and admired.

On the following day I rode through vast swamps, near the canal connecting the river Mukhavets with the Pina, in the southern part of the district. I spent the night in Gnevshchitsy, with Mr. G***.

I arrived to spend the night in the village of Moladava, with the former *Marszałek* of Pinsk S***, who was now very old and sick. I was greeted rather kindly by his wife and sister. The venerable old lady-hostess told me that they had only one son, from whom they hoped for support in their old age, who had been educated at the University; they had built two large stone houses in the village for him, while they themselves lived in a small wooden one; they had taken care to arrange their affairs in the best way for him, so that he would not want for anything, not only during his education at the University, but afterwards so that he would appear decently in the world and uphold the honour of their name. This was an excellent example of parenting of a son! Children who have such parents are most fortunate! But are they always worthy of it!

The headquarters of General [Ilya] Duka's cuirassier division was located in the town of Janove [*Ivanava*], on the eastern edge of the district. On an open field, outside the town, the cuirassiers, one by one and by ranks, learned the new paces of the march.

Here I met with the police chief. Within this company there was also an Assessor and a Secretary; I found their subtle body language amusing. The police chief boasted that all the *Powiat* nobility had begged him to remain in the service when he had begun to think about leaving; however, while observing strict justice, he did not show leniency to anyone.

Towards evening I arrived in the village of Gutov [*Hutava*], with a young landowner who had got married three days previously. His wife was a lovely, virile blonde. Two elderly men, relatives of the youngsters, were sitting with the company as a chaperon. Meanwhile, as they got more deeply involved with their cards, seriously engaging in the game, with almost every bid by the players, the young couple would kiss without pause. I envied their happiness, and having seen their passionate kissing, I wondered if I would see something like that myself in my dreams; a meagre supper after an exhausting journey, and cold accommodation quickly dispelled my dreams of voluptuousness. Besides, Ukrainian Cossacks had already spent the night in the village before my arrival.

At noon on 1st [13th] October, I arrived in the village of Perkhovili [*Perkovichi*], the estate of the *Marszałek* of Pruzhany V***. The proud title of *Marszałek* is arresting at first, as if with something important. This word originated in Poland from the French *Maréchal*, which means blacksmith, or with the addition of *de camp*, General; but for the Poles, Marshal, or *Marszałek*, only meant Leader of the Nobility, either district or governorate, their title had neither the first nor the second meaning. Whoever had once been a Leader of the Nobility, retained the title of *Marszałek* for life, and therefore there were very many of them in Poland; but ordinary nobles showed them particular respect, as they had towards senior nobility in the past.

On my travels, I had often met soldiers from the Chernigov *Opolchenie* [militia], who had been dismissed to their homes. With such joy they rushed to their wives! But would their women recognize such good fellows? It was not the Ukrainians who were the hearth-breakers,[13] but native Muscovites!

In Patriki Shlyakhetsky, some Polish Prince M*** did not want to accommodate me, but he could not help but let my talisman have a room. But so that he would not think of me as an army marauder, I refused his tea, demanding only statistics. Noticing such diplomacy in me, he became much more friendly, and admitted that the wife of Count L***[14], after her husband's attack on the Saxons, at Kobryn, had attacked his house, with a retinue of her Amazons, so decisively that she forced him to flee, and he had wandered for six days without shelter, almost without food; and therefore, had not been able to look at the military since then without a shudder. Meanwhile, musicians had appeared among the guests: his son played the violin decently, and his daughter the piano. The evening would have been pleasant for me if

---

13 In Ukrainian, що посгубили котлы, literally 'ruined kettles'

14 Ulyana Mikhailovna de Lambert, née Deeva

from the very beginning I had not had an unpleasant introduction to the Polish Prince.

Having finished the circumnavigation of most of the Kobryn district, I still had to visit a separate stretch of land, namely the Mokrany swamps. On the way there, in the noble village of Chadyničy, I had to spend the night due to a lack of horses. One angry noblewoman, dark as a Gypsy, not respecting my crumpled talisman, had not wanted to give me horses, boasting, however, that she had twenty of them in the stables. There was nothing to be done: one must sit like a sandpiper, contemplating its beak in an unfamiliar swamp and not according to ones wishes. Looking at these noble men and women, in gray *zipuni* [collarless caftans] and *onuchi* [puttees]: (the Polish noble farmer!) I was astonished at their strange progress. From these landowners and farmers, who ploughed and yelled for themselves, and took their rent from the peasants, initially, as small-holding farmers, then as *wspany* tenants, then as *mostsy pany*, and finally as *wielmoża Marszałek*. It so often happened that under one family name the older generation wore *zipuni* and *onuchi*, while the grandchildren were in tailcoats, speaking French and dancing the mazurka. It also frequently happened that these *wspany* served as lackeys to the *wielmoża pany*, under the *pogtsivym* (venerable title) of officiator; then, having accumulated several hundred zlotys in the course of their service, they become tenants, *pany*, and, in turn, invite the *wspany* into their service. This was the strange *perpetuum mobile* of noble honours.

Around Mokrany, every field had ditches up and down. The ground here is very low lying, and if it were not for the ditches, the fields would have always been inundated with water from the vast marshes in the vicinity; even now, if the sluices were opened, it would cause a flood. The landowner of this wet patch of the Kobryn *powiat* was the very respectable and kind old man Raisky. Entering a room in his vast house, I saw three fellows – officers, his sons. The eldest was a retired Captain of the Artillery who outwardly seemed ill, the middle was a Captain from the Life Guard Jäger Regiment, and the youngest was a Lieutenant from His Majesty's Suite in the Quartermaster's Department. They were home on leave. The welcome from them all was very good; they left me to supper, and I had a very pleasant time in their company. Although they also left me in their house for the night, I did not want to cause them unnecessary inconvenience, especially since, according to the information I had collected, I had no reason to dally here. I went to sleep at the post house.

The town of Dzivin, surrounded by forests and swamps, stands on sandy ground; the houses were wooden; in the middle of the square was a church. All this seemed quite beautiful to me from a distance, but when I entered the town, I could not find any accommodation for myself at all, and was forced to stay in an inn. The charm of the pleasant surroundings disappeared even sooner when I saw a crowd of Jews there. I climbed the bell tower in order to sketch the location. The position is tempting for a small detachment of troops, but because of the defiles going through the swamps to Kobryn, Radostovo and Mokrany, it would be dangerous if forced to retreat: only the route to Ratne is a little better, and Tormasov's army passed through there.

I arrived in Kobrin for the night, straight from Dzivin, about 40 *verstas* [27 miles], and went to the police chief. There I found these guests: the mayor, an army Major, two Assessors and the snub nosed Secretary. The evening began and ended with boston.[15] The hostess, in spite of her toothache, played willingly; the mayor often whistled at her; the daughter, a rather sweet brunette, engaged with the Assessors; the secretary, sipping punch, talked quietly in the corner with the police chief, who had returned from his journey. Five fingers and a fist seemed to have helped him because he had become quite hospitable; and this had not come from anything other than the pleasure in life.

The Chernigov *opolchenie*, returning to their homeland, had taken all the horses for the transport of their sick and their equipment, and therefore, I had to trudge to Bul'kova with the same horses with which I had travelled from Dzivin. My horses could barely move their legs: I regarded them without pity, and listened dispassionately to the curses of my desperate driver, because I was in a bad way myself.

Approaching Bul'kova, I had prepared greetings for the *Marszałkova*, imagining meeting again with the kind commissar and the affable blonde; imagined the snack with which they would greet me as a friend; on the contrary – it can be seen that we are only happy in our delusions, as one sophist said – the former commissar was not there. I was met by strangers; no one wanted to listen to my requests. I had wanted to enter to see the *Marszałkova* herself, but the servants announced that there was no access

---

15 An eighteenth-century card game, like whist

to her, because she had been forced to lie down to rest. Humouring me, the butler, in a blue frock coat, read my dilapidated talisman, which, from frequent passing through a thousand hands, had lost its cohesion, although I carefully wrapped it in paper covers; however, they directed that I be shown to a cottage near the Jew's inn. Having eaten nothing but six bagels all day, and being unable to get anything in the evening for money, I chewed a few crackers, which I had stumbled upon in the Kobryn magazine, for my non-commissioned officer, and lay down on the bare boards, putting my frock coat under my head and covered with my greatcoat. As a result of a day's hunger, I imagined a rich feast in my dreams, at which I gobbled down pasta, and washed it down with an excellent Burgundy; but waking up – alas! I felt the great emptiness in my stomach. Oh the animal needs of humanity! Is it possible that such a proud, ambitious, self-assured creature, having gone without for several days, would lose all its vitality, and humble itself like a lamb in front of anyone who could feed it! Why is the strength of the soul of this singular creature, this guest in an animal covering, as psychologists have defined it, why does this spirit, these qualities weaken and faint along with the body!..

It's easy to philosophize with an empty stomach; I experienced this when I got up early in the morning of 6th [18th] October, and, by my blessedness, for the sake of my reconnaissance I still had to stay in Bul'kova at the main post house until noon. The local peasants were so poor that they could not spare an edible chicken; and they had not seen beef for a long time. However, I did not get angry at this, and could judge that collations (dinners) and snacks could not be prepared for every passing guest. It would have been another matter, if I were some sort of His *Mosts*, or Excellency, or Reverence, then a hall, a dining room, a buffet would have been opened for me... then, beside myself with admiration, I would have extolled the hospitality of the *Marszałkova*, just as Princess L – B*** had, she having recently travelled here from Warsaw and under whom the *Feldjäger* [state courier] had been paid five chervonets for one journey, a domesticated moor watched over the bottles in the carriage trunk menacingly, while her Parisian poodle, with a velvet collar, rode with the courier. My companions, a non-commissioned officer and my batman, cursed Bul'kova and Mokrany, wishing them to sink into the ground, but they remembered Noble Chadyničy, and Dzivin with sympathy, where, in the former, the gentry had served them, and in the latter, the Jews.

173

Having lost faith in the talisman-like strength of my free passage document, which, from friction and passing through many hands, was oily, blackened and dilapidated, I fell into despair, but, fortunately, I arrived for the night in the village of Špitali from Bul'kova. Where I had begun, there I finished my reconnaissance, for general distribution. The landowner Ilakovich, a kind hospitable Russian person, treated me like an old acquaintance, and after the Dzivin, Kobryn and Bul'kova post houses, I broke my fast. He also had two control or customs inspectors from Krynka and Chereshev; they have come to initiate my host as intermediate supervisors against Jewish smugglers.

Riding through the Pruzhany district, via Veshki and Kivatichi, I rode to Gorodechno. Here I stopped on purpose to look at General Tormasov's position, in which he, on 27th July [8th August] 1812, with an 18,000 man army, had held out all day against 40,000 Austrians, under the command of Prince Schwarzenberg. The position would be very advantageous, only for a larger body of troops: to the front, near the Gorodechno inn, there is a swamp, across which, along the Pruzhany road, lies a causeway for 20 *sazhens* [140']. This swamp begins on the left flank, about six *verstas* [four miles] away, and, encircling it, goes along the front, past Poddubno and Gorodechno, to the Mukhavets. On the left flank, about four *verstas* [2⅔ miles] distant, begins the almost impenetrable Białowieża forest, or the dense Kovatichi forest, adjacent to Šarašova. On the right side of the position there are also impassable dense forests and swamps, along the river Mukhavets. It is known that the enemy initially launched a diversionary attack on the Gorodechno causeway, while General Reynier, with most of his forces, enveloped the left flank of our force's position, first at Poddubno, and then later, trying to cross the swamp. Although the enemy had some success at the latter village, the lack of coordination of operations, the separation of the forces and Reynier's indecision prevented success, and merely forced General Tormasov to stretch his troops, refusing his left flank as it was continuously enveloped by the enemy. With the onset of the next day, his position would have been disastrous if he had not decided to retreat to Kobryn by night, and onward, across the Dzivin swamps. Our troops could have endured here too, since from Kobryn to Dzivin, 40 *verstas* [27 miles] away, there is an almost continuous defile along causeways, through the swamps; but the wise Schwarzenberg, perhaps, himself was afraid to sit in the Kobryn swamps, especially since he had already learned of the approach of Admiral [Pavel] Chichagov with a land army, and was rushing towards Brest-Litovsk to engage Chichagov, leaving Tormasov to make his way through the swamps to Ratne.

The town of Pruzhany is more expansive than Kobryn, but in terms of buildings it is nothing more than a Jewish town. Pruzhany district is nicer than Kobryn district; one half of it represents grain-growing fields, and the other the vast forests of the Białowieża forest, where bison were found, a special kind of buffalo, which were forbidden to be slaughtered under pain of death, according to ancient Polish laws.

Approaching Śvislač, I felt almost the same emotions as when approaching my home town: having served for seven years in one company, I had become accustomed to them. I imagined a meeting of comrades, I wanted to find out about their welfare, and about my faithful, barking poodle, Paris. Thinking of him, I sighed in doubt that he was in one piece. For a long time Śvislač did not appear: I was losing patience; at last the Count Tyshkevich's palace – and the town – emerged from behind the forest... Everything was in the same place.

But where was my Paris? Where was my wordless friend? Alas! Paris had loved me like no other creature capable of speech could ever have loved. He had not been able to live separated from me: he pined and constantly looked for me where I used to walk with him; without me he would not take food from anyone, grew thin, became aggressive, and finally disappeared without a trace. Before that, being extremely weak, he had barely moved; but on the last evening, when it got dark and the retreat began to be beat, he jumped out of the window, broke into a run – to only he knows where. Hearing the story of the death of my wordless friend, I swallowed tears; but once alone in my room gave them free rein, and, under cover of the dark of night, wept as if I had lost a relative.[16] My moans echoed within the walls of the church, next to which I, sitting on a stone, surrendered to my pathos. Cold people! You who would laugh at a man of reason, indulging in the urges of his heart, who was crying in the solitude of the night – and about what? – about a dog! Yes, I cried for a dog, and not for so many so-called dear friends who were leaving this

---

16 Radozhitskii's note: This may seem ridiculous to some, but I ask you to recall that the renowned German writer and poet, [Ernst Theodor Amadeus] Hoffmann, could not bear life after the death of his beloved cat, Murr. Those who understand the depth of emotions can appreciate the bond we share with animals, whose friendship often proves more genuine than that of humans.

world! If the type of animal, to which I dedicated my tears, could show such an example of loyalty and unshakeable friendship to man, and even sometimes save him from death, then why should a person, in turn, not be grateful to the noble feelings of this wordless friend, albeit a bony and inferior organism! Why not ease the melancholy of the heart with a final debt of gratitude – tears! Unfortunate Paris! I said, if you loved me so much that you could not live apart from me, then your ghost should accept these tears of my gratitude to you, tears that flow to relieve the sadness of my heart! I was unintentionally responsible for your death. Having loved you a great deal, and fearing your loss by some mishap during my journey, I had decided on a short-term separation from you, having instructed my comrades to take care and cherish you. Why were you so devoted to me, and so sensitive yourself, that you were exhausted by the grief of separation from me! Truly, you were my only friend, with whom I shared my hours of relaxation, more pleasant than with the eloquent animals around me. You didn't know how to speak, but you knew how to feel, knew how to understand me, and anticipate my thoughts! For all that, no one knew how to stroke you and amuse you as I did. How fond was your farewell! I remember your last, sad look at me, when, after stroking you, I closed the door behind me with a sigh! Yes, I myself was sad, parting with a friend, and I almost shed a tear myself, anticipating separation from you forever. Noble creature! May your memory endure forever! I shall wash away your ashes with tears of gratitude for your loyalty and love for me. You touched my heart; you were the first to prove to me that even dumb animals like you can be loved as unselfish and educated friends; I had never shed so many tears for anyone before that time as I had for you!.. "It's a pity, sir!" said the church tutor, who had quietly approached me. "Sir must have lost a brother or a good friend; but we have no time for a funeral, come back in the morning; or I could take you to see the priest, perhaps..." – "Go to the devil!" I said blustering, got up from the stone, wiped away my tears with my hand, and went to my quarters, leaving the tutor in terrible bewilderment.

On 12th [24th] October, I began to polish and tidy up my sketches, and rewrite the Statistics for the Kobryn district.

Meanwhile, bad weather set in: snowy and windy. I was glad that I had time to finish my reconnaissance during tolerable and reasonably good weather.

Kobryn district lies in the southern part of the Grodno Governorate, between Pruzhany, Pinsk, Kovel and Brest-Litovsk; it stretches 105 *verstas* [70 miles] in length and 60 *verstas* [40 miles] wide. The highway from Brest-Litovsk to Pinsk divides it into two parts, of which the northern one is the best and most suitable for agriculture; but the southern part consists of almost continuous swamps covered with alder forest, in which the river Pina and the minor streams flowing into the Mukhavets have their sources. The river Mukhavets, emerging near Pruzhany, has a navigable stretch from Kobryn to Brest-Litovsk; the navigation begins at the town of Gorodets, where the Pina River connects with the Mukhavets, via a canal, 30 *verstas* [20 miles] long and 4 sazhen [28'] wide. The Yasel'da river flows partly along the northeastern edge of the district, watering the towns of Chomsk, Bezdezh and Motaĺ via Lake Dzhidin'ye. In the southeastern part of the district, 30 *verstas* [20 miles] distant, through forests and swamps, the source of the Pina River flows, even along the border with Volyn [*Volhynia*] to the river Pripyat. Kobryn is the district capital, its layout is better than Pruzhany; the highway from Brest-Litovsk to Northern Russia crosses it. The best towns after that are Antopal, Drahichyn, Ivanava, Chomsk, Motaĺ and Dzivin. There are a total of 370 named settlements and villages; there are 11,500 households, 37,000 males; 3,000 horses; 25,000 head of cattle. The main occupation of the inhabitants is agriculture; and as the inhabitants of the southern part, among the swamps, need bread, they float their timber to Brest-Litovsk, where they buy their own bread, and thus all shipping is limited. Significant land holdings are: the monastery at Tarakanovo, the landowners Brashevich, Orzeszki, Helvig, *Marszałkov* Ordina and Raisky. Today there are no wealthy people: the last war has ruined many. The minor gentry, owning one or two hearths or yards of unfortunate serfs, are a great multitude; all of them nestle mostly in the marshes, with the frogs and waders, enjoying almost complete independence, because they are in extreme poverty. Sometimes in one village of six cottages there might be seven *pani*; there may even be two *pani* for every serf. Almost every landowner's village has a farm and a steward from the swamp gentry. They receive an annual subsistence in kind, a couple of wild boars, or pigs, and several dozen zlotys (15 silver kopecks) a month. These savings, after several years in their service, with prudent discretion, would enable them to lease small villages themselves, which they then acquire by purchase, and are finally advanced from the poorest gentry to *pani* and *Marszałki*. On this basis, the Polish nobility progresses and multiplies, and therefore self-interest is their idol, expelling feelings of compassion and friendship from the heart of even the noblest: I am referring to minor nobles, or upstarts from the poor gentry. Their hospitality is based on mutual interests; these interests result in temporary friendship. The strongest or richest owner will try to oppress and rob their weakest neighbour: there is no end of snitching and denunciations. In these cases there is an abundant harvest for lawyers and Jews: the former confuse matters in order to suck the litigants for longer, and not a single landowner dares to dispose of his property without the latter. At any enterprise, a vodka tenant, *Pan* Hirsch, is called to the council, wearing a black velvet yarmulke, who, thrusting his hands behind his wide belt, proudly determines what will be and what will not be: without his will and the assistance of his associates, scattered throughout the taverns and farms, no craft or trade can advance. Moreover, it is rare to find a landowner, or indeed a peasant, who is never in debt to the Jews; for these and others Jews indulgently take distilleries and the right to distill as collateral from the former, or entire villages for rent, and take the grain ripening in the field from the latter. Landowners without money live in their villages out of necessity; anyone who has saved up a sufficient amount after two years, rushes to Warsaw to live with the patriots. The farmers' stewards and tenants who invest the latest profits from the estates of spendthrift patriots progress the fastest. Because of this, neither the landowners nor the peasants lives are pleasant; as a result of this the country is impoverished and miserable. The unskilled people are rude, lazy, and those living in the forests are almost as wild as their mossy environment. The tenant farmers treat them like mute beasts. Of the many landowners in the district, few are worshipped by the peasants for their mercy and meekness; only *Marszałek* Pusłowski in Chomsk, and *Marszałkova* Ordin in Vorotsevichi, are revered as good *pani*; the peasants of the latter in particular refer to her with affection as their kind mother. The pig is the favourite creature of ordinary Poles; no steward would take on the task of farm management for less than two boars a year. The psyche of the Polish nobility, consisting of the pushy gentry, is almost always stubborn. Not receiving a proper education, knowing nothing but Polish literacy and inventory calculation, they are often not thorough, impudent, and aggressive. As much as the character of the Poles is unseemly in some respects, so much to the contrary, there are many good features in the Poles. The married women are excellent hostesses; they rule the whole house and their husbands with particular prudence; their welcomes are friendly, albeit insincere. There are very few girls visible in the villages; most of them study in boarding houses, or live as companions to wealthy landowners. Girls, or *panna*, mature quickly here, and reveal in themselves a lot of sharpness and agility, which comes from their free association with men.

Upon my return, I learned that our forces were to be reorganized. Our 3rd Light Artillery Company of 11th Brigade was to be renamed 47th Company of 24th Brigade, and entered 3rd Infantry Corps, under the command of General [*Dmitry*] Dokhturov, in General Kaptsevich's Division, stationed in Białystok.

On 28th October [9th November], I completed the assignment given to me. I confess that I had to have quite a lot of patience in performing it. It didn't take as much for me to draw a clear map as to write a few dozen papers on dry subjects. My description consisted of three sections: in the first, all settlements, villages, farms were entered alphabetically, with statistics, or with a total opposite each, in columns, the number of souls, the number of horses, cattle, and the number of households; in the second section I described rivers, streams, lakes, canals, swamps, with roads and crossings passing over and around them; the third section included a description of all the offensive and defensive avenues of approach. To do this, I had to wargame on my map with two armies, choosing positions, and noting all the advantages and disadvantages of the locations, imagining them in reality. It was flattering for me, in the minutes of this imaginary command, to overwhelm a weak enemy with advancing forces, or to give him the means to exploit the location for a stubborn defence; to launch a cavalry attack on one flank, to plant marksmen on the other, to send assault columns forward from the centre, under the cover of batteries placed on high ground. Moving the troops around on paper in this way, I involuntarily recalled that I had been serving as a Lieutenant for a seventh year... But who was to blame for this, if not fate, if not for stupid fortune! She often smiles at Vanka and chases Alexei away...

In early [mid] November, with my detailed map and description of the Kobryn district, I went to Białystok, and presented myself to the Chief Quartermaster. For the fulfillment of this mission, he promised to have me promoted to the next rank, and in anticipation of this, he ordered me to go every day to the drawing room, where all the officers of the Suite, and the artillerymen assigned to them, were busy drawing a complete topographic map of the Grodno Governorate. Each officer was obliged, at the end of the survey of their assigned district, to enter his work on the general map.

Here I found an educated society of officers, each of whom had something original about him. Lieutenant Colonel D***, a kind, pious Christian Catholic, who refuted the new system of Philosophy, was a meek and honest man; he was conducting a scholarly dispute in writing with Captain G***, a natural born, well-bred Russian, a student of Literature under Merzlyakov,[17] and a part time author. They tried to convince each other with their hypotheses in many areas of Philosophy, Theology and Psychology; however, in spite of the eloquence of their mutual speculation, each remained with his own. Another Captain L***, an ardent Italian who called himself a Martinist, an admirer of Voltaire, knew his philosophy by heart and intended to walk the hidden paths in life. With fiery feelings and a sharp, although not always thorough mind, he could most accurately judge good from bad, noble from base; despising flattery, he was an oddity in the moral world. With a cheerful disposition, great erudition, and knowledge of the world, he was very friendly in company; but the ardour of his nature often led him into recklessness. Having been stationed in Åbo [*Turku*], he challenged one of his enemies to a duel through the newspapers; learned to fence in two months; finally, he met the enemy, and delivered a lethal thrust to Ensign D***, an Estonian nobleman, a great mathematician. During the Patriotic War, having been captured by the French, he walked 500 *verstas* [333 miles] to Borisov barefoot, in just a greatcoat. In Borisov, due to illness, he was abandoned by the enemy in a Jew's hut, where the compassionate Jew fed him on broth only, and where he sat with frostbitten feet, not getting up, for eighteen days. During this time, he scratched with a nail, across the entire wall above his bed doing mathematical calculations, and, according to him, he composed one formula by which in the simplest manner he could find the distance of the sun from the earth and from the most distant planets. Having found this formula, he was no less delighted than Archimedes having found the rule for the displacement of metals by plunging into his bath. He

---

17 Alexey Fedorovich Merzlyakov (1778 – 1830) was a Russian poet, critic, and translator

immediately invented a most convenient method for the internal defence of a bastion's facades. This great mathematician was an ardent defender of the most famous astronomers and geometricians. In his mathematical axioms, like Galileo, he was firm in the rules of strict morality, patient in adversity, very hardworking, and for that, despite his junior rank, he was respected by everyone. His job was to draw a geographic network on the map, with degrees of longitude and latitude of locations, and draw the rivers with a pen. According to the rules of Mathematics, he was convinced that everything in the world was done for the better; but how, with all his scholarship and honesty, he did not go far in the service and endured quite a few disasters, then, to comfort himself, he was convinced by the thought of a better life in the world to come, after death. He proved this by the fact that just as not all people fulfill their duties in this world, from which common calamities arise, there must be a better world, with the most perfect, blameless beings. Each has a certain amount of virtue (+), unhappiness (-), and all evil (x). In the society of such people, there was never a dull conversation. Having walked in on them for the first time, and listening to the conversation, I imagined that I must be in the midst of University Professors. Often the talk would start from trifles, and spread to all branches of science: about mathematics, about physics, about history and literature, or about military science, about politics, or about philosophy and theology. Everyone plotted or drew in his corner of the long table, listened to the speaker, refuted, contradicted, changed the subject, and spoke himself. I, for my part, wishing to maintain a liking for all the members of such a learned society, challenged each slightly, and swallowed a little from all; in fact, I did not participate sincerely in metaphysical imaginings, in the Scholasticism of Theology, or in the sophism of theoretical philosophy.

In our free time, after classes in the drawing room, we would spend evenings with good friends playing *boston* or occasionally lingering when someone caught our interest. On Sundays and holidays, we attended ballroom evenings and dances, either at the Casino or the Noble Assembly. Thus, the remainder of the year passed, divided between work and enjoyable diversions.

End of Volume Three